Inequality in School Discipline

Russell J. Skiba • Kavitha Mediratta • M. Karega Rausch
Editors

Inequality in School Discipline

Research and Practice to Reduce Disparities

palgrave
macmillan

Editors
Russell J. Skiba
Center for Evaluation and
Education Policy
School of Education
Indiana University
Bloomington, Indiana, USA

M. Karega Rausch
Center for Evaluation and
Education Policy
School of Education
Indiana University
Bloomington, Indiana, USA

Kavitha Mediratta
The Atlantic Philanthropies
New York, USA

ISBN 978-1-137-51256-7   ISBN 978-1-137-51257-4   (eBook)
DOI 10.1057/978-1-137-51257-4

Library of Congress Control Number: 2016940984

Cover illustration: © Shotshop GmbH / Alamy Stock Photo

Printed on acid-free paper

This Palgrave Macmillan imprint is published by Springer Nature
The registered company is Nature America Inc. New York

It is to the many individuals and organizations who have dedicated themselves to discovering more effective and socially just practices in education and juvenile justice, and to the children and youth who are the beneficiaries of those efforts, that we dedicate this book.

ACKNOWLEDGMENTS

This volume grew directly out of the efforts of the Discipline Disparities Research-to-Practice Collaborative, whose members committed three years to meetings, writing, and collaboration in order to identify the critical issues in the field, and commission the research projects that form the heart of this book. The Collaborative was composed of researchers, advocates, educators, policy analysts, juvenile justice representatives, and funders who contributed a disproportionate share of their professional lives to clarifying the issues, acting as review panels for research applications, writing and editing Collaborative publications, and most of all, building a hard-won consensus across disciplines. In particular, we are deeply grateful to the other members of the leadership team, Dan Losen and Tanya Coke, themselves intellectual leaders in this field, for their extraordinary effort and insight in helping establish the direction and activities of the Collaborative. Other members of the Discipline Disparities Collaborative include James Bell, Judith Browne-Dianis, Prudence Carter, Christopher Chatmon, Tanya Coke, Matt Cregor, Manuel Criollo, Jim Eichner, Eddie Fergus, Michelle Fine, Phillip Atiba Goff, Paul Goren, Anne Gregory, Damon Hewitt, Tammy Bang Luu, Pedro Noguera, Blake Norton, Mica Pollock, Stephen Russell, Leticia Smith-Evans Haynes, Lisa Thomas, Michael Thompson, and Ivory Toldson. We are extremely grateful to the numerous professional organizations, researchers, and policymakers at the federal and state level who contributed to the effort through their participation in stakeholder meetings and in the release and dissemination of the Collaborative briefing papers.[1]

We also gratefully acknowledge the funders who made this effort possible—the Atlantic Philanthropies, the Open Society Foundations, and a group of anonymous donors—who not only provided resources for the effort, but remained actively engaged throughout the lifespan of the Collaborative in moving the efforts and issues forward. A big thanks is also due to the staff of the Equity Project at Indiana University—Mariella Arredondo, Shana Ritter, Fatima McKenzie, Jillian DeHaan, Amara Lovato, and Natasha Williams—for their work on coordination and logistics in planning complex meetings and conferences in multiple cities across the nation.

This volume could not have been completed without the hard work, perseverance, and expertise of Jennifer Turrentine, who helped manage the organization of all aspects of the book from start to finish, doing whatever she had to do to keep it on track. We're grateful for the keen copyediting skills of Leigh Kupersmith, and for her ability to track down the hardest-to-find references and citations. Thanks also to the Palgrave Macmillan editorial team, Mara Berkoff, Milana Vernikova, and Sarah Nathan for their gracious and helpful assistance. Finally, words are not sufficient to express our gratitude to our partners and families, whose patience and support during the process never flagged.

The pace at which the public discourse on school discipline and inequity has changed in our nation has been remarkable. Finally, we acknowledge the ongoing efforts of individuals and organizations, too numerous to mention, who have made a long-term commitment to finding equitable and research-based alternatives to out-of-school suspension and expulsion. It is to many individuals and organizations who have dedication to discovering more effective and socially just practices in education and juvenile justice, and to the children and youth who are the beneficiaries of those efforts, that we dedicate this book.

NOTE

1. A complete listing of the institutional affiliations of all members and partner organizations as well as the products and publications of the Collaborative can be found at the Discipline Disparities website http://rtpcollaborative.indiana.edu/.

Contents

LIST OF CONTRIBUTORS

Mariella I. Arredondo, Ph.D., is an Associate Director of the Equity Project at Indiana University. Her research interests include the examination of impediments to educational equity, such as racial/ethnic disparities in exclusionary school discipline, as well as improving the educational access, survival, and outcomes of underserved students.

James Bell, Esq. is the Founder and Executive Director of the W. Haywood Burns Institute. Since 2001, Bell has spearheaded a national movement to address racial and ethnic disparities in public systems serving youth of color and their communities.

L. Boyd Bellinger is a Doctoral Student studying the social foundations of education in the Policy Studies in Urban Education department at the University of Illinois-Chicago. Boyd's research interests include the experience of LGBTQ young people with policing and surveillance both inside and outside of school contexts.

Kimberly M. Belmonte, M.A., is a Doctoral Student in the Critical Social/ Personality Psychology program at the Graduate Center, City University of New York. Her research interests focus on the intersection of justice, gender, and sexuality.

Jamilia J. Blake, Ph.D., is an Associate Professor in the School Psychology program in the Department of Educational Psychology at Texas A&M University. Her research interests surround children's peer relations and she is interested in exploring peer-directed aggression in ethnic/minority populations and females and the relation between peer-directed aggression and children's psychological/social adjustment, academic achievement, and familial risk and protective factors.

Jennifer F. Chmielewski, Ed.M., is a Doctoral Student in Critical Social/ Personality Psychology at the Graduate Center, City University of New York. Her research uses critical feminist theories and methods to explore women and girls' lived experiences of gender, desire, and sexual identity.

Eddie S.K. Chong holds an M.A. in Mental Health Counseling from Boston College (2014). His research relates to stigmatized groups across lifespans and cultures, and examines factors that foster community building and resilience of such groups.

Kathleen Clawson, Psy.D., is a School Psychologist in the Upper Darby School District. Her research interests include disproportionality in academic and behavioral outcomes.

Nicole Darcangelo is a Doctoral Student in the Educational Psychology program at the University of Illinois-Chicago. Darcangelo is interested in the intersections of race, gender, sexuality, and mental health within the school and prison nexus.

Michelle Fine, Ph.D., is a Distinguished Professor of Social Psychology, Women's Studies, and Urban Education at the Graduate Center, City University of New York (CUNY), and co-founder of the Public Science Project at the Graduate Center, CUNY. Her work addresses theoretical questions of social injustice that sit at the intersection of public policy and social research, particularly with respect to youth in schools and criminal justice.

Erik J. Girvan, J.D., Ph.D., is an Assistant Professor at the University of Oregon School of Law. Girvan teaches courses on the law and psychology of discrimination and the psychology of conflict. His research focuses on investigating practical, theory-driven ways to help reduce the effects of bias in the legal system and other related contexts.

Jack Glaser, Ph.D., is an Associate Professor at the Goldman School of Public Policy, University of California, Berkeley. He conducts research on stereotyping, prejudice, and discrimination, examining phenomena ranging from unconscious thoughts, feelings, and motives to discriminatory behaviors like racial profiling and hate crimes.

Phillip Atiba Goff, Ph.D., is an Associate Professor of Social Psychology at UCLA and Co-founder and President of the Center for Policing Equity. An expert in contemporary forms of racial bias and discrimination, Goff's research focuses on how contextual explanations play an under-explored role in producing racial inequality. He is also one of the four lead Principal Investigators on the National Justice Database, the first national-level data collection on police officer behavior in North America.

Chrystal Gray is a Ph.D. candidate in the School Psychology program at Indiana University. She works as a graduate assistant at the Equity Project at Indiana University. Her research interests include racial and gender disproportionality in school discipline and the evaluation of interventions used to reduce these disparities.

Anne Gregory, Ph.D., is an Associate Professor at the Graduate School of Applied and Professional Psychology at Rutgers University. Her research has focused on the persistent trend that African American adolescents are issued school suspension and expulsion at higher rates than adolescents from other groups.

Stacey S. Horn, Ph.D., is a Professor of Education and Developmental Psychology and Chair of the Department of Educational Psychology at the University of Illinois-Chicago. Her research focuses on issues of sexual prejudice among adolescents and adolescents' reasoning about peer harassment.

John Inglish, J.D., is an Education Specialist at the Oregon Department of Education. Formerly, he was a research associate at the University of Oregon where he directed Technical Assistance and Consulting Services in the College of Education. His work focuses on the intersection of law, public policy, and education, with an emphasis on restorative practices.

Angela Irvine, Ph.D., is a Vice President at Impact Justice, in Oakland, California. Irvine has more than 20 years of experience in education, health, and criminal justice policy and has served as the principal investigator of a national study of juvenile de-incarceration, and a national study of LGBT youth in the juvenile justice system.

Karen Junker, M.Div., is a Consultant and Trainer for the International Institute for Restorative Practices, and works in a variety of school districts throughout California. She is also a 6th grade math teacher with an expertise in community-building circles.

Kimberly Barsamian Kahn, Ph.D., is an Assistant Professor of Social Psychology at Portland State University. Kahn's research addresses contemporary forms of subtle racial bias, including implicit bias and social identity threats. Her work focuses on how racial stereotypes affect behavior within the criminal justice domain and in police–suspect interactions.

Eun Sook Kim, Ph.D., is an Assistant Professor of Educational and Psychological Studies in University of South Florida. She has a broad interest in research methodology and psychometrics including structural equation modeling, multilevel modeling, latent growth analysis, and propensity score analysis. Her focal research interests include measurement invariance testing in multilevel and longitudinal data.

Daniel J. Losen, J.D., is the Director of the Center for Civil Rights Remedies at UCLA's Civil Rights Project (CRP). On school-to-prison pipeline issues, Losen has conducted law and policy research; published books, reports, and articles; and provided guidance to policymakers, educators, and civil rights' advocates.

Harriet MacLean, Ed.D., is an Assistant Superintendent of Education Services for San Rafael City Schools in San Rafael, California. Her research interests include school culture and climate, academic motivation, and disproportionality in school discipline.

Miner P. Marchbanks III, Ph.D., is an Associate Research scientist for the Public Policy Research Institute at Texas A&M University. His expertise is in the use of advanced statistical methodologies to answer public policy questions. Statistical capabilities include maximum likelihood estimation, time-series analysis, and other advanced econometric techniques.

Timothy M. McCabe, M.S., is a Restorative Justice Program Manager at the Center for Dialogue and Resolution in Eugene, Oregon. His work focuses on creating opportunities for healing and learning with youth offenders and victims of crime. His recent projects include leading the Restorative Peer Court program and bringing restorative justice principles to schools.

Kavitha Mediratta, Ph.D., is the Head of Racial Equity Programmes at the Atlantic Philanthropies and leads the foundation's efforts to reform zero-tolerance school discipline policies and promote racial equity. Mediratta is one of the leading researchers on grassroots activism for public education reform in the USA.

Erica R. Meiners, Ph.D., is a Professor in the Department of Educational Leadership and Development at Northeastern Illinois University. Meiners's work is in the areas of prison/school nexus; gender, access, and technology; community-based research methodologies; and urban education.

Jean Phinney, Ph.D., is a Retired Professor of Psychology at California State University, Los Angeles. Her research interests include adolescent and young adults in first- and second-generation immigrants and restorative justice.

Mica Pollock, Ph.D., is a Professor of Education Studies and Director of the Center for Research on Educational Equity, Assessment, and Teaching Excellence (CREATE) at the University of California, San Diego. Pollock's work explores how diverse communities can come together in student support efforts. In projects based in schools, districts, cities, community organizations, and the government, Pollock has focused on how people might *communicate* so they can work together to support every young person's full human talent development.

V. Paul Poteat, Ph.D., is an Associate Professor in the Department of Counseling, Developmental, and Educational Psychology at Boston College. His research examines peer norms that perpetuate sexual prejudice and homophobic discrimination across adolescence and identifies factors that buffer against the negative effects of experiencing discrimination.

M. Karega Rausch, Ph.D., is the Former Associate Director and Research Associate with the Equity Project at Indiana University, has authored or co-authored more than 20 professional publications with an emphasis on racial/ethnic disproportionality in school discipline and special education. He is also a sought-after speaker and expert in charter school accountability.

Stephen T. Russell, Ph.D., is the Distinguished Professor and Fitch Nesbitt Endowed Chair in Family and Consumer Sciences in the John & Doris Norton School of Family and Consumer Sciences at the University of Arizona, and Director of the Frances McClelland Institute for Children, Youth, and Families.

Jillian R. Scheer Ph.D., is a Doctoral Student in Counseling Psychology at Boston College. Her research focuses on developmental and chronic trauma, experiences of LGBT youth and heterosexual youth allies in high school Gay Straight Alliances (GSAs), and trauma-informed care for survivors of domestic violence.

Marieka Schotland, Ph.D., is an Independent Consultant specializing in research and program evaluation in schools. Her research interests focus on school culture and climate, socio-emotional connections to school, and restorative justice.

Sarah Schriber, J.D., is the Policy Director at the Illinois Safe Schools Alliance, an organization that supports the safety and healthy development of LGB/T youth in schools and communities. Schriber's work focuses on ways to support LGB/T youth at different points along the school-to-prison pipeline through policy advocacy.

Allison L. Seibert, M.Ed., is an Associate Director of Advancement for Catholic Charities of Central Texas. Her work focuses on strengthening individuals, families, and communities through direct services, community collaboration, and social justice advocacy.

Russell J. Skiba, Ph.D., is a Professor in the School Psychology program at Indiana University and Director of the Equity Project at Indiana University. His research interests include racial and ethnic disparities in school discipline, school violence prevention, and special education disproportionality. He served as lead facilitator and project director of the Discipline Disparities Research-to-Practice Collaborative. Discipline Disparities Research-to-Practice Collaborative.

Danielle M. Smith, M.Ed., is a Doctoral Student in the School Psychology program at Texas A&M University. Her research interests center on the implications of trauma exposure in educational, criminological, and social/emotional contexts.

Leticia Smith-Evans Haynes, J.D., Ph.D., is an Interim Director of the Education Practice for the NAACP Legal Defense Fund. Haynes, a former elementary school teacher, frequently speaks and writes on eliminating racial, gender, and other disparities in education and has served as adjunct faculty at a number of educational institutions.

Shannon D. Snapp, Ph.D., is a Postdoctoral Research fellow at the University of Arizona with interests in health, well-being, sexuality, gender, and sociocultural contexts that support youth. Snapp holds M.A. and Ph.D. degrees in Developmental Psychology from Boston College.

Jeffrey R Sprague, Ph.D., is a Professor of Special Education and Director of the Institute on Violence and Destructive Behavior, University of Oregon. His work focuses on positive behavior interventions and supports, multi-tiered support systems, alternative education, juvenile delinquency prevention and treatment, and school safety.

Brett G. Stoudt, Ph.D., is an Assistant Professor in the Psychology Department with a joint appointment in the Gender Studies Program at John Jay College of Criminal Justice, as well as the Environmental Psychology Doctoral Program at the Graduate Center, City University of New York.

Claudia G. Vincent, Ph.D., is a Senior Research Assistant in the College of Education at the University of Oregon. Her primary research interests are disparate discipline outcomes across vulnerable student groups and blending positive behavior support with restorative practices to achieve greater equity in student outcomes.

Steve M. Wood, Ph.D., is an Assistant Research Scientist at PPRI working on projects related to criminal justice issues. He has over five years of experience conducting court-related research and specializes in research methodology, survey instrument development, focus groups, and multivariate statistical analysis techniques.

Aishatu R. Yusuf, M.P.A., has nearly 10 years of experience working in Social Policy. Yusuf's areas of interest include education, juvenile justice, disproportionality in school discipline, criminal justice, justice reforms for girls and women, and child welfare.

LIST OF FIGURES

LIST OF TABLES

PART I

Discipline Disparities: A Research-to-Practice Collaborative

CHAPTER 1

Introduction

Kavitha Mediratta and M. Karega Rausch

Our country recently witnessed the profound and life-altering consequences students face when engaging punitive disciplinary systems. Sitting
quietly at her desk at Spring Valley High School in Columbia, South
Carolina, Shakara[1]—a Black female teenager—was grabbed, thrown on
the ground and then dragged across the classroom and arrested by a White
male school resource officer for failing to comply with instructions to put
away her cell phone (Jarvie, 2015; Savali, 2015). The incident, which was
captured on video, left Shakara facing misdemeanor charges for "disturbing schools," a charge that carries a $1000 maximum fine and up to 90
days in jail, as well as a broken arm and injuries to her face, neck, ribs,
back, and left shoulder (Love, 2015).

While Shakara's case sparked national outrage, including an investigation from the US Department of Justice, it is one of many examples
of the excessive and racialized overuse of punitive discipline common in
schools (Ferris, 2015). Data from the US Department of Education show
that Black students, who comprise 16% of overall student enrollment in
US public schools, make up more than a quarter of students referred

K. Mediratta (✉)
Atlantic Philanthropies, New York, NY, USA

M.K. Rausch
The Equity Project, Indiana University, Bloomington, IN, USA

© The Author(s) 2016   3
R.J. Skiba et al. (eds.), *Inequality in School Discipline*,
DOI 10.1057/978-1-137-51257-4_1

to law enforcement from schools and 31% of those arrested for school-related incidents (CRDC, 2014). Nationally, 3.45 million students were suspended from school during the 2011–2012 school year; among those students, Black students were three times more likely to be suspended and expelled than their White peers. Students with disabilities also face increased risk of exclusionary discipline; in 2012, they were twice as likely to be suspended as those without disabilities and represented a quarter of students arrested and referred to law enforcement, although they represented only 13% of the nation's student population (CRDC, 2014).

Data like these have been the subject of increasing concern to policymakers, civil rights advocates, parents, students, and scholars. Reflecting this growing national awareness, one news report on Shakara's case observed: "The aggressive discipline [in Spring Valley] is just one example of the school-to-prison pipeline phenomenon, in which Black children are more likely to be criminalized for their behavior than their White peers" (Bellware, 2015). Professional associations such as the American Psychological Association (APA, 2008) have issued reports on the ineffectiveness of and risks associated with disciplinary exclusion, particularly for Black students. Prominent school districts, such as the Los Angeles Unified School District (Jones, 2013), San Francisco Unified School District, and the New York City Department of Education (Blad, 2014), and states such as Colorado (Marcus, 2012), Maryland (St. George, 2014), and California (Public Counsel, 2014) have revised their codes of conduct to focus on preventive alternatives to suspension and expulsion and curb the inequitable use of exclusionary discipline. At the federal level, the US Departments of Justice and Education led a national initiative on school discipline that resulted in federal civil rights guidance aimed at reducing the use of, and disparities in, suspension and expulsion, as well as expanded data collection and monitoring of disciplinary exclusion nationally. Federal agencies are also providing new funding for school-climate interventions, research on best practices, and judicially led multi-stakeholder coalitions to reform policy and practice (U.S. Department of Justice/Department of Education, 2014).

Yet, despite this growing sense of the need for a change and initial steps in some places to address the issue, the field lacks comprehensive analysis of why disciplinary exclusion and disparities have become so prevalent, and what can be done to reverse this trend. Why are some students subjected to harsher discipline than others, and why are suspensions, expulsions, and arrests so widely used? What should we do to change these patterns in schools?

This book intends to answer those questions by providing the most up-to-date and authoritative information on what has been learned from research, data, and practical experience about disciplinary disparities, and the latest findings regarding disparity-reducing approaches. We argue that there is a need to examine the roles of bias and inequality in educational and societal opportunities in the creation of disciplinary disparities in schools. In a context of increasing stakes for educational achievement, the work of disparity reduction could not be more important. Moreover, in light of growing evidence of disparate treatment by law enforcement authorities on the basis of race, we must explore how school-based authorities' perception of and response to youth behavior contribute to large and continuing disparities in school punishments.

THE DISCIPLINE DISPARITIES COLLABORATIVE

The chapters in this book draw from and were commissioned by the Discipline Disparities Research-to-Practice Collaborative (hereafter, Collaborative). The Collaborative is an inter-disciplinary, multi-sector, and highly diverse group of 28 nationally recognized researchers, advocates, content experts, and practitioners. Launched by the Equity Project at Indiana University and The Atlantic Philanthropies, with additional support from the Open Society Foundations and anonymous donors, the purpose of the Collaborative has been to explore and fill gaps in knowledge specific to disparities in school discipline, and to grow the evidence-base on effective practices, policies, and approaches that substantially reduce or eliminate disparities in discipline.

Initiated in 2011, the Collaborative engaged in more than seven multi-day face-to-face meetings with diverse stakeholders from across the country. That effort was intentional: we believed that such meetings would facilitate a deeper understanding of the context in which disciplinary disparities occur, ensure that our work was grounded in the lived experiences of key stakeholders, and also increase the likelihood that the Collaborative's research efforts would have real-world applicability and usefulness. The Collaborative met with (1) educators, including parents, teachers, principals, superintendents, and school board representatives; (2) state and national policymakers and policy analysts; (3) community-based organizations operating disciplinary and juvenile justice–reducing interventions; (4) local and national advocacy organizations; (5) juvenile justice specialists; and (6) researchers and equity trainers.

In addition to grounding the work, those meetings identified key areas in need of additional research. The Collaborative subsequently funded a set of research projects and produced briefing papers and forums to address the important questions and needs of practitioners, parents, advocates, and policymakers, and in particular, expand the availability and knowledge base of promising interventions that could reduce disparities in school discipline for students of color, girls, and lesbian, gay, bisexual and transgender (LGBT) youth.

This volume presents findings from the Collaborative's multi-year work. The chapters that follow document the continuing overuse of exclusionary discipline and law enforcement interventions for vulnerable students, and present evidence showing how removal from school for disciplinary purposes contributes to a range of negative school and life outcomes, including grade retention, school dropout, and involvement with the juvenile justice system. In addition to adding to the knowledge base on disparities for students of color and those with disabilities for whom the overuse of exclusionary discipline is increasingly recognized, the book also examines patterns and consequences of exclusionary discipline for students who are gender non-conforming or identify as LGBT, about which comparatively little is known. Finally, the book offers new strategies that policymakers and practitioners can use to reduce disparities.

School Discipline and Educational Equity: False Narratives on the Need for Exclusionary Discipline

School exclusion—out-of-school suspension, expulsion, and arrest—has become a central component of discipline in our nation's schools over the past several decades, and both its implementation and consequences fall disproportionally on certain groups. Some studies have suggested that at least a third of all students are now likely to experience an out-of-school suspension or expulsion at some point in their school career (Fabelo et al., 2011). The use of such measures is even higher for Black males, with one estimate suggesting that nearly 70% of these students experience at least one suspension or expulsion during their K-12 academic careers (Shollenberger, 2015).

Chapter 2 of this volume details the substantial negative consequences of the frequent and inequitable use of school exclusion in discipline. In brief, exclusionary discipline is associated with student and teacher perceptions of a more negative climate (Steinberg, Allensworth, & Johnson,

2015); lower levels of academic achievement (Arcia, 2006) and civic and voter participation (Kupchik & Caitlaw, 2013); and an increased risk of negative behavior over time (Tobin, Sugai, & Colvin, 1996), school drop-out or failure to graduate on time (Suh & Suh, 2007), and contact with the juvenile justice system (Fabelo et al., 2011). Indeed, the perceived and actual linkage between exclusionary discipline and justice system involvement led youth and civil rights advocates to coin the term "School-to-Prison Pipeline" that is now widely used (Mediratta, 2012).

But despite the growing evidence of the harms of exclusionary discipline and its ineffectiveness in increasing safety and academic success, belief in the efficacy of the approach is steadfast among wide-ranging sectors of the public. While the arguments for exclusionary discipline are varied, at least three meta-narratives appear to anchor its support among public school parents, policymakers, school leaders, and staff. These include (1) the narrative of safety and order, (2) the narrative of concentrated poverty, and (3) the narrative of culturally deficient norms of behavior among some students. We explore these narratives below, and present evidence from research and practice on each.

The Safety and Order Narrative

A common view of suspensions and other forms of punitive and exclusionary discipline is that they are necessary to maintain safety and order in schools (Wright, Morgan, Coyne, Beaver, & Barnes, 2014). Initially intended for violence and drug possession (Skiba & Knesting, 2001), exclusionary discipline approaches growing out of "zero tolerance" policies have become the predominant response to children's misbehavior. This expansion of exclusionary discipline echoes a "broken windows" theory of policing, where a swift and aggressive response to minor offenses is presumed to prevent more serious crimes (Kelling & Wilson, 1982). Suspensions, expulsions, and arrests are assumed to play a key role in "cracking down" on behavior that, if left unchecked, could undermine learning in the classroom. Proponents of the safety and order narrative generally believe that a trend of worsening student behavior both justifies and necessitates broad application of an exclusionary disciplinary strategy (MacDonald, 2012).

Implicit in this narrative, when viewed through the lens of disciplinary disparities, is that students of color, those with disabilities, and students whose sexual orientation or gender expression run counter to heteronormative assumptions in schools are more likely to have significant behavior problems compared to their peers. Stated differently, proponents of this narrative suggest that marginalized student groups are disproportionately more likely to be violent and disrespectful, and thus afford an increased need to be removed in order to protect the learning environment for other students. However, a growing body of research and practice contradicts these assumptions.

Myth #1: The increasing number of suspensions, expulsions, and arrests in schools is because student behavior in schools is growing worse. A stream of studies indicate that the largest contributor to the rise in use of exclusionary discipline is not a growth in seriously disruptive or violent behaviors, but in the use of these forms of discipline for more minor behaviors (APA, 2008). The use of exclusionary discipline, particularly for out-of-school suspension, is not restricted to serious or dangerous behavior, but rather appears to be most commonly used for more interactive day-to-day disruptions, especially defiance and non-compliance (Gregory & Weinstein, 2008; Skiba et al., 2011). Exclusionary disciplinary strategies have been used for lateness, dress code violations, and similar low-level offenses that do not pose a threat and could be handled differently and, in many schools, are dealt with through non-exclusionary means (Morgan, Salomon, Plotkin, & Cohen, 2014). Moreover, there remains no evidence that the racial disciplinary disparities can be explained by higher rates of disruptive behavior among Black and Latino students. If anything, available evidence suggests that, rather than being more disruptive, those students are punished more severely for similar infractions (Skiba et al., 2011).

Myth #2: Exclusionary discipline is necessary to maintain safety and order, and limiting its use will unleash chaos in schools. Experiences from schools and districts across the country suggest that reform of school disciplinary practice does not result in higher levels of disorder and disruptive behavior in schools. Rather, early findings suggest that school systems shifting away from suspensions toward non-punitive and non-exclusionary forms of discipline and behavior management have experienced higher ratings of safety and improved student attendance and achievement (Gonzalez, 2015). Indeed, rather than improving the learning climate for students who remain in the classroom, frequent use of student removal is associated with a less effective classroom and school climate (Steinberg et al., 2015) and lower academic achievement (Beck & Muschkin, 2012; Perry & Morris, 2014; Rocque, 2010).

The Concentrated Poverty Narrative

A second narrative posits that high rates of school exclusion and disciplinary disparities result from the systemic challenges faced by underresourced schools serving highly stressed neighborhoods that are characterized by concentrated poverty and weak school-community ties. Children in these neighborhoods come to school with wideranging behavioral and mental health needs that educators are underequipped to address, either because they lack sufficient training or access to appropriate services, or are overwhelmed by the sheer volume of demands. In the absence of alternative strategies and supports, educators with the best intentions have little choice but to rely on suspensions and expulsion to manage behavior in the classroom, even when the offending behaviors may be manifestations of students' underlying—and unmet—needs.

Implicit in this narrative are assumptions that disparities are (1) only a problem in schools and communities with challenging economic circumstances, and (2) that disinvestment in those schools and communities causes an over-reliance on punitive discipline. The implication is that educators in these more challenging contexts, characterized by a disproportionate number of students of color, students with disabilities, and other marginalized student groups, have virtually no other option but to remove students from the learning environment. Again, data and research evidence challenge the primacy of the poverty narrative.

Myth #3: Poverty, not race, is the main reason for disparities in discipline. Although poverty is a contributing factor to whether students are disciplined in school, numerous studies have shown that racial disparities in discipline remain significant even after controlling for poverty (see, for instance, Skiba, Michael, Nardo, & Peterson, 2002). That is, while the rate of disciplinary sanctions is often higher in schools serving larger numbers of low-income students in neighborhoods of concentrated poverty, disparities in discipline occur across a range of socioeconomic contexts. In fact, a number of studies have found that disparities in discipline are as great or greater in less segregated, well-resourced suburban districts (Skiba, Shure, & Williams, 2012).

Myth #4: Discipline disparities are caused primarily by conditions in under-resourced schools. While under-resourced and chaotic schools may rely on zero tolerance school discipline to impose order, evidence shows that one does not necessitate the other. National data have shown that, even in districts with challenging conditions, some schools make choices to reduce the use of exclusionary discipline (Losen, 2015). Moreover, differential use of exclusionary discipline is evident in urban schools as well: those schools do exhibit higher use of exclusionary discipline for *all* students and differentially higher rates for Black students (Mcloughlin & Noltemeyer, 2010).

The Cultural Deficiency Narrative

A third narrative sees exclusionary discipline as a necessary tool for establishing high behavioral expectations and fostering prosocial behavior and self-control among children who lack sufficient guidance in the home or suffer from adverse influences in their communities (Moscowitz, 2015; Updike, 2014). The "no-excuses" environment established by the frequent and consistent use of suspension, expulsion, and arrests is intended to communicate culturally mainstream norms for what is acceptable comportment in schools and to prevent "street" forms of behavior from flowing into and taking over the school environment (Mateu-Gelabert, 2007). The belief in the need for a tough line on misbehavior, which may be espoused by both educators of color and those who are White, assumes that student behavior is a function of deficiencies in the home rather than factors related to the school setting (Ferguson, 2000).

Implicit in this view is that disparities are not so much the result of White teachers punishing students of color while ignoring similar behavior from White students in the same class, but rather that conditions of racial isolation, economic deprivation, and family disruption create a situation wherein children of color and other marginalized students bring anti-social forms of behavior to school. That is, these children are viewed as disproportionately more likely to behave inappropriately in schools and, therefore, to require a tough disciplinary response. Here again, the predominance of research findings fail to support this view of children's cultural deficiencies as the predominant driver of disparities.

Myth #5: Discipline disparities result from the cultural norms that students bring to school, rather than decisions by educators and systems. In fact, research shows that educator perceptions of students *are* a strong driver in how they respond to student behavior and the likelihood of perceiving minor misbehavior as threatening and disruptive. For example, Ferguson's (2000) exploration of discipline disproportionality for Black boys documents how educators' beliefs in a "natural difference" and "criminal inclination" of Black males influenced their disciplinary decisions. And while White teachers may not be the only ones who struggle to manage behavior in the classroom, higher proportions of teachers of color are associated with lower rates of disproportionality in discipline (Mcloughlin & Noltemeyer, 2010; Roch, Pitts, & Navarro, 2010; Rocha & Hawes, 2009). These studies suggest that, whatever the reason, teachers of color may be more effective in preventing disturbance from escalating into office referral. As a result, while teachers of color may take a firm stance on behavior, they may not necessarily employ exclusionary discipline to do so.

Myth #6: Interpersonal bias on the part of educators toward students is the sole driver of disciplinary disparities. Although educators' perceptions play a role in disparities, it would be an error to ascribe fault solely to them. Disciplinary disparities are systemic and multi-determined by a host of policy and practice decisions and contextual variables (APA, 2008). For example, data indicate that Black, Latino, and Native American students are significantly more likely to have teachers with less experience and lower salaries than their colleagues in other schools, and to have less access to advanced courses and other supports, all of which can create conditions for disparities to occur (U.S. Department of Education, 2014).

The meta-narratives of safety and order, concentrated poverty, and cultural deficiency contribute to a deeply rooted and widespread belief that exclusionary discipline is both necessary and normal. Far from advancing equity, this line of reasoning asserts, emerging reforms are blaming educators for factors beyond their control, eroding their moral authority with students, and forcing them to endure unruly—even violent—behavior in their classrooms (Arum, 2005; Petrilli, 2014). Yet, an examination of the data suggests that these meta-narratives and associated claims of normativity are not well supported by evidence. While there is a considerable need to better understand the factors that contribute to—and might address—disproportionality in the use of exclusionary discipline, what we do know suggests that exclusionary discipline is neither effective nor necessary in schools. Suspensions, expulsions and arrests in schools have not been shown to improve student behavior, safety, or academic success, and their use contributes to disparities that further exacerbate inequities in schools.

ORGANIZATION OF THE BOOK

This volume consists of three sections, each organized around a central question. In Part I, Discipline Disparities, we explore the question of what we know about discipline disparities. Chap. 2 by Russell Skiba, Mariella Arredondo, Chrystal Gray, and M. Karega Rausch examines what has been learned in recent years from research on discipline disparities and the critical issues that remain unaddressed. The chapter reviews recent findings on the short- and long-term consequences of exclusionary discipline on students, analyzing the evidence on discipline disparities by race, gender, disability, and sexual orientation, and the factors that contribute to these disparities. It concludes with a discussion of what is known about interventions, noting that not all strategies for reducing the use of suspension, expulsion, and arrests are effective in closing disciplinary gaps.

In Chap. 3, Anne Gregory, James Bell, and Mica Pollack turn to the question of what educators can do, presenting a comprehensive framework for creating and implementing interventions to improve equity and fairness in the application of school discipline. The chapter offers strategies for improving teacher–student and student–student relationships, and building an equitable climate and culture in schools through a variety of methods, including structured decision-making processes and the training of administrators and police to reduce the influence of implicit stereotypes.

Part II of the book, Understanding and Addressing Disparities, presents the results of ten new studies on school discipline commissioned by the Disparities Collaborative, shedding further light on the question of what can be done to reduce disparities. Findings that extend our knowledge about disparities and describe new interventions to improve the climate for learning in schools and reduce discipline disparities are presented. Chapters in this section also show the importance of considering the additive and intersectional challenges faced by students coming from multiple marginalized backgrounds, when designing approaches to address disparities.

In Chap. 4, Paul Poteat, Jillian Scheer, and Eddie Chong examine evidence of sexual orientation-based discipline disparities in school suspension and juvenile justice system involvement among a sample of lesbian, gay, bisexual, and questioning (LGBQ) youth and heterosexual youth. The chapter proposes a conceptual model linking victimization and engagement in infractions to sexual orientation-based discipline disparities, and finds that disparities cannot be explained simply by greater levels of victimization and engagement in risky behavior by LGBQ students. Rather, LGBQ youth face greater odds of being disciplined when they engage in infractions, compared to their heterosexual peers.

Chapter 5 delves into the dynamics of teacher–student interactions. Jamilia Blake, Miner Marchbanks, Danielle Smith, and Allison Siebert examine how the racial and ethnic match between students and teachers, and particularly educators' stereotypes about and perceptions of Black students, affects the risk of exclusionary discipline. Examining data for over 900,000 students, this chapter presents evidence that the higher the student–teacher racial/ethnic congruence, the lower the risk of encountering school discipline. The chapter concludes with recommendations for schools and school systems to intensify efforts to recruit teachers of color, and provide professional development to improve educators' cultural competency and reduce their misperceptions regarding the behavior of students of color.

Turning to intervention strategies, Chap. 6 by Aishatu Yusuf, Angela Irvine, and James Bell discusses teacher perceptions of discipline reform in the Oakland Unified School district, in the context of one of the nation's most intensive programs for improving educational outcomes for African American males. The chapter describes a school-based professional development process through which teachers were helped to construct a decision-making tool to guide their decisions for disciplinary referrals. The chapter shares teachers' reflections on the reasons for and consequences of office referrals and suspensions, and alternative strategies they believe could be used to manage student behavior in the classroom.

In Chap. 7, Claudia Vincent, John Inglish, Erik Girvan, and Jeffrey Sprague explore an expanded form of the well-known school climate intervention, Positive Behavior Intervention and Supports (PBIS). The chapter examines a blended strategy of PBIS and restorative practices called School-wide Positive and Restorative Discipline (SWPRD), and reports findings from a pilot test in one high school showing greater use of restorative practices in classrooms; reduction of the impact of race/ethnicity and sexual orientation on student perceptions of fairness, bullying and harassment; and reduced number of office referrals and racial disparities.

In Chap. 8, Boyd Bellinger, Nicole Darcangelo, Stacey Horn, Erica Miners, and Sarah Schriber feature the voices of queer youth to illuminate the ways in which they are formally and informally sanctioned and pushed out of school. They investigate how these students' experiences with discipline relate to their identities and their experiences with bullying and harassment. The chapter highlights the need for schools to take a comprehensive and contextual approach to addressing the disparate impact of discipline on queer youth in order to uncover, understand, and respond to the ways in which institutional and inter-personal biases play out.

Chapter 9 reports on the potential of Restorative Practices (RP), a community-building conflict reduction strategy that is increasingly common in public schools, to narrow racial and gender disparities in school discipline. Drawing on a study of two high schools, Anne Gregory and Kathleen Clawson find that the strategy's potential to reduce discipline referrals for misconduct and defiance, and to narrow the gender and racial disparities in these actions, is related to the extent to which RP is consistently implemented in classrooms. Drawing on an analysis of 29 classrooms, the authors find that teachers who were perceived by students as consistently and frequently using RP issued fewer referrals for misconduct and defiance to male and female Black and Latino students, and had smaller gender and racial gaps in referrals.

In Chap. 10, Jennifer Chmieleswki, Kimberly Belmonte, Brett Stoudt, and Michelle Fine share findings from a multi-method collaborative research project examining disproportionate rates of discipline for lesbian, gay, bisexual, transgender and questioning (LGBTQ) students attending New York City public schools. The chapter presents evidence of how students are marginalized through overt discrimination in school discipline practices as well as by more subtle, yet insidious, policing of their gender and sexuality. It also presents data on the psychological impacts on LGBTQ youth as they negotiate school and community environments, and concludes with a set of intervention strategies identified by students participating in the research.

In Chap. 11, Kimberly Barsamian Kahn, Phillip Atiba Goff, and Jack Glaser follow the line of inquiry into policing practices and consider how masculinity threat (perceived threat to manhood) and implicit racial bias (unconscious racial prejudice) may affect authority figures' interactions with adolescents, in turn leading to disproportionate discipline outcomes for non-White adolescents. The chapter also presents the theory and development underpinning an emerging intervention program for authority figures, including school police officers, teachers, and school administrators, to reduce the impact of racial stereotypes and insecure masculinity on their decisions and actions.

In Chap. 12, Shannon Snapp and Stephen Russell share findings from focus groups with LGBTQ students and adult advocates and educators on school-based factors contributing to disparities. These factors include an overly punitive approach to discipline and security in schools, untrained and overextended school staff, explicit and implicit bias toward LGBTQ students, insufficient support in schools and implementation of policy and legislative reforms designed to help LGBTQ students, and lack of data on LGBTQ students' school experiences. The chapter presents recommendations, generated from interviewees, about what can be done to reduce disparities, including strategies for creating safe and affirming spaces for LGBTQ students and training school personnel to respond with sensitivity to LGBTQ issues.

The last chapter in this section, by Marieka Schotland, Harriet MacLean, Karen Junker, and Jean Finney, provides a window into one school's journey from punitive to restorative discipline. The chapter describes the reform strategy used at Davidson Middle School in California, detailing a multi-faceted approach of academic de-tracking, parent involvement, restorative circles, and anti-bullying and peer courts programs. The chapter presents findings from an analysis of observational and survey data and administrative records showing that the program was well integrated into the school, and associated with declines in the number of suspensions and disparities for Latino students in the school.

Part III of the book, Conclusions and Implications, considers the implications for education reform more broadly, reflecting on the significance of discipline disparities to educational equity. Daniel Losen and Leticia Smith-Evans Haynes place recent findings within a wider framework of federal and state policy, and offer a set of recommendations, drawn from the policy deliberations of the Collaborative, for reform at the district, state, and federal level. Finally, the concluding chapter by Russell Skiba summarizes the themes that cut across the chapters in the book, and offers recommendations for intervention, research, and policy to address the ongoing and critical problem of discipline disparities.

CONCLUSION

Today, many school leaders view exclusionary discipline as a normal and necessary part of what they do, often without awareness of the consequences. But this form of discipline is not educationally sound, does not make schools safer, and is not fairly distributed across students. While extreme incidents of mistreatment such as Shakara's more easily capture media attention, the stark differences in day-to-day school disciplinary treatment and outcomes for students of color, students with disabilities, and students who identify as LGBT or gender-non-conforming, are also indicators of a larger pattern of inequality and injustice that is just as worthy of national attention.

We cannot close the gaps in educational opportunity and achievement unless we also close the discipline gap. Working to better understand and eliminate racial, gendered, and sexuality-related disparities can help produce stronger and safer schools and communities. It is the goal of this book, and of the Discipline Disparities Collaborative in general, that, by deepening our understanding of such disparities and illuminating paths toward interventions to reduce them, we substantially contribute to policy and practice reform that will give our most marginalized children the greatest chance of success in school and in life.

NOTE

1. Shakara has been identified in media reports only by her first name.

REFERENCES

American Psychological Association Zero Tolerance Task Force. (2008). Are zero tolerance policies effective in the schools? An evidentiary review and recommendations. *American Psychologist, 63,* 852–862. doi:10.1037/0003-066X. 63.9.852

Arcia, E. (2006). Achievement and enrollment status of suspended students. *Education and Urban Society, 38,* 359–369.

Arum, R. (2005). *Judging school discipline. The crisis of moral authority.* Cambridge, MA: Harvard University Press.

Beck, A. N., & Muschkin, C. (2012). The enduring impact of race: Understanding disparities in student disciplinary infraction and achievement. *Sociological Perspectives, 55*(4), 637–662.

Bellware, K. (2015, October 28). Spring Valley School officer from violent arrest video fired. *Huffington Post.* Retrieved from http://www.huffingtonpost. com/entry/ben-fields-fired-spring-valley-high-school_5630dbede4b0c66bae 5a454f

Blad, E. (2014, September 23). Discipline debates turn to broad terms like 'defiance.' *Education Week.* Retrieved from http://www.edweek.org/ew/ articles/2014/09/24/05defiance.h34.html

Fabelo, A., Thompson, M. D., Plotkin, M., Carmichael, D., Marchbanks, M. P., & Booth, E. A. (2011). *Breaking schools' rules: A statewide study of how school discipline relates to students' success and juvenile justice involvement.* New York: Council of State Governments Justice Center, and College Station, TX: A&M University: Public Policy Research Institute. Retrieved from http://knowledgecenter.csg.org/kc/system/files/Breaking_School_Rules.pdf

Ferguson, A. (2000). *Bad boys: Public schools in the making of Black masculinity.* Ann Arbor, MI: University of Michigan Press.

Ferris, S. (2015, October 27). *Shocking South Carolina video no isolated case.* Center for Public Integrity. Retrieved from http://www.publicintegrity.org/2015/10/27/18687/shocking-south-carolina-video-no-isolated-case

Gonzalez, T. (2015). Socializing schools: Addressing racial disparities in discipline through restorative justice. In D. J. Losen (Ed.), *Closing the school discipline gap: Equitable remedies for excessive exclusion* (pp. 151–165). New York: Teachers College Press.

Gregory, A., & Weinstein, S. R. (2008). The discipline gap and African Americans: Defiance or cooperation in the high school classroom. *Journal of School Psychology, 46,* 455–475.

Jarvie, J. (2015, October 29). Girl thrown from desk didn't obey because the punishment was unfair, attorney says. *LA Times.* Retrieved from http://www.latimes.com/nation/la-na-girl-thrown-punishment-unfair-20151029-story.html

Jones, B. (2013, August 11). Back to school means big changes, challenges at LAUSD. *Los Angeles Daily News.* Retrieved January 1, 2014, from http://www.dailynews.com/20130811/back-to-school-means-big-changes-challenges-at-lausd

Kelling, G. L., & Wilson, J. Q. (1982, March). Broken windows: The police and neighborhood safety. *The Atlantic.* Retrieved from http://www.theatlantic.com/magazine/archive/1982/03/broken-windows/304465/

Kupchik, A., & Catlaw, T. J. (2013, January). *Discipline and participation: The long-term effects of suspension and school security on the political and civic engagement of youth.* Paper presented at the Closing the School Discipline Gap: Research to Practice conference, Washington, DC.

Losen, D. J. (2015). *Closing the school discipline gap: Equitable remedies for excessive exclusion.* New York: Teachers College Press.

Love, D. (2015, October 31). Her name is Shakara: Spring Valley High victim refused to comply with unfair punishment, as 100 students stage walkout for fired deputy. *Atlanta Blackstar.* Retrieved from https://atlantablackstar.com/2015/10/31/her-name-is-shakara-spring-valley-high-victim-refused-to-comply-with-unfair-punishment-as-100-students-stage-walkout-for-fired-deputy/

MacDonald, H. (2012, Summer). Undisciplined: The Obama administration undermines classroom order in pursuit of phantom racism. *City Journal.* Retrieved from http://www.city-journal.org/2012/22_3_school-discipline.html

Marcus, P. (2012, September 10). New law aims to curb "school to jail track". *The Colorado Statesman.* Retrieved from http://coloradostatesman.com/content/993726-new-law-aims-curb-%3Fschool-jail-track%3F

Mateu-Gelabert, P. (2007). Street codes in high school: School as an educational deterrent. *City and Community, 6*(3), 173–191. doi:10.1111/j.1540-6040.2007.00212.x.

Mcloughlin, C., & Noltemeyer, A. (2010). Research into factors contributing to discipline use and disproportionality in major urban schools. *Current Issues in Education, 13*(2). Phoenix, AZ: Mary Lou Fulton Teachers College, Arizona State University.

Mediratta, K. (2012). Grassroots organizing and the school-to-prison pipeline: The emerging national movement to roll back zero tolerance discipline policies in U.S. public schools. In S. Bahena, N. Cooc, R. Currie-Rubin, P. Kuttner, & M. Ng (Eds.), *Disrupting the school-to-prison pipeline* (pp. 211–236). Cambridge, MA: Harvard Education Review.

Morgan, E., Salomon, N., Plotkin, M., & Cohen, R. (2014). *The school discipline consensus report: Strategies from the field to keep students engaged in school and out of the juvenile justice system*. New York: The Council of State Governments Justice Center. Retrieved from https://csgjusticecenter.org/wp-content/uploads/2014/06/The_School_Discipline_Consensus_Report.pdf

Moscowitz, E. (2015, April 1). Turning schools into fight clubs. *Wall Street Journal*. Retrieved from http://www.wsj.com/articles/eva-moskowitz-turning-schools-into-fight-clubs-1427930575

Perry, B. L., & Morris, E. W. (2014). Suspending progress: Collateral consequences of exclusionary punishment in public schools. *American Sociological Review, 79*(6), 1067–1087. doi:10.1177/0003122414556308.

Petrilli, M. (2014). *On school discipline, let's not repeat all our old mistakes*. Washington, DC: Thomas Fordham Institute. Retrieved from http://edexcellence.net/articles/on-school-discipline-let%E2%80%99s-not-repeat-all-our-old-mistakes

Public Counsel. (2014, September 27). *California enacts first-in-the-nation law to eliminate student suspensions for minor misbehavior* [Press release]. Retrieved from http://www.publiccounsel.org/press_releases?id=0088

Roch, C. H., Pitts, D. W., & Navarro, I. (2010). Representative bureaucracy and policy tools: Ethnicity, student discipline, and representation in public schools. *Administration & Society, 42*(1), 38–65.

Rocha, R. R., & Hawes, D. P. (2009). Racial diversity, representative bureaucracy, and equity in multiracial school districts. *Social Science Quarterly, 90*(2), 326–344. doi:10.1111/j.1540-6237.2009.00620.x.

Rocque, M. (2010). Office discipline and student behaviors: Does race matter? *American Journal of Education, 116*(4), 557–581.

Savali, K. W. (2015). Assaulted by white cop: Do we matter yet? *The Root*. Retrieved from http://www.theroot.com/articles/news/2015/10/assault_at_spring_valley_high_school_black_girl_choked_dragged_by_white.html

Shollenberger, T. L. (2015). Racial disparities in school suspension and subsequent outcomes: Evidence from the National Longitudinal Survey of Youth

1997. In D. J. Losen (Ed.), *Closing the school discipline gap: Equitable remedies for excessive exclusion* (pp. 31–43). New York: Teachers College Press.

Skiba, R. J., Horner, R. H., Chung, C. G., Rausch, M. K., May, S. L., & Tobin, T. (2011). Race is not neutral: A national investigation of African American and Latino disproportionality in school discipline. *School Psychology Review, 40*, 85–107.

Skiba, R. J., & Knesting, K. (2001). Zero tolerance, zero evidence: An analysis of school disciplinary practice. In R. J. Skiba & G. G. Noam (Eds.), *New directions for youth development (no. 92: Zero tolerance: Can suspension and expulsion keep schools safe?)* (pp. 17–43). San Francisco: Jossey-Bass.

Skiba, R. J., Michael, R. S., Nardo, A. C., & Peterson, R. (2002). The color of discipline: Sources of racial and gender disproportionality in school punishment. *Urban Review, 34*, 317–342. doi:10.1023/A:1021320817372.

Skiba, R. J., Shure, L., & Williams, N. (2012). Racial and ethnic disproportionality in suspension and expulsion. In A. L. Noltemeyer & C. S. Mcloughlin (Eds.), *Disproportionality in education and special education* (pp. 89–118). Springfield, IL: Charles C. Thomas Publisher, Ltd.

St. George, D. (2014, January 28). Maryland school board approves new discipline regulations. *The Washington Post.* Retrieved from https://www.washingtonpost.com/local/education/maryland-approves-new-school-discipline-regulations/2014/01/28/c11ad4de-8385-11e3-bbe5-6a2a3141e3a9_story.html

Steinberg, M. P., Allensworth, E., & Johnson, D. W. (2015). What conditions jeopardize and support safety in urban schools? The influence of community characteristics, school composition and school organizational practices on student and teacher reports of safety in Chicago. In D. J. Losen (Ed.), *Closing the school discipline gap: Equitable remedies for excessive exclusion* (pp. 118–131). New York: Teachers College Press.

Suh, S., & Suh, J. (2007). Risk factors and levels of risk for high school dropouts. *Professional School Counseling, 10*(3), 297–306.

Tobin, T., Sugai, G., & Colvin, G. (1996). Patterns in middle school discipline records. *Journal of Emotional and Behavioral Disorders, 4*, 82–94.

U.S. Department of Education, Office of Civil Rights. (2014, March 21). *Civil rights data collection data snapshot: School discipline.* Retrieved from https://www2.ed.gov/about/offices/list/ocr/docs/crdc-discipline-snapshot.pdf

Updike, N. (Producer). (2014). Is this working? [Radio series episode]. In J. Snyder (Senior Producer), *This American life.* Chicago: WBEZ. Retrieved from http://www.thisamericanlife.org/radio-archives/episode/538/transcript

Wright, J. P., Morgan, M. A., Coyne, M. A., Beaver, K. M., & Barnes, J. C. (2014). Prior problem behavior accounts for the racial gap in school suspensions. *Journal of Criminal Justice, 42*, 257–266.

What Do We Know About Discipline Disparities? New and Emerging Research

Russell J. Skiba, Mariella I. Arredondo, Chrystal Gray, and M. Karega Rausch

Since first identified by the Children's Defense Fund (1975) 40 years ago, disproportionality in punishment for African American students has been consistently documented in a range of exclusionary discipline practices, including office disciplinary referrals, suspensions, expulsions, school arrests, and corporal punishment (American Psychological Association, 2008; Bradshaw, Mitchell, O'Brennan, & Leaf, 2010; Eitle & Eitle, 2004; Gregory & Weinstein, 2008; Hinojosa, 2008; Rocque, 2010; Theriot, 2009). Although expanding research has led to a more sophisticated understanding of the extent and causes of disciplinary disparities for African American students, the research base has been more limited concerning the extent of, and reasons for, disparities for other student groups, such as Hispanic/ Latino and Native American students, girls, students with disabilities, and LGBT students. An even more significant gap has been a lack of research attention to the identification of strategies, interventions, or programs to reduce or eliminate disparities in discipline. This chapter, based on the New

R.J. Skiba (✉)• M.I. Arredondo • C. Gray • M.K. Rausch
The Equity Project, Indiana University, Bloomington, IN, USA

© The Author(s) 2016
R.J. Skiba et al. (eds.), *Inequality in School Discipline*,
DOI 10.1057/978-1-137-51257-4_2

Research briefing paper of the Discipline Disparities Research-to-Practice Collaborative series (Skiba, Arredondo, & Rausch, 2014), describes findings from new research, identifies remaining gaps in the literature, and offers recommendations for future research on discipline disparities.

We organize the chapter into two sections:

1. *What Have We Learned? Key New Research Findings* describes research by leading scholars from across the nation on disproportionality in school discipline.
2. *Future Research Needs.* Despite considerable knowledge generated in recent years, significant gaps remain, especially in identifying and evaluating intervention strategies that reduce inequity in discipline for all students.

WHAT HAVE WE LEARNED? KEY NEW RESEARCH FINDINGS

Who Is at Risk?

Students of color, especially Black males, are at higher risk for office referrals, suspension, and expulsion. African American students continue to be more likely than White students to be disciplined and excluded from school. The latest data from the US Department of Education Office for Civil Rights (US DoE, 2014a) shows that Black students are nearly 3.5 times more likely than White students to receive out-of-school suspension (OSS), and that such disparities begin as early as pre-school. They are suspended for longer periods of time (Balfanz, Byrnes, & Fox, 2015), and punished more harshly than White students for the same offenses (Anyon et al., 2014).

In particular, Black males are significantly more likely than other groups to be excluded from school for disciplinary reasons after receiving an office discipline referral. Black males are significantly more likely to be removed from the classroom for office disciplinary referrals, even after controlling for individual, classroom, or school factors (Bradshaw et al., 2010; Skiba et al., 2011; Wallace, Goodkind, Wallace, & Bachman, 2008). Once removed from the classroom, Black males are 3.3 times more likely to be suspended or expelled (Wallace et al., 2008). Nationally, nearly one-third of Black male high school and middle school students receive a suspension in a given year, while only one in ten of their White male peers are suspended (Cornell, Shin, Ciolfi, & Sancken, 2013). Black males are also more likely to be suspended earlier in their school career and experience harsher punishments than other youth (Shollenberger, 2015).

Disproportionality in discipline extends to other racial/ethnic groups as well. Examining Office Disciplinary Referrals (ODRs) in two Southwestern school districts, Whitford and Levine-Donnerstein (2014) found that American Indian students were 1.92 times more likely to receive ODRs than White students. Findings of disproportionality have been somewhat inconsistent for Hispanic/Latino students (see e.g., Peguero & Shekarkhar, 2011). Recent research, however, has begun to identify patterns by school level, with little or no disproportionality for Latinos at the elementary level, but a significantly higher likelihood of suspension and expulsion at the middle and high school level (Losen & Gillespie, 2012; Skiba et al., 2011).

Other groups are at higher risk as well. Students with disabilities are also at a high risk for disproportionate discipline. Even after controlling for poverty, students with disabilities are suspended almost twice as frequently as their non-disabled peers (Losen & Gillespie, 2012) and for longer periods of time (Balfanz et al., 2015). Disability and race intersect to increase a student's risk of exclusion. Across the nation, 25% of Black students with disabilities were suspended out-of-school at least once in 2009–2010, a rate higher than every other racial/ethnic group and 16% higher than White students with a disability (Losen & Gillespie, 2012). Native American students with disabilities in Utah were found to be 11 times more likely than White students to be expelled (Walsh, 2015).

Gender intersects with race to increase the risk of school exclusion. Males are more likely to be suspended than females (Anyon et al., 2014; Toldson, McGee, & Lemmons, 2015), and Black males are consistently the most at risk for exclusionary discipline and arrest (Darensbourg, Perez, & Blake, 2010). Yet, Black girls are also at a high risk of suspension and expulsion. Black females have been found to be suspended out of school at rates significantly higher than other females, and sometimes higher than White and Hispanic/Latino males (Finn & Servoss, 2015; Toldson et al., 2015).

Finally, Lesbian, Gay, Bisexual, and Transgender (LGBT) students and students who are gender nonconforming may also experience exclusionary discipline, hostile school climates, and contact with the juvenile justice system more often than their peers. In a nationally representative sample of 7th through 12th grade students, adolescents reporting same-sex attraction had significantly higher odds of being expelled from school, even after controlling for self-reported rates of misbehavior, age, gender, race, and socioeconomic status (Himmelstein & Bruckner, 2011). Findings from a mixed-methods study documenting the experiences of discipline for LGBT and gender-nonconforming youth indicate that they experience high rates of exclusionary discipline, disciplinary consequences for violating gender norm policies, and a hostile school climate that provokes fighting to protect oneself against bullying (Snapp, Burdge, Licona, Moody, & Russell, 2015).

What Causes Disciplinary Disparity?

Racial/ethnic differences in the use of suspension and expulsion are not due to poverty or different rates of misbehavior. A common explanation of inequity in discipline is that students of color and other marginalized groups who face severe disadvantages due to poverty, family circumstances, and/ or the lack of support are assumed to engage in student behavior that runs counter to school norms, resulting in higher rates or severity of disruptive behavior at school, and hence differential exposure to discipline. Although factors associated with poverty do make a contribution to the likelihood of discipline (see Hinojosa, 2008), poverty has not been found to be the sole or even primary cause of racial disparities in discipline. Multivariate studies controlling for socioeconomic status have consistently found that Black–White differences in out-of-school suspension persist regardless of controls for poverty (Anyon et al., 2014; Balfanz et al., 2015; Skiba et al., 2011; Wallace et al., 2008); that is, while Black students in the most extreme poverty situations are more likely than their White peers to be suspended, Black students are also over-represented in suspension across the rest of the economic spectrum as well. Thus, race makes a contribution to Black disproportionality in discipline that is *independent of poverty.*

Nor is there evidence that students of color engage in more severe or higher rates of disruption that could justify higher rates of punishment. Racial/ethnic disparities in school discipline tend to be most commonly found, not in more serious or safety-threatening behaviors, but rather in more subjective infractions, such as defiance or disrespect, where interpretation rather than objective criteria are at play (Gregory & Weinstein, 2008; Skiba, Michael, Nardo, & Peterson, 2002). Even after controlling for behavioral ratings of misbehavior, classroom teachers still refer a higher rate of students of color to the office (Bradshaw et al., 2010). Survey data from 8th and 10th grade students indicate that Black males reported receiving more suspensions than any other group, despite a similar or lower use of drugs, alcohol, and weapons in school compared to other students (Toldson et al., 2015). Thus, while factors associated with economic inequality certainly play a role in understanding school discipline, neither socioeconomic status nor differential rates of misbehavior are sufficient to explain large and consistent racial/ethnic discipline gaps in schools.

School practices contribute to disparities. Educator perspectives and practices have consistently emerged as significant predictors of rates of referral and disproportionality in suspension. In a series of multilevel analyses, Skiba and colleagues (2014) found that while the type of infraction, student characteristics, and school characteristics predicted the likelihood of out-of-school suspension, school characteristics such as principal perspective on discipline were stronger predictors of racial discipline disparities than type of behavior or student characteristics, suggesting that efforts to reduce disciplinary disparity may be more effective if focused on altering school factors. A study among urban schools in Chicago found that students felt less safe in schools with high suspension rates; in contrast, strong relationships among students, teachers, parents, and administrators were associated with lower suspension rates and a more positive sense of safety and school climate (Steinberg, Allensworth, & Johnson, 2015).

Disparities in discipline have consistently been found to begin at the classroom level (Gregory, Skiba, & Noguera, 2010) and to be related to differences in teachers' classroom management. In a nationally representative sample of 364 elementary and secondary schools, Skiba et al. (2011) found that Black students are twice as likely to receive office disciplinary referrals at the elementary level and up to four times as likely in middle school.

Differential processing at the administrative level also makes a contribution to racial and ethnic disparities in suspension and expulsion. Drawing from a national sample, Skiba et al. (2011) reported that, although minor infractions in general receive less serious consequences, Black and Latino students were more likely than White students to receive suspension and/or expulsion for the same. A number of studies have reported that Black students commonly receive more severe consequences for the same or similar infraction (Finn & Servoss, 2015; Nicholson-Crotty, Birchmeier, & Valentine, 2009; Toldson et al., 2015).

The role of implicit bias and stereotype. Finally, the data has begun to suggest that implicit bias and stereotypes may play a role in discipline disparities. As Kahn, Goff, and Glaser note (this volume), research has shown that implicit racial bias is widespread in our society; evidence of its possible role in school discipline is beginning to emerge. In a simulation study,

Okonofua and Eberhardt (2015) presented teachers with descriptions of behavioral incidents in which only the name was changed between names more associated with either White or African American students. For the first infraction, there were few differences in the ways teachers treated students based on their presumed racial identity. For a second infraction, however, teachers were more troubled, more likely to regard the incident as part of a pattern, and more likely to recommend suspension in cases associated with African American rather than White names. Such results suggest the importance of further research on the role of stereotypes in discipline, and, in particular, how those stereotypes might play themselves out in classroom interactions that lead to suspension and expulsion.

Consequences of Discipline Disparities

Suspension is often the first step in a chain of events leading to negative short- and long-term consequences, including academic disengagement, decreased academic achievement, and dropping out of school. Given that the opportunity to learn is among the strongest predictors of academic achievement (Brophy, 1988; Greenwood, Horton, & Utley, 2002), it is not surprising that removing students from school for disciplinary reasons is associated with negative academic outcomes. In a longitudinal study in a metropolitan school district, Perry and Morris (2014) found that the pervasive threat of punishment in schools with high rates of out-of-school suspension (OSS) hinders academic achievement, even for non-suspended students. In a longitudinal study across the state of Florida, 73% of students suspended in 9th grade failed subsequent academic courses, compared to 36% of non-suspended students (Balfanz et al., 2015). Examining a national dataset, Flannery, Frank, and Kato (2012) found that increased exposure to OSS has a strong effect on later occurrences of truancy over time. Eventually, this accumulation of loss of educational opportunity places students at increased risk of dropout: Balfanz et al. (2015) found that being suspended even once in 9th grade is associated with a 20% increase in dropping out, even after controlling for demographics, attendance, and course performance.

Suspension is a risk factor for future contact with the justice system. Shollenberger (2015) found that that more than one-third (32%) of males suspended for ten or more days by age 12 had been confined in a correctional facility by the time they were in their late twenties. Notably, student reports of engagement in delinquency or crime occurred only after the first time they were suspended from school. Fabelo et al. (2011) reported that suspension and expulsion for a discretionary school violation nearly tripled a student's likelihood of juvenile justice involvement within the subsequent year. Examining the association between exclusionary discipline and truancy with arrest, Monahan, VanDerhei, Bechtold, & Cauffman (2014) found that the likelihood of arrest increased in the same month that a suspension or expulsion occurred, particularly among youth who did not have a history of misbehavior and did not associate with delinquent peers.

The disproportionate confinement of African American males in secure juvenile detention facilities mirrors their experience with school discipline disparities. In an examination of school discipline and juvenile justice for Black and White youth aged 10–17 in 53 counties in Missouri, Nicholson-Crotty et al. (2009) reported racial disproportionality in OSS to be a strong predictor of similar levels of racial disparity in juvenile court referrals, even when controlling for levels of delinquent behavior, poverty, and other demographic variables.

The School-to-Prison Pipeline. The data on the significant negative impacts of suspension and expulsion, especially for marginalized groups, provides clear and disturbing evidence that the process that has been termed the *school-to-prison pipeline* (see Mediratta, 2012) is all too real. Exclusion from school through suspension and expulsion reduces school engagement and school achievement, increasing the chances of truancy and school dropout. In turn, these outcomes add to the risk of involvement in the juvenile justice system. At every step in the pipeline, students of color, students with disabilities, and, it is beginning to appear, LGBT and gender nonconforming students are at increased risk for those negative outcomes. There are indeed personal and community factors, such as poverty, single-parent households, low-achievement, or repeat offending that increase a student's risk of school failure, dropout or delinquency. But the research evidence makes clear that out-of-school suspension and expulsion are *in and of themselves* risk factors for a host of negative school and life outcomes, regardless of levels of poverty, achievement, or previous behavioral history (Skiba, Arredondo, & Williams, 2014).

SOLUTIONS AND INTERVENTIONS

Emerging data indicate that schools and school systems have the power to change their rates of exclusion. Alternative discipline approaches have been implemented in school districts across the country, helping reduce suspension and expulsion, and improve school safety, climate, and academic outcomes. While the specific effects on disciplinary disproportionality are still emerging, such strategies, organized below by classroom and school intervention, address important components of school climate and discipline that may lead to disparity reduction.

Classroom Instruction and Behavior Supports

Relationship-building. Interventions that focus on strengthening teacher–student relationships can lead to a reduction in the use of exclusionary discipline, particularly for African American students. My Teaching Partner (MTP) is a professional development program that involves teachers who have been successful in building positive relationships in their classroom as mentors to others (Allen, Pianta, Gregory, Mikami, & Lun, 2011). In a randomized controlled trial, Gregory, Allen, Mikami, Hafen, and Pianta (2015) found that MTP reduced teachers' reliance on exclusionary discipline with all of their students, and that the effect was most pronounced for African American students.

Relationships are also a central component of Restorative Practices (RP)—informal and formal processes implemented throughout the school building that aim to proactively build relationships and a sense of community (preventing conflict), and to repair harm after wrongdoing has occurred (see Gregory and Clawson, Vincent and colleagues, and Schotland and colleagues, this volume). Studying implementation of RP in the Denver Public Schools, Gonzalez (2015) reported that suspension rates were reduced by nearly 47% for all racial and ethnic groups across the district: In particular, African American suspension rates dropped from 17.6 to 10.4%, and Hispanic/Latino rates dropped from 10.18 to 4.74%. Examination of teacher and student reports of RP in two high schools found that individual teachers with better RP implementation tended to have less disproportionality in discipline (Gregory, Clawson, Davis, & Gerewitz, 2015).

Social emotional instruction. Social and emotional learning (SEL) approaches building social and emotional skills through the inculcation of knowledge, attitudes, and skills to recognize and manage emotions, develop empathy for others, establish positive relationships, make responsible decisions, and handle challenging situations constructively (CASEL, 2015). The implementation of SEL in Cleveland, with a student population comprising 81% African American and Latino students, yielded improved student attendance district-wide, a decline in negative behavioral incidents per school by almost 50%, and a nearly 60% district-wide reduction in use of out-of-school suspension, although disciplinary disparities remained (Osher, Poirier, Jarjoura, Brown, & Kendziora, 2015). Again, more explicit attention to race, culture, and difference in the implementation of SEL may be necessary in order to reduce racial/ethnic disparities.

Culturally responsive classroom approaches. Elements of culturally responsive approaches to classroom management and behavior supports have been identified in case studies and ethnographic observation studies (see Chelowa, Goodman, West-Olatunji, & Amatea, 2014; Cramer & Bennett, 2015; Milner & Tenore, 2010; Monroe & Obidah, 2004), including (1) teacher communication of awareness of issues of race and respect for students' perspectives and cultural heritage; (2) classrooms characterized by high expectations, strong interpersonal support, and a sense of family and community; (3) instruction that is culturally relevant; and (4) high levels of meaningful parental engagement. While these studies have demonstrated the power of culturally responsive approaches for improving classroom climate and student well-being, much more research is needed in order to examine how specific elements of culturally responsive pedagogy and behavior supports affect student outcomes.

School-Level Interventions

Positive Behavior Interventions and Supports. The Positive Behavior Interventions and Supports (PBIS) framework has been found to create positive reductions in the use of exclusionary discipline, although the evidence suggests that specific attention to issues of race, culture, and difference may be necessary if PBIS is to reduce disciplinary disparities. A five-year randomized controlled study of PBIS implementation in 35 middle schools (Vincent, Sprague, CHiXapkaid, Tobin, & Gau, 2015) showed significant improvement in the implementation of more positive disciplinary environments in treatment vs. control schools. Yet, effects on disciplinary disparities were mixed, with reductions in disciplinary exclusion rates for Hispanic/Latino and Native American/Alaska Native students, but not for African American students. Such results have led to proposals for revised PBIS models that include cultural considerations (Sprague, Vincent, Tobin, & CHiXapkaid, 2013), incorporating local cultural values and norms that can better address the specific needs of the school and community population (McIntosh, Moniz, Craft, Golby, & Steinwand-Deschambeault, 2014). Examining school-wide Positive Behavior Interventions and Supports practices in schools in Oregon with low suspension rates for Native Americans, Vincent et al. (2015) found that schools that imbued culturally responsive practices aligned with American Indian culture into a PBIS framework were successful in reducing inequities in discipline practices.

Threat assessment. Systematic approaches to threat assessment may also hold promise for reducing the use of exclusion and affecting discipline disparities. The Virginia Threat Assessment Guidelines (Cornell & Sheras, 2006) is a school-based process developed to help school administrators, mental health staff, and law enforcement officers assess and respond to threat incidents involving students in K-12 and prevent student violence across schools. Use of the Threat Assessment Guidelines in the state of Virginia was associated with reductions in both long-term suspensions and short-term suspensions that were greater than in schools not using the Guidelines (Cornell & Lovegrove, 2015). Furthermore, the intervention was associated with reductions in suspensions for all racial groups, as well as a reduction in disproportionality between Black and White males, even after controlling for school size and poverty (Cornell et al., 2013).

FUTURE RESEARCH NEEDS

Recent research has extended what we know about disparities in school discipline. Even with these advances, however, significant gaps remain, particularly in our knowledge of the extent of, and reasons for, such disparities and how schools and school systems should address them.

Building Knowledge on the Extent of and Reasons for Disparities

While much is known about discipline disparities and African American students, the knowledge base for other student groups and the impact of school security technology on disparities is not nearly as robust. A number of key questions remain, some addressed by the Discipline Disparities Collaborative and the research contained in this volume, some still relatively unexamined:

What are the patterns of, and reasons for, exclusionary discipline for students who are LGBT, gender nonconforming, American Indian, female, and English language learning? Where do race/ethnicity, gender, disability, and sexual orientation intersect? In addition to confirming the substantial risk of discipline for African American males, the number of other groups found to be at risk for differential discipline is striking. A closer examination of disproportionality for these groups and the way in which students' intersecting identities increase their risk for exclusion and punishment is an important direction for future research.

What is the impact of increased law enforcement and security technology in schools on disciplinary disparities? Despite dramatic increases in the presence of law enforcement and school security technology in recent years (Kupchik & Ward, 2013), there are insufficient research studies of the effectiveness of these measures on school discipline and school safety, and their differential use and impact by race, disability, or sexual orientation. As many states and schools consider increasing the use of such methods (Theriot, 2009), an understanding of the conditions under which security technology and increased police presence enhance school security, or may contribute to disciplinary disparities, is critical.

Building Knowledge of Effective Interventions and Systems Change

The development of evidence-based interventions, and especially the conditions under which such interventions are most effective, is arguably the most important contribution that research can make in guiding practice toward replacing ineffective disciplinary strategies with more evidence-based alternatives. Key questions for future research include the following:

What school factors and interventions show the most promise for reducing disparities? Research on effective interventions for reducing exclusionary discipline is growing, but research on approaches that specifically focus on reducing disparities is still emerging. Identifying evidence-based and practical disparity-reducing interventions, such as those explored in five chapters in this volume, is a critical need as pressure increases for schools to address high rates of disciplinary removal (IDEA, 2004; US DoE, 2014b).

Disparities in school suspension and expulsion appear to begin with differential rates of office referrals from teachers (Gregory & Weinstein, 2008; Skiba et al., 2011), but the micro-level processes that cause this are not well-understood. Well-designed classroom observational studies that identify and describe classroom practices and processes that contribute to disciplinary disparities will provide greater guidance for classroom-based intervention. In particular, further research is needed on the extent to which implicit bias may contribute to disparities in office referrals, suspension, or expulsion (see e.g., Pollock, 2009; Kahn & colleagues, this volume).

Interventions designed to reduce use of exclusionary discipline overall do not necessarily also reduce disparities (Vincent et al., 2015). Gregory, Bell, and Pollock (this volume) identify equity-based principles of conflict prevention and intervention. Guidance is needed on how educators can effectively talk about race/ethnicity, difference, and power in a way that produces positive change rather than reinforces stereotypes (see Buehler, 2012; Carter, Skiba, Arredondo, & Pollock, 2014; Howard, 2010; Pollock, 2009).

How do school-based practitioners respond to state, district, and school disciplinary policy changes? A growing number of states and school districts have instituted policy changes to reduce the use of exclusionary discipline for minor misbehaviors (see Losen and Smith-Evans Haynes, this volume). Research is needed on the extent to which these and other policy changes impact disproportionality in discipline at the local level, and to better understand how those policies influence the decisions, behaviors, and perspectives of local decision makers. In particular, research is needed describing connections between under-resourced schools and disproportionality, and how new and/or existing resources—such as funding allocations, human capital development and distribution systems, and federal, state, and local accountability and support systems—might be best utilized to create greater equity.

CONCLUSION

Our understanding of the extent of disparities in school discipline has significantly advanced over the past 40 years, and recent research has further expanded our understanding of the nuances of disciplinary disparities. Yet, significant gaps remain, including a robust description of the nature of disparities for a number of student groups.

Developing research-validated strategies and interventions that can reduce or eliminate disciplinary gaps is an urgent priority and perhaps the most important and challenging need in the field. As the consequences of ineffective exclusionary practices, and the impact of those practices on marginalized groups, become increasingly evident, pressure will increase to replace ineffective practices and reduce disciplinary disparities. Given an increasing understanding of the severe consequences on students' lives of disproportionate rates of discipline, it is critical that future research seeks to identify effective research-based strategies that can guide practitioners as they seek to implement more effective and equitable school discipline practices.

REFERENCES

Allen, J. P., Pianta, R. C., Gregory, A., Mikami, A. Y., & Lun, J. (2011). An interaction-based approach to enhancing secondary school instruction and student achievement. *Science, 333*(6045), 1034–1037. doi:10.1126/science. 1207998.

American Psychological Association Zero Tolerance Task Force (2008). Are zero tolerance policies effective in the schools? An evidentiary review and recommendations. *American Psychologist, 63*, 852–862. doi:10.1037/0003-066X.63.9.852.

Anyon, Y., Jenson, J. M., Altschul, I., Farrar, J., McQueen, J., Greer, E., Simmons, J. (2014). The persistent effect of race and the promise of alternatives to suspension in school discipline outcomes. *Children and Youth Services Review, 44*, 379–386.

Balfanz, R., Byrnes, V., & Fox, J. (2015). Sent home and put off-track: The antecedents, disproportionalities, and consequences of being suspended in the 9th grade. In D. J. Losen (Ed.), *Closing the school discipline gap: Equitable remedies for excessive exclusion* (pp. 17–30). New York: Teachers College Press.

Bradshaw, C. P., Mitchell, M. M., O'Brennan, L. M., & Leaf, P. J. (2010). Multilevel exploration of factors contributing to the overrepresentation of Black students in office disciplinary referrals. *Journal of Educational Psychology, 102*(2), 508–520.

Brophy, J. E. (1988). Research linking teacher behavior to student achievement: Potential implications for instruction of Chapter 1 students. *Educational Psychologist, 23*, 235–286. doi:10.1207/s15326985ep2303_3.

Buehler, J. (2012). 'There's a problem, and we've got to face it': How staff members wrestled with race in an urban high school. *Race Ethnicity and Education, 16*(5), 1–24.

Carter, P., Skiba, R. J., Arredondo, M. I., & Pollock, M. (2014). *You can't fix what you don't look at: Acknowledging race in addressing racial discipline disparities.* Bloomington, IN: The Equity Project at Indiana University. Retrieved from http://www.indiana.edu/~atlantic/wp-content/uploads/2014/12/Acknowledging-Race_121514.pdf

Chelowa, B., Goodman, R. D., West-Olatunji, C., & Amatea, E. (2014). A qualitative examination of the impact of culturally responsive educational practices on the psychological well-being of students of color. *Urban Review, 46,* 574–596. doi:10.1007/s11256-014-0272-y.

Children's Defense Fund (1975). *School suspensions: Are they helping children?* Cambridge, MA: Washington Research Project.

Collaborative for Academic, Social, and Emotional Learning (CASEL). (2015). *What is social and emotional learning?* Chicago: Author. Retrieved from http://www.casel.org/social-and-emotional-learning

Cornell, D., & Lovegrove, P. (2015). Student threat assessment as a method of reducing student suspensions. In D. J. Losen (Ed.), *Closing the school discipline gap: Equitable remedies for excessive exclusion* (pp. 180–191). New York: Teachers College Press.

Cornell, D., & Sheras, P. (2006). *Guidelines for responding to student threats of violence.* Longmont, CO: Sopris West.

Cornell, D., Shin, C., Ciolfi, A., & Sancken, K. (2013). *Prevention v. punishment: Threat assessment, school suspensions, and racial disparities.* Charlottesville, VA: Legal Aid Justice Center and University of Virginia. Retrieved from https://www.justice4all.org/wp-content/uploads/2013/12/Prevention-v-Punishment-Report-FINAL.pdf

Cramer, E. D., & Bennett, K. D. (2015). Implementing culturally responsive positive behavior interventions and supports in middle school classrooms. *Middle School Journal, 46,* 18–24.

Darensbourg, A., Perez, E., & Blake, J. J. (2010). Overrepresentation of African American males in exclusionary discipline: The role of school-based mental health professionals in dismantling the school to prison pipeline. *Journal of African American Males in Education, 1*(3), 196–211.

Eitle, T. M. N., & Eitle, D. J. (2004). Inequality, segregation, and the overrepresentation of African Americans in school suspensions. *Sociological Perspectives, 47,* 269–287. doi:10.1525/sop.2004.47.3.269.

Fabelo, T., Thompson, M. D., Plotkin, M., Carmichael, D., Marchbanks, M. P., & Booth, E. A. (2011). *Breaking schools' rules: A statewide study of how school discipline relates to student's success and juvenile justice involvement.* New York: Council of State Governments Justice Center, and College Station, TX: Texas A&M University, Public Policy Research Institute. Retrieved from http://knowledgecenter.csg.org/kc/system/files/Breaking_School_Rules.pdf

Finn, J. D., & Servoss, T. J. (2015). Misbehavior, suspensions, and security measures in high school: Racial/ethnic and gender differences. In D. J. Losen (Ed.), *Closing the school discipline gap: Equitable remedies for excessive exclusion* (pp. 45–58). New York: Teachers College Press.

Flannery, K. B., Frank, J. L., & Kato, M. M. G. (2012). School disciplinary responses to truancy: Current practice and future directions. *Journal of School Violence, 11*(2), 118–137. doi:10.1080/15388220.2011.653433.

Gonzalez, T. (2015). Socializing schools: Addressing racial disparities in discipline through restorative justice. In D. J. Losen (Ed.), *Closing the school discipline gap: Equitable remedies for excessive exclusion* (pp. 151–165). New York: Teachers College Press.

Greenwood, C. R., Horton, B. T., & Utley, C. A. (2002). Academic engagement: Current perspectives on research and practice. *School Psychology Review, 31,* 328–349.

Gregory, A., Allen, J. P., Mikami, A. Y., Hafen, C. A., & Pianta, R. C. (2015). The promise of a teacher professional development program in reducing the racial disparity in classroom exclusionary discipline. In D. J. Losen (Ed.), *Closing the school discipline gap: Equitable remedies for excessive exclusion* (pp. 166–179). New York: Teachers College Press.

Gregory, A., Clawson, K., Davis, A., & Gerewitz, J. (2015). The promise of restorative practices to transform teacher-student relationships and achieve equity in school discipline. *Journal of Educational and Psychological Consultation, 25,* 1–29.

Gregory, A., Skiba, R. J., & Noguera, P. A. (2010). The achievement gap and the discipline gap: Two sides of the same coin? *Education Researcher, 39*(1), 59–68.

Gregory, A., & Weinstein, R. S. (2008). The discipline gap and African Americans: Defiance or cooperation in the high school classroom. *Journal of School Psychology, 46*(4), 455–475. doi:10.1016/j.jsp.2007.09.001.

Himmelstein, K. E. W., & Bruckner, H. (2011). Criminal-justice and school sanctions against non-heterosexual youth: A national longitudinal study. *Pediatrics, 127*(1), 49–57. doi:10.1542/peds.2009-2306.

Hinojosa, M. S. (2008). Black-white differences in school suspension: Effect of student beliefs about teachers. *Sociological Spectrum, 28*(2), 175–193. doi:10.1080/02732170701796429.

Howard, T. C. (2010). *Why race and culture matter in schools: Closing the achievement gap in America's classrooms.* Multicultural education series. New York: Teachers College Press.

Individuals with Disabilities Education Act (IDEA). (2004). Public Law 108-446 (20 U.S.C. 1400 et seq.).

Kupchik, A., & Ward, G. (2013). Race, poverty, and exclusionary school security: An empirical analysis of U.S. elementary, middle, and high schools. *Youth Violence and Juvenile Justice.* Retrieved from http://yvj.sagepub.com/content/early/2013/09/16/1541204013503890

Losen, D. J., & Gillespie, J. (2012). *Opportunities suspended: The disparate impact of disciplinary exclusion from school.* Los Angeles, CA: The Center for Civil Rights Remedies at The Civil Right Project/Proyecto Derechos Civiles.

McIntosh, K., Moniz, C. A., Craft, C. B., Golby, R., & Steinwand-Deschambeault, T. (2014). Implementing school-wide positive behavioural interventions and supports to better meet the needs of Indigenous students. *Canadian Journal of School Psychology, 29,* 236–257. doi:10.1177/0829573514542217.

Mediratta, K. (2012). Grassroots organizing and the school to prison pipeline: The emerging national movement to roll back zero tolerance discipline policies in U.S. public schools. In S. Bahena, N. Cooc, R. Currie-Rubin, P. Kuttner, & M. Ng (Eds.), *Disrupting the school to prison pipeline* (pp. 211–236). Cambridge, MA: Harvard Education Press.

Milner, H. R., & Tenore, F. B. (2010). Classroom management in diverse class-rooms. *Urban Education, 45*, 560–603. doi:10.1177/0042085910377290.

Monahan, K. C., VanDerhei, S., Bechtold, J., & Cauffman, E. (2014). From the school yard to the squad car: School discipline, truancy, and arrest. *Journal of Youth and Adolescence, 43*(7), 1110–1122. doi:10.1007/s10964-014-0103-1.

Monroe, C. R., & Obidah, J. E. (2004). The influence of cultural synchronization on a teacher's perceptions of disruption: A case study of an African American middle-school classroom. *Journal of Teacher Education, 55*(3), 256–268. doi:10.1177/0022487104263977.

Nicholson-Crotty, S., Birchmeier, Z., & Valentine, D. (2009). Exploring the impact of school discipline on racial disproportion in the juvenile justice system. *Social Science Quarterly, 90*(4), 1003–1018. doi:10.1111/j.1540-6237.2009.00674.x.

Okonofua, J. A., & Eberhardt, J. L. (2015). Two strikes: Race and the disciplining of young students. *Psychological Science, 26*(5), 617–624. doi:10.1177/0956797615570365.

Osher, D., Poirier, J. M., Jarjoura, G. R., Brown, R., & Kendziora, K. (2015). Avoid simple solutions and quick fixes: Lessons learned from a comprehensive district-wide approach to improving conditions for learning. In D. J. Losen (Ed.), *Closing the school discipline gap: Equitable remedies for excessive exclusion* (pp. 192–206). New York: Teachers College Press.

Peguero, A. A., & Shekarkhar, Z. (2011). Latino/a student misbehavior and school punishment. *Hispanic Journal of Behavioral Sciences, 33*(1), 54–70. doi:10.1177/0739986310388021.

Perry, B. L., & Morris, E. W. (2014). Suspending progress: Collateral consequences of exclusionary punishment in public schools. *American Sociological Review, 79*(6), 1067–1087. doi:10.1177/0003122414556308.

Pollock, M. (2009). *Colormute: Race talk dilemmas in an American school.* Princeton, NJ: Princeton University Press.

Rocque, M. (2010). Office discipline and student behaviors: Does race matter? *American Journal of Education, 116*(4), 557–581.

Shollenberger, T. L. (2015). Racial disparities in school suspension and subsequent outcomes: Evidence from the National Longitudinal Survey of Youth 1997. In D. J. Losen (Ed.), *Closing the school discipline gap: Equitable remedies for excessive exclusion* (pp. 31–43). New York: Teachers College Press.

Skiba, R. J., Arredondo, M. I., & Rausch, M. K. (2014). *New and developing research on disparities in discipline.* Bloomington, IN: The Equity Project at Indiana University. Retrieved from http://rtpcollaborative.indiana.edu/briefing-papers/

Skiba, R. J., Arredondo, M. I., & Williams, N. T. (2014). More than a metaphor: The contribution of exclusionary discipline to a school-to-prison pipeline. *Equity and Excellence in Education, 47*(4), 546–564.

Skiba, R. J., Chung, C. G., Trachok, M., Baker, T. L., Sheya, A., & Hughes, R. L. (2014). Parsing disciplinary disproportionality: Contributions of infraction, student, and school characteristics to out-of-school suspension and expulsion. *American Educational Research Journal, 51*(4), 640–670.

Skiba, R. J., Horner, R. H., Chung, C. G., Rausch, M. K., May, S. L., & Tobin, T. (2011). Race is not neutral: A national investigation of African American and Latino disproportionality in school discipline. *School Psychology Review, 40*(1), 85–107.

Skiba, R. J., Michael, R. S., Nardo, A. C., & Peterson, R. L. (2002). The color of discipline: Sources of racial and gender disproportionality in school punishment. *The Urban Review, 34,* 317–342. doi:10.1023/A:1021320817372.

Snapp, S., Burdge, H., Licona, A. C., Moody, R., & Russell, S. T. (2015). Students' perspectives on LGBTQ-inclusive curriculum. *Equity and Excellence in Education, 48,* 249–265. doi:10.1080/10665684.2015.1025614.

Sprague, J. R., Vincent, C. G., Tobin, T. J., & CHiXapkaid (2013). Preventing disciplinary exclusions of students from American Indian/Alaska Native backgrounds. *Family Court Review, 51,* 452–459.

Steinberg, M. P., Allensworth, E., & Johnson, D. W. (2015). What conditions support safety in urban schools? The influence of school organizational practices on student and teacher reports of safety in Chicago. In D. J. Losen (Ed.), *Closing the school discipline gap: Equitable remedies for excessive exclusion* (pp. 118–131). New York: Teachers College Press.

Theriot, M. T. (2009). School resource officers and the criminalization of student behavior. *Journal of Criminal Justice, 37*(3), 280–287.

Toldson, I. A., McGee, T., & Lemmons, B. P. (2015). Reducing suspensions by improving academic engagement among school-age Black males. In D. J. Losen (Ed.), *Closing the school discipline gap: Equitable remedies for excessive exclusion* (pp. 107–117). New York: Teachers College Press.

U.S. Department of Education. (2014a). *Civil rights data collection: Data snaphot (school discipline) 2011-12.* Available at http://ocrdata.ed.gov. Data notes are available at http://ocrdata.ed.gov/downloads/DataNotes.docx

U.S. Department of Education. (2014b). *Guiding principles: A resource guide for improving school climate and discipline.* Washington, DC: Author. Retrieved from http://www2.ed.gov/policy/gen/guid/school-discipline/guiding-principles.pdf

Vincent, C. G., Sprague, J. R., CHiXapkaid, Tobin, T. J., & Gau, J. M. (2015). Effectiveness of schoolwide positive behavior interventions and supports in reducing racially inequitable disciplinary exclusion. In D. J. Losen (Ed.), *Closing the school discipline gap: Equitable remedies for excessive exclusion* (pp. 207–221). New York: Teachers College Press.

Wallace Jr., J. M., Goodkind, S., Wallace, C. M., & Bachman, J. G. (2008). Racial, ethnic, and gender differences in school discipline among U.S. high school students: 1991-2005. *The Negro Educational Review, 59*(1–2), 47–62.

Walsh, V. (2015). *Disparities in discipline: A look at school disciplinary actions for Utah's American Indian students.* Social Science Electronic Publishing, Inc. Available at SSRN: http://ssrn.com/abstract=2609177.

Whitford, D. K., & Levine-Donnerstein, D. (2014). Office disciplinary referral patterns of American Indian students from elementary school through high school. *Behavioral Disorders, 39*(2), 78–88.

CHAPTER 3

How Educators Can Eradicate Disparities in School Discipline

Anne Gregory, James Bell, and Mica Pollock

Despite efforts in recent years to reform disciplinary policy and practice in US public schools, the number of students issued out-of-school suspensions continues to be extremely high and disparities in suspension rates continue to worsen (Losen, 2015), indicating that students in some groups are missing school far more often and disproportionately compared to other groups. These disparities are also true of referrals to law enforcement and school-based arrests (Krezmien, Leone, Zablocki, & Wells, 2010; U.S. Department of Education, 2014).

Punitive school discipline matters tremendously to the educational opportunity of young people: even a single suspension or referral to the juvenile court system increases the odds of low achievement and dropping out of school altogether (Kirk & Sampson, 2013). Moreover, educators' beliefs and approaches to discipline are key factors in the prevalence of disciplinary actions that exclude students from the classroom (Skiba et al.,

A. Gregory (✉)
Graduate School of Applied and Professional Psychology, Rutgers, The State University of New Jersey, Piscataway, NJ, USA

J. Bell
W. Haywood Burns Institute, Oakland, CA, USA

M. Pollock
Education Studies, Center for Research on Educational Equity, Assessment, and Teaching Excellence, University of California, San Diego, CA, USA

© The Author(s) 2016
R.J. Skiba et al. (eds.), *Inequality in School Discipline*,
DOI 10.1057/978-1-137-51257-4_3

2014). Effective school discipline is critical in building school climates that are both safe and productive. The key question for educators is how to initiate a change in school disciplinary approach so that more young people remain engaged in learning in school.

PRINCIPLES AND PROGRAMS TO REDUCE DISPARITIES IN SCHOOL DISCIPLINE

This chapter provides a synthesis of current research and best practices in reducing disparities in school discipline.[1] What follows are starting points that educators—including teachers, administrators, paraprofessionals, and support personnel—might use to begin shifting disciplinary conflicts and consequences toward a more positive school climate, benefitting both educators and students. We offer intervention strategies to help educators build strong and effective relationships with students and avoid the criminalization of child and adolescent behaviors, reducing student exposure to the juvenile justice system. By criminalization we mean the tendency for adults to perceive student appearance, body language, or behavior as inordinately threatening or defiant of authority and rules, leading them to issue excessively punitive sanctions, including suspension and justice system referrals, rather than to engage the student in school-based prevention and intervention.

Effective schools consider discipline to be part of their overall approach to establishing conditions for successful teaching and learning, rather than blaming educators or students when disciplinary conflicts or disparities arise. Thus, we need sophisticated ways to think about school safety and discipline that can promote orderly and healthy instructional climates while reducing time spent out of school, inequitable discipline, and criminalization. When guided by the principles of equity and prevention, effective discipline can foster an environment characterized by healthy relationships and academic engagement across classrooms, hallways, and lunchrooms (Gregory, Cornell, & Fan, 2011). Disciplinary interventions can be used to resolve conflict *and* educate students, rather than push them out of school.

MOVING BEYOND PUNITIVE DISCIPLINE TO CONFLICT PREVENTION AND CONFLICT INTERVENTION

In this chapter, we present research-based principles to support educators in shifting their approach to discipline, grouped into the categories of "Conflict Prevention" and "Conflict Intervention." The likelihood of conflict is reduced (prevention) when schools create diverse communities of motivated, invested, and engaged student and staff learners. When conflict does occur, however, it can be addressed through constructive and equitable intervention that provides tools to address the source of conflicts and identify appropriate alternatives, thereby building stronger school climates.

Principles of Conflict Prevention

Research suggests that to prevent unnecessary conflict and reduce disproportionate discipline for particular groups of students, educators should provide the following:

- *Supportive Relationships*: Authentic connections forged with all students.
- *Academic Rigor*: The potential of all students is promoted through high expectations and high-level learning opportunities.
- *Culturally Relevant and Responsive Teaching*: Instruction responds respectfully to students' lives.
- *Bias-free Classrooms and Respectful School Environments*: Inclusive, positive classroom and school environments are established in which all students feel fairly treated.

Principles of Conflict Intervention

Research suggests that when discipline problems arise, educators should engage in the following:

- *Inquiry into the Causes of Conflicts*: Equity-focused inquiry is used regularly to identify "hot spots" of disciplinary conflict or differential treatment for particular groups.
- *Problem-solving Approaches to Discipline*: Solutions aim to uncover sources of behavior or teacher-student conflict and address the identified needs.
- *Inclusion of Student and Family Voice and Perspectives on Conflict Causes and Solutions*: Student and family voices are integrated into conflict resolution.
- *Re-integration of Students after Conflict*: Students are supported to re-enter a community of learners after conflict has occurred.

In the following pages, we describe how each principle relates to disparities in school discipline, and offer strategies and sample programs to help guide schools in enacting the same.

Prevention Through Supportive Relationships

Through caring and supportive relationships, school staff can prevent conflict, communicate high expectations for student engagement in learning, and demonstrate fair and consistent application of school rules (Gregory et al., 2011; Osher et al., 2012). All too often, however, supportive relationships are not evenly distributed among student groups. Compared to White students, Black and Latino students report finding fewer adults in school who are supportive and fair (Hughes, 2011; Voight, Hanson, O'Malley, & Adekanye, 2015). Similar patterns also are evident for lesbian, gay, bisexual and transgender (LGBT) students. In a national survey of LGBT students from over 3000 school districts, almost half reported that school staff did nothing when they heard homophobic remarks (Kosciw, Greytak, Bartkiewicz, Boesen, & Palmer, 2012).

Knowing Students Well Goes a Long Way

Effective educators get to know their students well, especially those students whose lived experience differs substantially from their own. Given that America's teaching force is predominantly middle class and disproportionately White, differences in lived experience can be pronounced for low-income students and those of color. Educators' connectedness to their individual students, as well as their knowledge of events in students' communities, can help to bridge the "identity gulf" and prevent misjudgments, unintentionally hurtful comments ("microaggressions"), and overly harsh reactions to child and adolescent misbehavior (Sue, 2010). Getting to know the strengths of students' communities has similar effects. Administrators highlight how essential it is for school leaders to regularly engage with families and community leaders outside of school in order to build trust and open lines of communication (Henderson, Johnson, Mapp, & Davies, 2007; Pollock, in press).

Supportive relationships can also reduce negative stereotyping and implicit bias (see Kahn and colleagues, this volume). When students and educators get to know each other well, understanding, empathy and trust can develop (Gregory & Ripski, 2008), helping students feel accepted and honored for who they are, even when who they are differs radically from the teachers' own experience and identity. In addition, knowing students as individuals who belong to diverse communities counteracts stereotypes (Pollock, in press).

How Can Schools Engage in Supportive Relationships with Youth?

- *Systematically identify student strengths, integrate "getting to know you" activities into instruction, and avoid defining and labeling students by their deficits.* Examples of strength-based, relationship-building activities include: daily morning circles or check-ins about students' thoughts, feelings, and experiences; assigned autobiographies or portfolios of students' interests, skills, and accomplishments, which can be developed interactively, online, or using multimedia (Oneville Project, 2012); positive notes home, and teacher attendance at student events outside of the classroom.

- *Improve interactions among educators and students through professional development programs.* One example of a relationship-building professional development program is the My Teaching Partner-Secondary (MTP-S) program. Teachers, paired with a coach for an entire school year, reflect on video recordings of their classroom instruction and interactions with students. A recent study of the program showed the Black-White gap in student discipline referral was largely eliminated for teachers in the program (see www.mtpsecondary.net; Gregory, Allen, Mikami, Hafen, & Pianta, 2015).

- *Implement professional development to increase and maintain cultural competence.* Increasing educator "cultural competence"—the ability to connect with and respond respectfully and skillfully to students' lived experiences—has been shown to be key to good school-student relationships (Monroe & Obidah, 2004). Professional development can help educators understand lived experiences outside of what is familiar to them (e.g., learning about others' experiences with immigration, poverty, English Language Learning, racism, homophobia; Singleton & Linton, 2006).

PREVENTION THROUGH ACADEMIC RIGOR

When students are deeply engaged in and excited about academic activities, school discipline referrals are less likely (Fredricks, Blumenfeld, & Paris, 2004). Yet, academic rigor is not evenly distributed in our school system today (Weinstein, 2002). Within schools, remedial and honors levels are often racially divided and characterized by widely divergent norms of control (Howard, 2008). In many lower-tracked classrooms, boredom, frustration, and shame can contribute to student-teacher conflict, while high-achieving classrooms are often characterized by lively teacher-student interactions, where independent learning activities and enriching materials are prioritized over tight management of behavior (Noguera & Wing, 2006). It is not surprising that students in lower-tracked classrooms, often students of color and low-income students, become less engaged and less on-task.

Educators might also inadvertently send messages that some groups are expected to succeed, while others are destined for failure (Weinstein, 2002). Students are astute at inferring such messages from adults' voice, tone, or body language, as well as from the instructional tasks and material they are given. If differential messages are internalized, students can lose confidence in their own academic abilities, and become less invested in schooling. Discipline struggles often result.

How Can Schools Provide Academic Rigor to Historically Underserved Youth?

- *Promote high expectations and assist students in meeting those expectations.* Schools effective in preventing conflict communicate high expectations through high-level and engaging instruction that includes access to necessary learning supports (Mehan, 2012). For instance, the Preuss School in San Diego (Mehan, 2012) established single-track, college-preparatory curricula to build a college-bound culture for its students—all of whom are low income, and primarily students of color—providing flexible supports and remediation programming through expanded school days. A nearby partner school, Gompers Preparatory Academy in San Diego, similarly transformed a high-suspension, chaotic campus into a college-prep environment with high expectations for every student (Mehan, 2012). Gompers has met its goal of 100% graduation and college acceptance for several years running.

PREVENTION THROUGH CULTURAL RELEVANCY AND RESPONSIVENESS

When students' identities and cultures are integrated into curriculum and instruction as well as the norms and ethos of the school, they feel safer and report less victimization and discrimination (Gay, 2006). They also feel more connected to school and report higher academic achievement (Cammarota, 2007). Weinstein, Tomlinson-Clarke, and Curran (2004) assert that culturally competent pedagogy is characterized by teachers' (1) awareness of their own ethnocentrism (the tendency to see one's own cultural norms as neutral, universal, normal and correct); (2) knowledge of students' cultural backgrounds and communities; (3) understanding of broader social, economic, and political contexts that open or close opportunity and access; and (4) demonstrated commitment to building caring classrooms.

How Can Schools Offer Cultural Relevancy and Responsiveness to Youth?

- *Recognize and affirm diversity through school events and course materials.* More effective schools integrate student racial, ethnic, cultural, gender, and sexual identities and experiences into school curricula, school-wide events, library resources, and other forums and activities (Burdge, Snapp, Laub, Russell, & Moody, 2013; Moll, 2010).
- *Critical self-reflection on interactions with students.* Through a process of self-reflection and careful observation of their instructional style, educators can ask themselves: Am I reacting negatively, or in an unfair way, to a behavior that is simply unfamiliar to me? The Double-Check program (Bottiani et al., 2012) is a structured professional development experience in which instructional coaches observe teachers and offer performance feedback that helps them reflect on the degree to which they offer positive behavioral supports in a culturally competent manner (Hershfeldt et al., 2010). "Personal autobiographies" and book discussion groups (Nieto, 2008) can help educators acknowledge their own personal and community histories, and consider how those backgrounds may create assumptions about what behavior in school is normal and desirable.

PREVENTION THROUGH BIAS-FREE CLASSROOMS AND RESPECTFUL SCHOOL ENVIRONMENTS

When some student groups experience school as uncaring, culturally irrelevant or non-responsive, they may be detecting unfair treatment driven by implicit bias—biases that we hold without being aware of them. Research on implicit bias shows that, regardless of racial background, many people associate faces that look "White" with words like "smart" and faces that look Black with criminality (Banaji & Greenwald, 2013). Goff, Jackson, Di Leone, Culotta, and DiTomasso (2014) found that Black boys are generally viewed as less childlike than White peers (older and more culpable), and that characteristics typically associated with childhood (innocence) are less frequently applied to Black boys relative to White boys. Although operating outside conscious awareness, implicit bias can impact decision-making. In juvenile justice, unconscious attitudes toward darker skin have been shown to influence more punitive responses to the behavior of darker-skinned youth (Graham & Lowery, 2004). These attitudes may fuel the prevalence of harsher sanctions for students of color.

Although research on the effects of implicit bias in schools is sparse, there is no reason to believe administrators and teachers are exempt from processes that affect the decision-making of professionals in a range of work settings (Banaji & Greenwald, 2013). In schools, implicit bias may fuel negative reactions on the part of administrators and staff to students' hair, dress, speech, or even body language, in a way that undermines students' positive relationships to school (Ferguson, 2001; Okonofue & Eberhardt, 2015). More research and intervention is needed to help educators prevent their unconscious biases from driving disciplinary decisions (McIntosh, Girvan, Horner, & Smolkowski, 2014).

Schools serving communities that educators are unfamiliar with or believe to be unsafe may resort to a security infrastructure, including police, scanners and other technology, to establish a safe and orderly environment. Although some schools and school districts may feel strongly that such approaches are necessary, it is unclear how much such measures actually contribute to better learning climates. The overuse of security measures such as law enforcement presence, daily checkpoints, random searches, and drug-sniffing canines in lower-income schools serving predominantly communities of color has been linked to negative student outcomes (Tanner-Smith & Fisher, 2015), including higher rates of school-based referrals to juvenile court (Theriot, 2009). These security techniques have also been shown to reduce the level of trust between educators and students (Finn & Servoss, 2015), and are associated with increased student disengagement from school, as students begin to see school as a hostile "prison-like" environment (Kupchik, 2010).

How Can Schools Pursue Bias-Free Discipline and Respectful Interactions with Youth?

- *Create opportunities for staff to reflect critically on how stereotyping and implicit bias can affect students in their schools.* Educators can become more aware of when snap judgments about student behavior may be in play and ask themselves whether they have considered the whole context when they respond to students (McIntosh et al., 2014). Educators can also examine the potential of bias in their responses to student behavior: Am I overreacting to youth from particular groups when I discipline my students?

- *Communicate trust and respect throughout the school.* Data have consistently demonstrated the centrality of a positive climate and proactive prevention to promoting safe and productive schools (e.g., Gregory et al., 2011; Heilburn, Cornell, & Lovegrove, 2015). Schools that emphasize the development of positive relationships tend to be experienced by teachers and students as safer and more supportive (Gregory, Cornell, Fan, Sheras, & Shih, 2010), while schools relying heavily on security technology tend to suspend at higher rates (Finn & Servoss, 2015).

- *Increase awareness about how the structure and history of racism impacts schooling.* Educators can learn about the structural nature and historical context of racism in order to understand how racial bias is influenced by our collective experiences rather than personal flaws, and consider how implicit biases about race can affect decision-making (Pollock, in press). School staff can take the Implicit Association Tests (IAT), a free online assessment of implicit bias, and discuss the results (See https://implicit.harvard.edu/implicit/takeatest.html).

INTERVENTION AND REGULAR INQUIRY INTO THE CAUSES OF CONFLICTS

Some conflict in schools is inevitable. However, it is possible for schools to handle conflict equitably with clear, fair, and consistent enforcement of rules, a focus on developing student and educator skills in constructive resolution of conflict, and processes for re-engagement and reparation of trust and community for all those involved in disputes.

Regular analysis of data is important to resolving disciplinary problems in fair and equitable ways. Disaggregating data can help educators identify and address ways in which discipline practices may impact some student groups more than others. For instance, one middle school principal led a discussion with staff on the data for dress code violations, helping them to see that rules against short skirts were not enforced to the same degree as rules against the baggy pants worn by many of the male students of color (Morris, 2005).

Sharing data with communities and families can yield far-reaching solutions to disciplinary problems, for both individual students and for school districts. Families, advocates, and students in the Los Angeles Unified School District (LAUSD) took action when they realized the sheer number of students of color given suspensions under the category "Willful Defiance," which can be applied for a range of behaviors that are subjectively interpreted by educators (Watanabe, 2013). As a result, the LAUSD school board revised the district's school discipline policy and passed the School Climate Bill of Rights, abolishing the category "Willful Defiance" (Watanabe, 2013). The new policy encourages schools to address low-level conflict proactively, rather than lumping all negative interactions into the "defiance" category.

Ensuring equitable discipline also requires a commitment to understanding the experience of historically marginalized groups of students at school and in their communities and society at large (Carter, Skiba, Arredondo, & Pollock, 2014). Actively engaging students in the inquiry process can help to reveal overlooked needs, such as the experiences of LGBT students. Once these needs are identified, schools can develop responsive programming, such as ongoing discussions of culturally responsive practice or anti-bias LGBT training for school staff.

How Can Schools Conduct Equity-Driven Inquiry to Intervene in Discipline Patterns Involving Students?

- *Review discipline data regularly.* To intervene in existing discipline patterns and prevent unnecessary discipline, educators can review discipline data regularly to conduct equity audits. At the school and district level, educators can track and disaggregate discipline data by offense type, student characteristics (e.g., student race/ethnicity, gender, disability status), teacher/school, location of offense, referral to law enforcement, and whether students receive a school-based ticket or arrest.

- *Analyze discipline data intersectionally.* Consider students who belong to multiple subgroups simultaneously to identify how school discipline is impacting subpopulations. Research suggests, for example, that gender non-conforming students of color are particularly over-disciplined, often after being the victim of bullying (Snapp, Hoenig, Fields, & Russell, 2015; also see Bellinger et al., this volume; Poteat et al., this volume).
- *Investigate important discretionary points in the discipline process in order to understand how best to intervene.* Specific reasons why students are being referred for "defiance," "disrespect," or "insubordination" can be closely examined by school data teams, in order to more precisely describe the offense (e.g., use of inflammatory language toward adult). Educators can then consider which consequences for the specific infraction are actually merited, with exclusion from instruction being used as a last resort (see also Yusuf et al., this volume).
- *Harness youth leadership in the inquiry process itself.* Educators can also create groups of student participatory researchers who help analyze the disparities data, offer interpretations, and generate interventions with and for educators (Chmielewski et al., this volume; Jones & Yonezawa, 2002). (Also see www.publicscienceproject.org)

INTERVENTION AND PROBLEM-SOLVING APPROACHES TO DISCIPLINE

In contrast to a punitive, zero-tolerance approach to conflict, a problem-solving approach identifies contextual contributions to school discipline issues so that responses to conflict are sufficiently nuanced. A multi-faceted understanding of rule-breaking would incorporate multiple perspectives (disputants, supporters) and multiple sources of information (Cornell, Sheras, Gregory, & Fan, 2009). A problem-solving approach helps teachers and administrators understand the greater context around any behavior or response by inquiring into the "why" of a student's behavior or teacher's response and eliciting relevant information (e.g., a student is angry or stressed because he is up at night caring for a younger sibling, a teacher is angry because she is in the midst of a divorce).

How Can Schools Use Problem-Solving Approaches to Respond to Conflict and Support Youth?

- *Assess needs and provide appropriate supports.* Educators can learn problem-solving approaches to conflict that include the following steps: (1) inquiry into the "why" of the behavior or incident; (2) inquiry into classroom, school, family or community issues that may aggravate the behavior; (3) provision of a period of reflection for student and school staff member; (4) facilitation of a restoration process that supports students in sharing their experience (including disputants and those affected in the school community); and (5) provision of appropriate services for those students suffering from traumatic events or other, more serious mental health issues. One problem-solving program is the Virginia Threat Assessment Guidelines (Cornell et al., 2009), in which staff are trained to conduct a systematic investigation into the circumstances and underlying problems that culminate in a student making threats. Schools using threat assessment have safer school environments (e.g., less bullying) and issued fewer suspensions to both Black and White students who made threats (Cornell et al., 2009; Cornell & Lovegrove, 2015).
- *Through problem-solving, identify the needs of vulnerable groups in the school.* Some rule-breaking behavior may be a consequence of traumatic experiences (Gorman-Smith, 2003). Schools that identify such needs can provide services to address the consequences of trauma, and may also identify a school-wide need to enhance student and staff social and emotional skills. Given the frequent stressors in daily school life, school staff may need support to manage emotions (their own and that of the students), to address cultural differences, and to constructively resolve conflict (Pollock, 2008).

INTERVENTION AND INCLUSION OF STUDENT AND FAMILY VOICE

Typically, students and staff who are affected by a rule infraction do not have a forum to discuss their experience of the events. The offended parties rarely have the opportunity to face the person who harmed them (Zehr, 2002). Seldom are students given an authentic opportunity to participate in "righting wrongs." By institutionalizing procedures that tap into both student and staff experience after a rule infraction, all parties involved can learn essential social and emotional skills—perspective-taking, empathy, and problem-solving—that are essential for lifelong success in work settings (Costello, Wachtel, & Wachtel, 2010). When students feel their opinions are valued, they tend to be more engaged and invested (Hafen et al., 2012).

How Do Schools Integrate Student and Family Voice into School Discipline?

- *Explicitly integrate student and parent voice in resolving conflict.* Conflict resolution programs and restorative justice programs systematically integrate student and family voice after an incident. Student accountability is achieved when all parties involved take responsibility for their actions, recognize the impact of their actions on others, and offer ways to repair the harm (Costello et al., 2010). Conflict resolution or restorative justice programming can help schools ensure that voices of marginalized students and their families are systematically included in educational programming and provide a relationship-based process to resolve disputes (restorative conferences; see www.safersanerschools.org). Recent research suggests that restorative practices hold promise for reducing racial disparities in discipline (González, 2015; Gregory, Clawson, Davis, & Gerewitz, 2015; Jain, Bassey, Brown, & Kalra, 2014).
- *Establish forums with youth, parent and community-led organizing groups, and families.* Youth-, parent- and community-led movements are at the core of many important reforms on school discipline across the nation. Local organizing groups, such as *Padres y Jovenes Unidos* in Denver, CADRE in Los Angeles, and Voices of Youth in Chicago Education, have helped highlight the negative impact of punitive discipline on students and supported schools to develop better ways of managing student behavior (Rogers & Terriquez, 2013). Schools can proactively reach out to such groups in their own communities to better understand the needs and concerns of students who are issued discipline sanctions at disproportionate rates. Youth organizing has been documented as a powerful approach to youth development and community change (Shah, 2011): By learning to identify problems on their campuses or in their communities and determining solutions to address them, youth become critical thinkers.

INTERVENTION THROUGH REINTEGRATING STUDENTS AFTER CONFLICT

After receiving a punitive disciplinary action, students can become increasingly alienated from the school community. Students re-entering school from a ten-day suspension or from juvenile detention are often placed back into school with little guidance or support to reconnect successfully (Seigle, Walsh, & Weber, 2014). The burden to make up instructional time often falls on the returning student. If the young person is engaged with the justice system while on probation or is facing current charges because of school behavior, the effect of school absence is exacerbated. With lost instructional time accruing, students can fall irrevocably behind in their academics, fueling racial and gender gaps in school achievement. To minimize lost instructional time, students need to be actively re-engaged in the process of learning and in the school community after an incident has occurred.

How Can Schools Reintegrate Students?

- *Develop reintegration rituals and connect support services to students* after short absences, as well as longer-term absences due to suspension or juvenile detention. One approach is to create a "transition center" that supports collaboration between the probation department, mental health/child welfare services, and the school district (Seigle et al., 2014). Such collaboration can facilitate access to wraparound support services to young people exiting juvenile hall.
- *Link schools with youth advocate and mentoring programs that support youth as they re-enter communities after they have been detained in the justice system.* Well-trained and matched mentors can help youth navigate the stressors and demands that occur for those who have missed instruction from their local schools for extended periods of time (see e.g., the Youth Empowerment Project, Community Reintegration Program, New Orleans, LA).

CONCLUSION

Districts and schools across the nation are engaging in long-term change to transform their approach to school discipline: equity-oriented principles of conflict prevention and intervention can help guide that change.

Schools that prevent punitive discipline responses and increase students' access to supportive relationships, academic rigor, and culturally relevant and responsive teaching are more likely to reach their educational goals. These schools teach social and emotional skills and coping strategies, and build positive relationships between educators, students, and parents. When conflict and rule-breaking arise, effective schools engage in problem-solving to identify underlying contributors to the problem, while integrating student and family perspectives into how to repair the harm. When students are excluded from the learning environment, effective schools systematically reintegrate them back into the community and their coursework. Schools enacting equity-oriented principles also regularly use data, such as school disciplinary records and student surveys, to track their progress in resolving conflict and educating young people.

Efforts to undertake an equity-oriented transformation in school discipline are already underway across the nation. States are considering new legislation to reduce the overuse of school suspension for non-safety related student misbehavior (Clough, 2014). Districts are collaborating with students, parents and advocates to rewrite student codes of conduct to undo zero-tolerance policies that mandate rigid, exclusionary responses to student behavior (Green, 2013). Urban districts are implementing restorative approaches to school discipline to reduce their use of suspension (Encarnacao, 2013). These efforts reflect the growing recognition that educators can disrupt discipline disparities, which have been seen as inevitable and unchangeable for too long, and replace them with strategies and programs that build a safe, healthy, and academically rigorous school climate for all students.

NOTE

1. This chapter is based on the briefing paper designed for educators, drafted for the Discipline Disparities Research-to-Practice Collaborative (see preface). The full brief can be found online at http://www.indiana.edu/~atlantic/wp-content/uploads/2014/12/Disparity_Intervention_Full_121114.pdf

REFERENCES

Banaji, M. R., & Greenwald, A. G. (2013). *The blindspot.* New York: Random House.

Bottiani, J. H., Bradshaw, C. P., Rosenberg, M. S., Hershfeldt, P. A., Pell, K. L., & Debnam, K. J. (2012). Applying double check to response to intervention:

Culturally responsive practices for students with learning disabilities. *Insights on Learning Disabilities: From Prevailing Theories to Validated Practices, 9*(1), 93–107.

Burdge, H., Snapp, S., Laub, C., Russell, S. T., & Moody, R. (2013). *Implementing lessons that matter: The impact of LGBTQ-inclusive curriculum on student safety, well-being, and achievement*. San Francisco: Gay-Straight Alliance Network, and Tucson, AZ: Frances McClelland Institute for Children, Youth, and Families at the University of Arizona.

Cammarota, J. (2007). A social justice approach to achievement: Guiding Latina/o students toward educational attainment with a challenging, socially relevant curriculum. *Equity & Excellence in Education, 40*, 87–96. doi:10.1080/10665680601015153.

Carter, P., Skiba, R. J., Arredondo, M. I., & Pollock, M. (2014). *You can't fix what you don't look at: Acknowledging race in addressing racial discipline disparities*. Discipline Disparities: Research-to-Practice Collaborative. Retrieved from http://rtpcollaborative.indiana.edu/briefing-papers/

Clough, C. (2014). Brown signs bill limiting 'willful defiance' suspensions, expulsions. *LA School Report*. Retrieved from http://laschoolreport.com/brown-signs-bill-limiting-willful-defiance-suspensions-expulsions/

Cornell, D., & Lovegrove, P. (2015). Student threat assessment as a method of reducing student suspension. In D. J. Losen (Ed.), *Closing the school discipline gap: Equitable remedies for excessive exclusion* (pp. 180–191). New York: Teachers College Press.

Cornell, D., Sheras, P., Gregory, A., & Fan, X. (2009). A retrospective study of school safety conditions in high schools using the Virginia Threat Assessment Guidelines versus alternative approaches. *School Psychology Quarterly, 24*, 119–129. doi:10.1037/a0016182.

Costello, B., Wachtel, J., & Wachtel, T. (2010). *Restorative circles in schools: Building community and enhancing learning. A practical guide for educators*. Bethlehem, PA: International Institute for Restorative Practices (IIRP).

Encarnacao, J. (2013, September 3). Sharp drop in suspensions as Boston schools try 'restorative' approach. *Boston Herald.com*. Retrieved from http://bostonherald.com/news_opinion/local_coverage/2013/09/sharp_drop_in_suspensions_as_boston_schools_try_restorative

Ferguson, A. (2001). *Bad boys: Public schools in the making of Black masculinity*. Ann Arbor, MI: University of Michigan Press.

Finn, J. D., & Servoss, T. J. (2015). Security measures and discipline in American high schools. In D. J. Losen (Ed.), *Closing the school discipline gap: Equitable remedies for excessive exclusion* (pp. 44–58). New York: Teachers College Press.

Fredricks, J. A., Blumenfeld, P. C., & Paris, A. H. (2004). School engagement: Potential of the concept, state of the evidence. *Review of Educational Research, 74*, 59–109. doi:10.3102/00346543074001059.

Gay, G. (2006). Connections between classroom management and culturally responsive teaching. In C. M. Evertson & C. S. Weinstein (Eds.), *Handbook of classroom management* (pp. 343–372). Mahway, NJ: Erlbaum.

Goff, P. A., Jackson, M. C., Di Leone, B. A., Culotta, C. M., & DiTomasso, N. A. (2014). The essence of innocence: Consequences of dehumanizing Black children. *Journal of Personality and Social Psychology, 106*, 526–545. doi:10.1037/a0035663.

González, T. (2015). Socializing schools: Addressing racial disparities in discipline through restorative justice. In D. J. Losen (Ed.), *Closing the discipline gap: Equitable remedies for excessive exclusion* (pp. 151–165). New York: Teachers College Press.

Gorman-Smith, D. (2003). The ecology of community and neighborhood and risk for antisocial behavior. In C. Essau (Ed.), *Conduct disorders: Risk and intervention* (pp. 117–136). New York: Lawrence Earlbaum Associates.

Graham, S., & Lowery, B. S. (2004). Priming unconscious racial stereotypes about adolescent offenders. *Law and Human Behavior, 28*, 483–504. doi:10.1023/B:LAHU.0000046430.65485.1f.

Green, E. (2013, September 2). Code of conduct allows principals to not suspend students for certain weapons. *Baltimore Sun.* Retrieved from http://articles. baltimoresun.com/2013-09-02/news/bs-md-ci-student-conduct-code-20130827_1_school-principals-jimmy-gittings-school-support-networks

Gregory, A., Allen, J., Mikami, A., Hafen, C., & Pianta, R. (2015). The promise of a teacher professional development program in reducing racial disparity in classroom exclusionary discipline. In D. J. Losen (Ed.), *Closing the discipline gap: Equitable remedies for excessive exclusion* (pp. 166–179). New York: Teachers College Press.

Gregory, A., Clawson, K., Davis, A., & Gerewitz, J. (2014). The promise of restorative practices to transform teacher-student relationships and achieve equity in school discipline. For a special issue on *Restorative Justice in the Journal of Educational and Psychological Consultation, 25*, 1–29. doi:10.1080/10474412.2014.929950

Gregory, A., Cornell, D., & Fan, X. (2011). The relationship of school structure and support to suspension rates for Black and White high school students. *American Educational Research Journal, 48*(4), 904–934. doi:10.3102/0002831211398531.

Gregory, A., Cornell, D., Fan, X., Sheras, P., & Shih, T. (2010). Authoritative school discipline: High school practices associated with lower student bullying and victimization. *Journal of Educational Psychology, 102*, 483–496.

Gregory, A., & Ripski, M. (2008). Adolescent trust in teachers: Implications for behavior in the high school classroom. *School Psychology Review, 37*, 337–353.

Hafen, C. A., Allen, J. P., Mikami, A. Y., Gregory, A., Hamre, B., & Pianta, R. C. (2012). The pivotal role of adolescent autonomy in secondary classrooms.

Journal of Youth and Adolescence, 41, 245–255. doi:10.1007/s10964-011-9739-2.

Heilburn, A., Cornell, D., & Lovegrove, P. (2015). Principal attitudes regarding zero tolerance and racial disparities in school suspensions. *Psychology in the Schools, 52,* 489–499. doi:10.1002/pits.21838.

Henderson, A. T., Johnson, V., Mapp, K. L.,., & Davies, D. (2007). *Beyond the bake sale: The essential guide to family/school partnerships.* New York: The New Press.

Hershfeldt, P. A., Sechrest, R., Pell, K. L., Rosenberg, M. S., Bradshaw, C. P., & Leaf, P. J. (2010). Double-check: A framework of cultural responsiveness applied to classroom behavior. *Teaching Exceptional Children Plus, 6,* 1–18.

Howard, T. C. (2008). Who really cares? The disenfranchisement of African American males in pre K-12 schools: A critical race theory perspective. *Teachers College Record, 110,* 954–985.

Hughes, J. N. (2011). Longitudinal effects of teacher and student perceptions of teacher-student relationship qualities on academic adjustment. *Elementary School Journal, 112,* 38–60. doi:10.1086/660686.

Jain, S., Bassey, H., Brown, M. A., & Kalra, P. (2014). *Restorative justice in Oakland schools. Implementation and impact: An effective strategy to reduce racially disproportionate discipline, suspensions, and improve academic outcomes.* Retrieved May 27, from http://www.ousd.org/cms/lib07/CA01001176/Centricity/Domain/134/OUSD-RJ%20Report%20revised%20Final.pdf

Jones, M., & Yonezawa, S. (2002). Student voice, cultural change: Using inquiry in school reform. *Equity and Excellence in Education, 35,* 245–254.

Kirk, D. S., & Sampson, R. L. (2013). Juvenile arrest and collateral educational damage in the transition to adulthood. *Sociology of Education, 86,* 36–62. doi:10.1177/0038040712448862.

Kosciw, J. G., Greytak, E. A., Bartkiewicz, M. J., Boesen, M. J., & Palmer, N. A. (2012). *The 2011 National School Climate Survey. The experiences of lesbian, gay, bisexual and transgender youth in our nation's schools.* New York: Gay, Lesbian, and Straight Education Network (GLSEN).

Krezmien, M. P., Leone, P. E., Zablocki, M. S., & Wells, C. S. (2010). Juvenile court referrals and the public schools: Nature and extent of the practice in five states. *Journal of Contemporary Criminal Justice, 26,* 273–293.

Kupchik, A. (2010). *Homeroom security: School discipline in the age of fear.* New York: NYU Press.

Losen, D. J. (2015). *Closing the school discipline gap: Equitable remedies for excessive exclusion.* New York: Teachers College Press.

McIntosh, K., Girvan, E. J., Horner, R. H., & Smolkowski, K. (2014). Education not incarceration: A conceptual model for reducing racial and ethnic disproportionality in school discipline. *Journal of Applied Research on Children: Informing Policy for Children at Risk, 5,* 1–44.

Mehan, H. (2012). *In the front door: Creating a college-bound culture of learning.* Herdon, VA: Paradigm Publishers.

Moll, L. C. (2010). Mobilizing culture, language, and educational practices: Fulfilling the promises of Mendez and Brown. *Educational Researcher, 39,* 451–460. doi:10.3102/0013189X10380654.

Monroe, C. R., & Obidah, J. E. (2004). The influence of cultural synchronization on a teacher's perceptions of disruption: A case study of an African American middle-school classroom. *Journal of Teacher Education, 55*(3), 256–268. doi:10.1177/0022487104263977.

Morris, E. W. (2005). "Tuck in that shirt!" Race, class, gender, and discipline in an urban school. *Sociological Perspectives, 48,* 25–48. doi:10.1525/sop.2005.48.1.25.

Nieto, S. (2008). *Affirming diversity: The sociopolitical context of multicultural education* (5th ed.). New York: Allyn & Bacon Publishers.

Noguera, P., & Wing, J. (2006). *Unfinished business: Closing the racial achievement gap in our schools.* San Francisco: Jossey-Bass.

Okonofue, J. A., & Eberhardt, J. L. (2015). Two strikes: Race and the disciplining of young students. *Psychological Science, 26,* 617–624. doi:10.1177/0956797615570365.

Oneville Project. (2012). *Eportfolios.* Retrieved from http://wiki.oneville.org/main/Eportfolio

Osher, D., Coggshall, J., Colombi, G., Woodruff, D., Francois, S., & Osher, T. (2012). Building school and teacher capacity to eliminate the school-to-prison pipeline. *Teacher Education and Special Education: The Journal of the Teacher Education Division of the Council for Exceptional Children, 35,* 284–295.

Pollock, M. (in press). *Schooltalking: Communicating for equity in schools.* New York: The New Press.

Pollock, M. (2008). *Because of race: How Americans debate harm and opportunity in our schools.* Princeton, NJ: Princeton University Press.

Rogers, J., & Terriquez, V. (2013). *Learning to lead: The impact of youth organizing on the educational and civic trajectories of low-income youth.* Los Angeles: Institute for Democracy, Education, and Access.

Seigle, E., Walsh, N., & Weber, J. (2014). *Core principles for reducing recidivism and improving other outcomes for youth in the juvenile justice system.* New York: Council of State Governments Justice Center.

Shah, S. (2011). *Building transformative youth leadership: Data on the impacts if youth organizing.* New York: Funders' Collaborative on Youth Organizing.

Singleton, G. E., & Linton, C. (Eds.) (2006). *Courageous conversations about race: A field guide for achieving equity in schools.* Thousand Oaks, CA: Corwin Press.

Skiba, R. J., Chung, C. G., Trachok, M., Baker, T. L., Sheya, A., & Hughes, R. L. (2014). Parsing disciplinary disproportionality: Contributions of infraction, student, and school characteristics to out-of-school suspension and expulsion. *American Educational Research Journal, 51*(4), 640–670.

Snapp, S., Hoenig, J. M., Fields, A., & Russell, S. T. (2015). Messy, butch, and queer: LGBTQ youth and the school-to-prison pipeline. *Journal of Adolescent Research, 30*, 57–82. doi:10.1177/0743558414557625.

Sue, D. W. (2010). *Microaggressions in everyday life: Race, gender, and sexual orientation.* Hoboken, NJ: John Wiley & Sons, Inc.

Tanner-Smith, E. E., & Fisher, B. W. (2015). Visible school security measures and student academic performance, attendance, and postsecondary aspirations. *Journal of Youth and Adolescence, 45*(1), 195–210. doi:10.1007/s10964-015-0265-5.

Theriot, M. T. (2009). School resource officers and the criminalization of student behavior. *Journal of Criminal Justice, 37*(3), 280–287.

United States Department of Education (2014). *Guiding principles: A resource guide for improving school climate and discipline.* Author: Washington, DC.

Voight, A., Hanson, T., O'Malley, M., & Adekanye, L. (2015). The racial school climate gap: Within-school disparities in students' experiences of safety, support, and connectedness. *American Journal of Community Psychology, 56*, 252–267.

Watanabe, T. (2013, May 14). LA Unified bans suspension for willful defiance. *Los Angeles Times.* http://articles.latimes.com/2013/may/14/local/la-me-lausd-suspension-20130515

Weinstein, R. S. (2002). *Reaching higher: The power of expectations in schooling.* Cambridge, MA: Harvard University Press.

Weinstein, C. S., Tomlinson-Clarke, S., & Curran, M. (2004). Toward a conception of culturally responsive classroom management. *Journal of Teacher Education, 55*, 25–38.

Youth Empowerment Project. (2011). *Community Reintegration Program.* New Orleans, LA: Author. Retrieved from http://www.youthempowermentproject.org/

Zehr, H. (2002). *The little book of restorative justice.* Intercourse, PA: Good Books.

PART II

Understanding and Addressing Disparities: What We Are Learning and What We Can Do

CHAPTER 4

Sexual Orientation-Based Disparities in School and Juvenile Justice Discipline Practices: Attending to Contributing Factors and Evidence of Bias

V. Paul Poteat, Jillian R. Scheer, and Eddie S.K. Chong

INTRODUCTION

There is substantial evidence that sexual minority youth (lesbian, gay, bisexual, or questioning [LGBQ] youth) face elevated physical and mental health risks compared to heterosexual youth as a result of discrimination (Coker, Austin, & Schuster, 2010; Russell, Everett, Rosario, & Birkett, 2014). Despite a sizable literature base on health risks, less attention has focused on understanding whether discrimination shapes sexual orientation-based disparities in other areas, such as school discipline practices. Punitive and exclusionary discipline sanctions, ranging from school suspension to incarceration, are directed disproportionately toward certain marginalized youth populations, for example, African American youth (Gregory, Skiba, & Noguera, 2010; Wallace, Goodkind, Wallace, & Bachman, 2008). Are discipline sanctions also directed disproportionately toward LGBQ

V.P. Poteat (✉) • J.R. Scheer
Counseling, Developmental, and Educational Psychology Department, Boston College, Boston, MA, USA

E.S.K. Chong
University of Maryland, College Park, MD, USA

© The Author(s) 2016   61
R.J. Skiba et al. (eds.), *Inequality in School Discipline*,
DOI 10.1057/978-1-137-51257-4_4

youth compared to heterosexual youth? If so, what underlying factors and processes may account for such sexual orientation-based disparities?

Recent studies indicate the existence of sexual orientation-based discipline disparities. As one example, using items from the nationally representative Add Health study, Himmelstein and Brückner (2011) found that non-heterosexual youth were more likely than heterosexual youth to indicate that they had been stopped by police, arrested before the age of 18, expelled from school, and had a juvenile conviction. These disparities were evident even when controlling for minor to violent transgressive behaviors (e.g., intoxication, stealing, threatening someone with a weapon). Findings of Himmelstein and Brückner (2011) run parallel to those documented among youth of color, which show that the latter are more likely to be overrepresented across various types of discipline sanctions (Piquero, 2008; Ray & Alarid, 2004; Shaw & Braden, 1990; Skiba, Michael, Nardo, & Peterson, 2002; Wehlage & Rutter, 1986). Other recent studies have documented disciplinary bias against LGBQ youth within schools (Snapp, Hoenig, Fields, & Russell, 2015). These findings suggest that discipline disparities based on sexual orientation may well be occurring and emphasize the need for greater attention to this issue. In this chapter, we propose a theoretically based model to inform emerging research on sexual orientation-based disparities in school suspension and juvenile justice system involvement.

A Theoretical Basis for Sexual Orientation-Based Discipline Disparities

Our model hypothesizes that peer victimization predicts engagement in various behavioral infractions that ultimately lead to sexual orientation-based discipline disparities. In effect, this model aims to explain the connection between victimization and discrimination in producing disproportional rates of discipline for LGBQ youth compared to heterosexual youth. There is much evidence that victimization on the basis of sexual orientation predicts youths' substance use, truancy, and self-protective strategies such as carrying a weapon (Gastic, 2008; Luk, Wang, & Simons-Morton, 2010; Simon, Dent, & Sussman, 1997; Tharp-Taylor, Haviland, & D'Amico, 2009). Because victimized LGBQ students are in school and also because they are minors, some of the behaviors associated with or resulting from victimization (e.g., alcohol use or truancy) constitute punishable infractions by school and juvenile justice systems. As such, the very ways in which some youth—whether heterosexual or LGBQ—cope with victimization (e.g., truancy to avoid victimization, carrying a weapon for self-defense) increases their risk for school discipline or criminal justice sanctions. In the next section, we bring together theories from the LGBQ health disparities literature and the juvenile justice literature to clarify ways in which these factors may give rise to sexual orientation-based discipline disparities.

Minority Stress Theory

We propose that minority stress theory (Meyer, 2003), a model drawn from health disparities literature, could partially explain disparities in disciplinary outcomes, by considering the discrimination experienced disproportionately by LGBQ youth relative to heterosexual youth. That is, LGBQ individuals experience multiple stressors, such as discrimination, due to their marginalized sexual orientation identity in society. As a result of experiencing stressors at greater rates, LGBQ individuals are at a greater risk of negative health outcomes than heterosexuals.

There is robust support for this theory as applied to LGBQ youth. LGBQ youth indeed report more frequent peer victimization than heterosexual youth (Russell et al., 2014). In turn, peer victimization predicts a range of concerns for LGBQ youth, such as alcohol use, depression, carrying a weapon for self-defense, and school truancy (Marshal et al., 2008; Newcomb, Heinz, Birkett, & Mustanski, 2014; Panfil, 2014; Poteat, Mereish, DiGiovanni, & Koenig, 2011). Our model ultimately links such victimization and several of these behavioral health disparity outcomes to disparities in disciplinary outcomes.

Differential Behavior or Differential Selection and Processing

Two perspectives from the juvenile justice literature may shed additional light on discipline disparities: the differential behavior perspective and the differential selection and processing perspective (Piquero, 2008). The differential behavior perspective focuses on the behavior of students themselves, suggesting that discipline disparities between groups are due to the differential rates at which members of each group commit infractions. The differential behavior perspective tends to place responsibility for group-based discipline disparities on a group's members and their higher rates of illicit behavior. Applying minority stress theory to this perspective suggests that the discipline of LGBQ students may be a three-stage process: (1) LGBQ youth are more likely than heterosexual youth to be victimized, as stipulated by minority stress theory; (2) higher rates of victimization among LGBQ youth predict higher rates of infractions (e.g., alcohol use) among LGBQ youth; and, (3) because they engage in these infractions at differential rates, LGBQ youth will be more likely than heterosexual youth to face punitive discipline. Minority stress theory adds a critical extension to the differential behavior perspective by drawing attention to precipitating experiences of disproportionately higher rates of discrimination experienced by LGBQ youth. Thus, it calls attention to broader social conditions and biases that prompt these behaviors in the first place, and highlights how these behaviors can represent coping strategies and protective behaviors.

The differential behavior perspective has had mixed support, however, in accounting for race-based discipline disparities (Gregory et al., 2010); it also seems insufficient on its own to explain sexual orientation-based discipline disparities. If LGBQ youths' higher rates of infractions were the primary cause of their disproportionate discipline, then sexual orientation-based discipline disparities should be minimal when controlling for different rates of engagement in these infractions. Yet Himmelstein and Brückner (2011) found that discipline disparities between heterosexual and non-heterosexual youth remained even when introducing such controls in their analyses. As a result of such findings, researchers have also considered a second explanation for discipline disparities, the differential selection and processing perspective.

The latter (Piquero, 2008) focuses on the role of bias in the process of delegating punishment. It states that discipline disparities between groups exist because members of one group are more likely to be punished or punished more harshly for the same infraction than members of another group. This pattern has been found for youth of color in outcomes ranging from classroom office referrals to court sanctions (Piquero, 2008; Skiba, Arredondo, & Williams, 2014a; Wehlage & Rutter, 1986). In effect, the differential selection and processing perspective suggests that discipline disparities may be partly reflective of discrimination at an institutional level by adults who are more likely to discipline LGBQ youth because of their sexual orientation. There is growing documentation of discriminatory institutional policies and practices directed against LGBQ youth (e.g., harsher punishment for showing public displays of same-sex affection or for taking a same-sex partner to prom; Chesir-Teran & Hughes, 2009; Snapp et al., 2015) and lawsuits filed by LGBQ youth have shown that they have often faced discrimination from authority figures at school (Cianciotto & Cahill, 2012). Thus, this perspective captures the emphasis of minority stress theory on the role of discrimination in explaining disparities, suggesting that LGBQ youth may be more likely to face discipline than heterosexual youth who engage in the same infractions at similar rates.

Currently, there has been insufficient study of school discipline sanctions and LGBQ youth to suggest which perspective—differential behavior or differential selection/processing—best explains sexual orientation-based discipline disparities. Notably, minority stress theory is not aligned exclusively with either the differential behavior or differential selection/processing perspective. Discrimination is relevant to the differential behavior perspective, in that greater peer or adult victimization faced by LGBQ youth may prompt greater engagement in infractions and ultimately lead to sexual orientation-based discipline disparities. Discrimination is also relevant to the differential selection/processing perspective, in that adults may discriminate against LGBQ youth by differentially selecting and punishing them more so than heterosexual youth for the same infractions. Instead of treating the differential behavior perspective and the differential selection/processing perspectives as mutually exclusive, we consider the extent to which both, with their shared connection to discrimination, may relate to sexual orientation-based discipline disparities.

In the sections that follow, we present our recent findings related to the issues we have raised above. First, we document the existence of sexual orientation-based disparities in school suspension and juvenile justice system involvement among a large sample of youth. Second, we present results from models that compare two ways in which victimization and engagement in infractions are connected to sexual orientation-based discipline disparities. The first model considers the differential behavior perspective: we tested whether higher rates of victimization among LGBQ youth than heterosexual youth would predict the former's engagement in more infractions, and whether this differential engagement would account for why LGBQ youth were more likely than heterosexual youth to be suspended or involved in the juvenile justice system. The second model considers the differential selection/processing perspective: we tested whether LGBQ youth who engaged in infractions had greater odds of experiencing punitive discipline than heterosexual youth who engaged in the same infractions.

METHODS

Data Source

We used data from the 2012 Dane County Youth Assessment (DCYA) in Wisconsin, modeled on the Youth Risk Behavior Survey (YRBS; Centers for Disease Control and Prevention, 2009). The DCYA was collected by Dane County Human Services and supported by several community partners. In city-based high schools with large student populations, 50% of the school's students were randomly selected by the school systems to complete the survey. In all other schools, surveys were administered to the entire student body, as this was more feasible in smaller schools. The survey was administered electronically in computer labs during school hours. The data were collected from 13,645 youth across 22 high schools in rural, suburban, and urban schools. There was an even distribution of male and female students (50% in each group). Students were predominantly White (73.7%), followed by students who identified as biracial or multi-racial (7.3%), Black (5.3%), Hispanic (5.1%), Non-Hmong Asian (2.7%), Hmong-identified Asian (1.6%), Middle Eastern (0.6%), Native American (0.6%), and 3.1% identified other self-reported racial or ethnic identities. As expected, most students identified as heterosexual (93.6%), followed by students who identified as bisexual (3.2%), questioning their sexual orientation (2.0%), and those who identified as gay or lesbian (1.2%). From this total sample of youth, our analysis included all LGBQ youth (n = 869) and a comparison sample of 869 heterosexual youth who were selected through matching on a number of demographic and behavioral indices. These indices included students' gender identity, age, grade level, race/ethnicity, whether they received a free or reduced-price lunch, the grades they reported typically earning, and self-reported bullying behavior.[1]

Variables

The survey assessed a broad range of factors; here we describe the measures used for the current study. Participants completed a four-item measure (Espelage & Holt, 2001) of peer victimization (e.g., "I got hit or pushed by other students"). Infractions were represented by five items assessing cigarette, alcohol, and marijuana use, as well as whether students had been truant in the last 30 days (0 = not truant; 1 = truant at least once) or carried a weapon onto school property in the last 30 days (0 = did not carry a weapon to school; 1 = carried a weapon to school at least one day). Finally, we assessed school suspension with the item, "During this school year, how many times have you been suspended from school?" We assessed juvenile justice system involvement with the item, "Have you ever been in juvenile corrections/prison for more than 30 days?" Responses for both items were dichotomized (0 = not suspended, 1 = suspended at least once; 0 = no juvenile corrections/prison involvement, 1 = has been in juvenile corrections/prison in the past year).

Analytic Approach

In order to test for sexual orientation-based discipline disparities, we compared the likelihood of suspension or involvement in the juvenile justice system for LGBQ youth as opposed to heterosexual youth through odds ratios based on logistic regression. We then tested several models comparing the differential behavior and the differential selection/processing perspectives using structural equation modeling. For the purpose of this chapter, we forego a technical presentation of the analyses (e.g., model fit indices or detailed invariance tests); however, detailed statistical output is reported in Poteat, Scheer, and Chong (2016). Figures 4.1 and 4.2 provide a conceptual diagram of these models.

In our differential behavior-based model, we hypothesized that (a) LGBQ youth would report more victimization than heterosexual youth; (b) victimization would be associated with committing infractions; and, (c) infractions would be associated with the likelihood of having been suspended and involved in the juvenile justice system. The model tests whether discipline disparities can be accounted for based on LGBQ

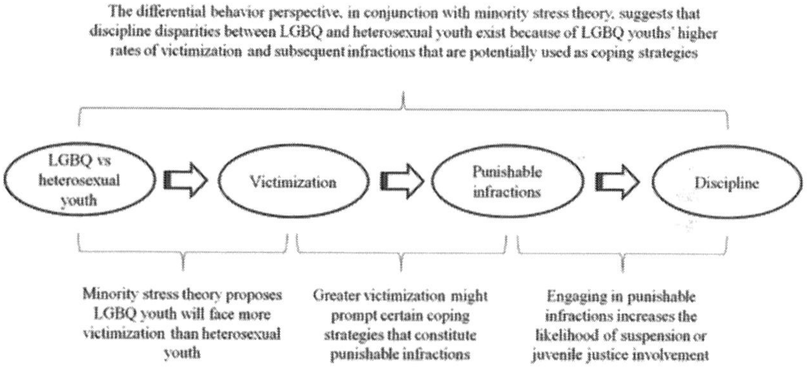

Fig. 4.1 A model reflecting how the differential behavior perspective, in conjunction with minority stress theory, could account for sexual orientation-based discipline disparities

The differential selection/processing perspective, in conjunction with minority stress theory, suggests that discipline disparities between LGBQ and heterosexual youth exist because LGBQ youth are more likely to be disciplined than heterosexual youth who commit the same infractions, due to bias against LGBQ youth

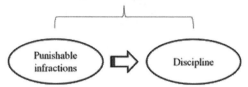

Fig. 4.2 A model reflecting how the differential selection/processing perspective, in conjunction with minority stress theory, could account for sexual orientation-based discipline disparities

youths' higher rates of victimization and infraction engagement, that is, differential behavior. In this scenario, the link between sexual orientation and discipline is expected to be explained through these preceding intermediary processes of victimization and infractions. As part of the analyses, we calculated *indirect effects*, which represent this process. Significant and sizable indirect effects of sexual orientation on suspension and juvenile justice system involvement through the proposed path of victimization and infraction engagement would support the differential behavior perspective.

In our differential selection/processing-based model, we hypothesized that LGBQ youth who engaged in infractions would be more likely to report having been suspended or involved in the juvenile justice system than heterosexual youth who had engaged in these infractions. Stronger associations between infraction engagement and discipline experiences for LGBQ youth than heterosexual youth would reflect differential selection/processing rather than differential behavior, because this discrepancy would show that, even when comparing LGBQ and heterosexual youth who are engaging in infractions at similar rates, LGBQ youth are still more likely to have been suspended or involved in the juvenile justice system.[2]

RESULTS: EVIDENCE OF SEXUAL ORIENTATION-BASED DISCIPLINE DISPARITIES

LGBQ youth were more than twice as likely as heterosexual youth to report that they had been suspended from school in the past school year (OR =2.41, $p < 0.001$), and more than nine times as likely as heterosexual youth to report that they had been involved in the juvenile justice system in the past year (OR =9.21, $p < 0.001$). Having found evidence that these disparities existed, we then compared whether the differential behavior or differential selection/processing perspective best explained the connections between our set of variables.

Differential Behavior Perspective

As we hypothesized, LGBQ youth reported more victimization than heterosexual youth (β = 0.14, $p < 0.01$). In turn, having been victimized predicted that students engaged in more infractions (β = 0.19, $p < 0.01$). Students who engaged in infractions were more likely to have been suspended (β = 0.41, $p < 0.01$) and to have been involved in the juvenile justice system (β = 0.33, $p < 0.01$). Although each of these single paths was significant, the true test of the differential behavior perspective is reflected in the overall contribution of indirect effects in the model: Are the observed differences in discipline outcomes between LGBQ and heterosexual students accounted for by the intermediary differences in victimization and infraction engagement between the two groups? The indirect effects provided only limited support for this question; indirect effects of sexual orientation on disciplinary experiences through victimization and infractions were significant but small in size (β = 0.01, $p < 0.05$, for both disciplinary outcomes).

Differential Processing Perspective

We tested whether heterosexual youth and LGBQ youth who engaged in comparable levels of infractions were equally likely to have been suspended or involved in the juvenile justice system. To do so, we forced the associations between infractions and each disciplinary outcome to be equal for both heterosexual and LGBQ youth. This constraint was not supported, in that the fit of the model was poor under conditions of forced equivalence. Instead, the results showed that there was a stronger association between infraction engagement and suspension for LGBQ youth than for heterosexual youth (β = 0.47 and 0.40, respectively) and a stronger association between infraction engagement and juvenile justice involvement for LGBQ youth than for heterosexual youth (β = 0.57 and 0.12, respectively). As such, the results offered support for the differential selection/ processing perspective.

How Do Our Results Relate to Theory?

Our findings provide additional evidence that discipline disparities exist between LGBQ youth and heterosexual youth. Consistent with the findings of Himmelstein and Brückner (2011), we found evidence of disparities in school suspension and juvenile justice system involvement. These findings are also consistent with research on discipline disparities for youth of color (Gregory et al., 2010; Wallace et al., 2008). Further, our findings suggest how multiple factors relate to and could potentially lead to these disparities. We drew from minority stress theory to clarify the role of discrimination in contributing to disparities faced by marginalized populations, while also giving attention to both the differential behavior and the differential selection/processing perspectives from the juvenile justice literature. In all, our findings underscore the need for further research on the experiences of LGBQ youth and to further assess and address ways in which discrimination is associated with disproportionately high rates of punitive disciplinary outcomes for LGBQ youth.

These disparities are of concern because punitive and exclusionary discipline can carry longer-term consequences. LGBQ youth who are restricted from attending school may be even less likely to return than heterosexual youth because they already perceive their school as hostile (Goodenow, Szalacha, & Westheimer, 2006). Indeed, exclusionary discipline may be linked to disparities in academic achievement (Gregory et al., 2010; Skiba et al., 2014b).

Building on this initial evidence of discipline disparities, our findings provide some indication of the relative extent to which the differential behavior and the differential selection/processing perspectives might explain these disparities in conjunction with minority stress theory. Consistent with research on youth of color (Gregory et al., 2010), we documented only minimal support for the differential behavior perspective. This perspective stipulates that differences between heterosexual and LGBQ youth on discipline outcomes are largely explained by their differential engagement in these infractions; minority stress theory would further argue that these differential behaviors are partly on account of having experienced more discrimination. Although LGBQ youth reported greater victimization, which in turn was associated with greater engagement in infractions, these variables accounted for few of the initial differences between LGBQ and heterosexual youth in discipline experiences.

This latter finding was indicated by the small contribution of indirect effects to the model. In other words, discipline disparities between LGBQ and heterosexual youth could not be wholly explained simply because LGBQ youth reported greater victimization and engagement in infractions than heterosexual youth.

We found stronger support for the differential selection/processing perspective. When LGBQ and heterosexual youth engaged in infractions, the odds were greater for LGBQ youth to have experienced discipline than for heterosexual youth. These findings parallel those for youth of color, showing that they are more likely to be penalized than White youth in school discipline practices and the criminal justice system, even when controlling for their offenses or the severity of the crime (Shook & Goodkind, 2009; Skiba et al., 2002; Wordes, Bynum, & Corley, 1994). Minority stress theory would suggest that the stronger association between engaging in infractions and discipline for LGBQ youth could reflect bias from, for example, adults who may have responded to these infractions more harshly. Indeed, LGBQ youth in other studies have reported that they have faced institutional practices that differentially punished their behaviors as compared to heterosexual youth, and that they have experienced discrimination from authorities at school (Chesir-Teran & Hughes, 2009; Cianciotto & Cahill, 2012; Snapp et al., 2015). Still, our data did not allow us to explore whether the youth perceived their discipline to be a result of bias. Thus, future research needs to give more direct attention to discrimination that LGBQ youth experience from adults, not only discrimination experienced from peers. By focusing on multiple sources of discrimination, future research could provide a clearer indication of the ways in which sexual orientation-based bias may be evident throughout the process that leads to differential disciplinary outcomes for LGBQ youth.

The fact that the infractions of substance use, truancy, and carrying a weapon on school property were even more strongly associated with punitive discipline for LGBQ youth than heterosexual youth highlights a major predicament faced by the former. As noted, some LGBQ youth drink as a means to cope with chronic discrimination, skip school to avoid victimization, or carry a weapon for self-defense (Birkett, Russell, & Corliss, 2014; Panfil, 2014; Rosario, Schrimshaw, & Hunter, 2011). Often, youth use these strategies because they face rejection, victimization, or receive inadequate support from other sources such as families, peers, teachers, or community agencies (Bos & Sandfort, 2015; Darwich, Hymel, & Waterhouse, 2012; Poteat, Espelage, & Koenig, 2009; Ryan, Huebner, Diaz, & Sanchez, 2009). Nevertheless, using these protective or coping strategies creates further risk of discipline, discrimination, and other health or academic concerns. Thus, these findings add weight to the need for researchers and interventionists to address the circumstances that prompt youths' engagement in these behaviors and how these behaviors are subsequently addressed.

IMPLICATIONS FOR RESEARCH

As evidence of sexual orientation-based discipline disparities continues to accumulate, it is becoming clear that future research needs to consider them in greater detail. As this occurs, we recommend that future studies consider the diversity within the LGBQ community based on points of intersectionality; that is, how do youths' sexual orientation identities intersect with their other social identities, such as race, gender identity or expression, or social class? For example, it would be helpful for research to consider the unique experiences of LGBQ youth of color. Indeed, LGBQ youth of color can experience heightened discrimination because of their multiple marginalized statuses (Mustanski, Garofalo, & Emerson, 2010; Russell et al., 2014). Future research could identify types of institutional bias from adults that may result in harsher discipline toward LGBQ youth of color than youth who are not members of marginalized groups.

In a similar manner, researchers might consider discipline experiences based on gender identity and expression. Himmelstein and Brückner's (2011) findings suggested that sexual orientation-based discipline disparities were more pronounced for females than males on outcomes such as school expulsion or adult criminal convictions. Snapp et al. (2015) also highlighted disciplinary bias based on gender expression: gender nonconforming youth reported discrimination from adults at school by being punished for behaviors such as wearing clothes aligned with their self-affirmed gender.

Longitudinal data would help to identify the longer-term implications of discipline among LGBQ youth. Some LGBQ youth may be caught in an increasingly detrimental process due to the stressors they experience, the strategies they use to cope, and the discipline they face. Some discipline experiences could act as significant stressors for LGBQ youth in addition to those they already face, such as parental rejection. This could exacerbate the existing health and academic concerns that initially led them to experience these forms of discipline. Consequently, this process could prompt LGBQ youth who have limited access to other support services to engage in these behaviors at even greater rates (e.g., greater substance use), which could lead to more severe sanctions in a recursive process with compounded negative effects.

IMPLICATIONS FOR PRACTICE

Our results and those of other researchers have begun to underscore the potential role of bias in accounting for the experiences of LGBQ youth. Within this frame, schools and juvenile justice systems might consider whether behaviors typically labeled as infractions may reflect coping and protective strategies by LGBQ youth. Adults might consider strategies to probe the underlying causes of these behaviors and help youth address the varied stressors that might underlie some of these behaviors. Overall, supportive approaches might produce better longer-term outcomes for LGBQ youth than a penalizing or exclusionary approach, by addressing some of the precipitating causes, such as discrimination, mental health concerns, or use of less-effective coping strategies.

Professional training could raise attention to the disproportionate victimization and discrimination faced by LGBQ youth and uncover ways to create an inclusive environment and how to respect and affirm students' sexual orientation as well as their gender identity and expression (Gender Spectrum, n.d.; GLSEN, n.d.; GSA Network, n.d.; Ollis, 2013). School systems might also consider ways in which to monitor how disciplinary cases are handled and identify any potential patterns of bias based on students' sexual orientation or gender identity or expression. Because this remains an under-studied area and because LGBQ youth often face invisibility in schools (Russell, Kosciw, Horn, & Saewyc, 2010), ongoing school-based data collection could be helpful for schools to identify discipline bias that their LGBQ students may experience. Taken together, these strategies might help to address discipline-related issues faced by LGBQ youth.

Conclusion

In this chapter, we presented evidence of sexual orientation-based discipline disparities in school suspension and juvenile justice system involvement among LGBQ and heterosexual youth, while identifying the ways in which peer victimization and infraction engagement contributed to the same through the frameworks of minority stress theory and the differential behavior and differential selection/processing perspectives. Although the results of our models indicated weak support for the differential behavior perspective, there was stronger support for the differential selection/processing perspective. Minority stress theory provided an overarching framework for both perspectives, highlighting the way in which discrimination can contribute to discipline disparities. Based on these findings, we offered several suggestions for future research and practice. We believe that interdisciplinary collaborations across multiple fields (e.g., psychology, education, law) will significantly advance ongoing efforts in this area. Ultimately, we believe that work in the area of sexual orientation-based discipline disparities will be integral as part of larger efforts to ensure the safety of LGBQ youth at school and their access to educational opportunities.

Notes

1. We followed standard procedures (Austin, 2011) for forming propensity scores for all individuals. We then matched heterosexual youth to LGBQ youth based on their identical propensity scores. When there were more heterosexual youth than LGBQ youth with the same propensity score, we randomly selected the heterosexual youth with that score to be matched with the LGBQ youth with that same score. There were a few cases where there was not a heterosexual youth with an identical propensity score as an LGBQ youth; in these situations we selected a heterosexual youth with the closest value to the LGBQ youth. We then performed balance diagnostics to ensure comparability of the heterosexual and LGBQ samples on these variables.
2. The analytical approach to test this conceptual model involved a multiple group comparison of LGBQ youth and heterosexual youth, in which we conducted a series of invariance tests (Chen, 2007; Cheung & Rensvold, 2002; Kline, 2011). The technical nature of these analyses extends beyond the scope of this chapter, but a full description of the methods and detailed presentation of the results can be found in Poteat, Scheer, & Chong (2015).

REFERENCES

Austin, P. C. (2011). An introduction to propensity score methods for reducing the effects of confounding in observational studies. *Multivariate Behavioral Research, 46,* 399–424.

Birkett, M., Russell, S. T., & Corliss, H. L. (2014). Sexual orientation disparities in school: The mediational role of indicators of victimization in achievement and truancy because of feeling unsafe. *American Journal of Public Health, 104,* 1124–1128. doi:10.2105/AJPH.2013.301785.

Bos, H., & Sandfort, T. (2015). Gender nonconformity, sexual orientation, and Dutch adolescents' relationship with peers. *Archives of Sexual Behavior, 44,* 1269–1279.

Centers for Disease Control and Prevention. (2009). *Youth Risk Behavior survey.* Retrieved September 10, 2012, from http://www.cdc.gov/yrbss

Chen, F. F. (2007). Sensitivity of goodness of fit indexes to lack of measurement invariance. *Structural Equation Modeling, 14,* 464–504.

Chesir-Teran, D., & Hughes, D. (2009). Heterosexism in high school and victimization among lesbian, gay, bisexual, and questioning students. *Journal of Youth and Adolescence, 38,* 963–975. doi:10.1007/s10964-008-9364-x.

Cheung, G. W., & Rensvold, R. B. (2002). Evaluating goodness-of-fit indexes for testing measurement invariance. *Structural Equation Modeling, 9,* 233–255. doi:10.1207/S15328007SEM0902_5.

Cianciotto, J., & Cahill, S. (2012). *LGBT youth in America's schools.* Ann Arbor, MI: University of Michigan Press.

Coker, T. R., Austin, S. B., & Schuster, M. A. (2010). The health and health care of lesbian, gay, and bisexual adolescents. *Annual Review of Public Health, 31,* 457–477. doi:10.1146/annurev.publhealth.012809.103636.

Darwich, L., Hymel, S., & Waterhouse, T. (2012). School avoidance and substance use among lesbian, gay, bisexual, and questioning youth: The impact of peer victimization and adult support. *Journal of Educational Psychology, 104,* 381–392. doi:10.1037/a0026684.

Espelage, D. L., & Holt, M. K. (2001). Bullying and victimization during early adolescence: Peer influences and psychosocial correlates. *Journal of Emotional Abuse, 2,* 123–142. doi:10.1300/J135v02n02_08.

Gastic, B. (2008). School truancy and the disciplinary problems of bullying victims. *Educational Review, 60,* 391–404. doi:10.1080/00131910802393423.

Gay, Lesbian, and Straight Education Network (GLSEN). (n.d.). *Educator Resources.* Retrieved from http://www.glsen.org/educate/resources

Gender Spectrum. (n.d.). *Resources.* Retrieved from http://www.genderspectrum.org/resources

Goodenow, C., Szalacha, L., & Westheimer, K. (2006). School support groups, other school factors, and the safety of sexual minority adolescents. *Psychology in the Schools, 43*, 573–589. doi:10.1002/pits.20173.

Gregory, A., Skiba, R. J., & Noguera, P. A. (2010). The achievement gap and the discipline gap two sides of the same coin? *Educational Researcher, 39*, 59–68. doi:10.3102/0013189X09357621.

GSA Network. (n.d.). *Resources*. Retrieved from http://www.gsanetwork.org/resources

Himmelstein, K. E. W., & Brückner, H. (2011). Criminal-justice and school sanctions against nonheterosexual youth: A national longitudinal study. *Pediatrics, 127*(1), 49–57. doi:10.1542/peds.2009-2306.

Kline, R. B. (2011). *Principles and practice of structural equation modeling* (3rd ed.). New York: Guilford Press.

Luk, J. W., Wang, J., & Simons-Morton, B. G. (2010). Bullying victimization and substance use among U.S. adolescents: Mediation by depression. *Prevention Science, 11*, 355–359. doi:10.1007/s11121-010-0179-0.

Marshal, M. P., Friedman, M. S., Stall, R., King, K. M., Miles, J., Gold, M. A., Morse, J. (2008). Sexual orientation and adolescent substance use: A meta-analysis and methodological review. *Addiction, 103*, 546–556. doi:10.1111/j.1360-0443.2008.02149.x.

Meyer, I. H. (2003). Prejudice, social stress, and mental health in lesbian, gay, and bisexual populations: Conceptual issues and research evidence. *Psychological Bulletin, 129*, 674–697. doi:10.1037/0033-2909.129.5.674.

Mustanski, B. S., Garofalo, R., & Emerson, E. M. (2010). Mental health disorders, psychological distress, and suicidality in a diverse sample of lesbian, gay, bisexual, and transgender youths. *American Journal of Public Health, 100*, 2426–2432.

Newcomb, M. E., Heinz, A. J., Birkett, M., & Mustanski, B. (2014). A longitudinal examination of risk and protective factors for cigarette smoking among lesbian, gay, bisexual, and transgender youth. *Journal of Adolescent Health, 54*, 558–564. doi:10.1016/j.jadohealth.2013.10.208.

Ollis, D. (2013). Planning and delivering intervention to promote gender and sexuality. In I. Rivers & N. Duncan (Eds.), *Bullying: Experiences and discourses of sexuality and gender* (pp. 145–161). London: Routledge.

Panfil, V. R. (2014). Gay gang- and crime-involved men's experiences with homophobic bullying and harassment in schools. *Journal of Crime and Justice, 37*, 79–103. doi:10.1080/0735648X.2013.830395.

Piquero, A. R. (2008). Disproportionate minority contact. *The Future of Children, 18*, 59–79. doi:10.1353/foc.0.0013.

Poteat, V. P., Espelage, D. L., & Koenig, B. W. (2009). Willingness to remain friends and attend school with lesbian and gay peers: Relational expressions of prejudice among heterosexual youth. *Journal of Youth and Adolescence, 38,* 952–962. doi:10.1007/s10964-009-9416-x.

Poteat, V. P., Mereish, E. H., DiGiovanni, C. D., & Koenig, B. W. (2011). The effects of general and homophobic victimization on adolescents' psychosocial and educational concerns: The importance of intersecting identities and parent support. *Journal of Counseling Psychology, 58,* 597–609. doi:10.1037/a0025095.

Poteat, V. P., Scheer, J. R., & Chong, E. S. K. (2016). Sexual orientation-based disparities in school and juvenile justice discipline: A multiple group comparison of contributing factors. *Journal of Educational Psychology., 108,* 229–241. doi:10.1037/edu0000058.

Ray, K. E. B., & Alarid, L. F. (2004). Examining racial disparity of male property offenders in the Missouri juvenile justice system. *Youth Violence and Juvenile Justice, 2,* 107–128. doi:10.1177/1541204003262228.

Rosario, M., Schrimshaw, E. W., & Hunter, J. (2011). Cigarette smoking as a coping strategy: Negative implications for subsequent psychological distress among lesbian, gay, and bisexual youths. *Journal of Pediatric Psychology, 36,* 731–742. doi:10.1093/jpepsy/jsp141.

Russell, S. T., Kosciw, J., Horn, S., & Saewyc, E. (2010). Safe schools policy for LGBTQ students. *Society for Research in Child Development Social Policy Report, 24*(4), 1–25.

Russell, S. T., Everett, B. G., Rosario, M., & Birkett, M. (2014). Indicators of victimization and sexual orientation among adolescents: Analyses from youth risk behavior surveys. *American Journal of Public Health, 104,* 255–261. doi:10.2105/AJPH.2013.301493.

Ryan, C., Huebner, D., Diaz, R. M., & Sanchez, J. (2009). Family rejection as a predictor of negative health outcomes in White and Latino lesbian, gay, and bisexual young adults. *Pediatrics, 123,* 346–352.

Shaw, S. R., & Braden, J. P. (1990). Race and gender bias in the administration of corporal punishment. *School Psychology Review, 19,* 378–383.

Shook, J. J., & Goodkind, S. A. (2009). Racial disproportionality in juvenile justice: The interaction of race and geography in pretrial detention for violent and serious offenses. *Race and Social Problems, 1,* 257–266. doi:10.1007/s12552-009-9021-3.

Simon, T. R., Dent, C. W., & Sussman, S. (1997). Vulnerability to victimization, concurrent problem behaviors, and peer influence as predictors of in-school weapon carrying among high school students. *Violence and Victims, 12,* 277–289.

Skiba, R. J., Michael, R. S., Nardo, A. C., & Peterson, R. L. (2002). The color of discipline: Sources of racial and gender disproportionality in school punishment. *The Urban Review, 34,* 317–342. doi:10.1023/A:1021320817372.

Skiba, R. J., Arredondo, M., & Williams, N. T. (2014a). More than a metaphor: The contribution of exclusionary discipline to a school-to-prison pipeline. *Equity and Excellence in Education, 47*(4), 546–564.

Skiba, R. J., Chung, C. G., Trachok, M., Baker, T. L., Sheya, A., & Hughes, R. L. (2014b). Parsing disciplinary disproportionality: Contributions of infraction, student, and school characteristics to out-of-school suspension and expulsion. *American Educational Research Journal, 51*, 640–670.

Snapp, S. D., Hoenig, J. M., Fields, A., & Russell, S. T. (2015). Messy, butch, and queer LGBTQ youth and the school-to-prison pipeline. *Journal of Adolescent Research, 30*, 57–82. doi:10.1177/0743558414557625.

Tharp-Taylor, S., Haviland, A., & D'Amico, E. J. (2009). Victimization from mental and physical bullying and substance use in early adolescence. *Addictive Behaviors, 34*, 561–567. doi:10.1016/j.addbeh.2009.03.012.

Wallace Jr., J. M., Goodkind, S., Wallace, C. M., & Bachman, J. G. (2008). Racial, ethnic, and gender differences in school discipline among U.S. high school students: 1991–2005. *The Negro Educational Review, 59*(1–2), 47–62.

Wehlage, G., & Rutter, R. (1986). Dropping out: How much do schools contribute to the problem? *The Teachers College Record, 87*, 374–392.

Wordes, M., Bynum, T. S., & Corley, C. J. (1994). Locking up youth: The impact of race on detention decisions. *Journal of Research in Crime and Delinquency, 31*, 149–165. doi:10.1177/0022427894031002004.

CHAPTER 5

Does Student–Teacher Racial/Ethnic Match Impact Black Students' Discipline Risk? A Test of the Cultural Synchrony Hypothesis

Jamilia J. Blake, Danielle M. Smith, Miner P. Marchbanks III, Allison L. Seibert, Steve M. Wood, and Eun Sook Kim

INTRODUCTION

Black students comprise 16% of the US public school population, but represent 32–42% of students' exclusionary discipline sanctions, and 27–31% of law enforcement referrals and school-based arrests (U.S. Department of Education, 2014). These statistics mirror 40 years of overrepresentation of Black students in the school discipline system (Children's Defense Fund, 1975; Skiba, Michael, Nardo, & Peterson, 2002; Wallace, Goodkind, Wallace, & Bachman, 2008).

While a number of explanations have been offered to explain racial/ethnic disparities in school discipline, the cultural synchrony hypothesis provides a unique theoretical framework to explain how student–teacher

J.J. Blake, Ph.D. (✉) • D.M. Smith, M.Ed. • M.P. Marchbanks III, Ph.D.
A.L. Seibert, M.Ed. • S.M. Wood, Ph.D.
Education & Human Development, Texas A&M University,
College Station, TX, USA

E.S. Kim, Ph.D.
University of South Florida, Tampa, FL, USA

© The Author(s) 2016
R.J. Skiba et al. (eds.), *Inequality in School Discipline*,
DOI 10.1057/978-1-137-51257-4_5

racial/ethnic incongruence might affect the allocation of school discipline sanctions to Black students (Blake, Butler, Lewis, & Darensbourg, 2011; Irvine, 1990; Monroe & Obidah, 2004). By considering how the incongruence between the racial/ethnic diversity of the teaching workforce and US student population contribute to cultural misunderstandings in the classroom, the cultural synchrony hypothesis asserts that a cultural divide exists between students and teachers (Aud et al., 2013; Goldring, Gray, & Bitterman, 2013; Irvine, 1990; Kena et al., 2014). This divide, which is rooted in a lack of shared cultural understanding between teachers and students of differing race/ethnicities, may explain Black students' elevated discipline rates. The purpose of this chapter is to determine whether the cultural synchrony hypothesis can serve as a theoretical framework for explaining Black students' elevated risk for exclusionary discipline, using a statewide dataset of secondary school students' discipline records.

Cultural Synchrony Hypothesis

Research suggests that school personnel perceive and evaluate Black students more negatively than students of other races across academic and behavioral domains (Downey & Pribesh, 2004; Tenenbaum & Ruck, 2007). Academically, teachers perceive Black students' performance as lower than that of White students, making Black students less likely to be recommended for honors courses and more likely to be placed in special education than students from other racial/ethnic groups (Francis, 2012; Oates, 2009; Skiba, Poloni-Staudinger, Gallini, Simmons, & Feggins-Aziz, 2006). Behaviorally, Black students are frequently rated as having more overt externalizing behaviors (e.g., physical aggression, destruction of property), being more disruptive to the classroom environment, and having more emotional problems than their White peers (Bates & Glick, 2013; Cullinan & Kauffman, 2005; Francis, 2012). The cultural synchrony hypothesis asserts that educators' negative evaluations of Black students are fueled by stereotypes of Black adults, who are depicted in the media as violent, threatening, hypersexualized, and in need of socialization (Blake et al., 2011; Blake, Butler, & Smith, 2015; Rome, 2004; West, 1995). These negative evaluations have been shown to intensify when teachers do not share the racial/ethnic background of their students (Bates & Glick, 2013; Dee, 2005; Downey & Pribesh, 2004; Takei & Shouse, 2008).

Taking into consideration the lack of racial/ethnic diversity within the teaching workforce, the cultural synchrony hypothesis asserts that many educators may be unfamiliar with the culture and learning styles of their racially and ethnically diverse students, particularly their Black students (Goldring et al., 2013; Irvine, 1990; Landsman & Lewis, 2011). By extension, the social and behavioral norms that Black students experience and translate to their classroom behaviors may be unfamiliar to their teachers (Goldring et al., 2013; Graves & Howes, 2011). As a result, teachers may unknowingly apply media-driven stereotypes about Black culture to understand the ambiguous actions of Black students that are distinct from White, middle-class culture (e.g., use of slang, questioning of authority rather than assuming legitimacy based on position/title).

Teachers' subconscious application of stereotypes may influence the administration of school discipline to Black youth for behaviors that are considered benign among White students, yet perceived as more threatening and potentially harmful when committed by Black students (Blake et al., 2015; Francis, 2012; Neal, McCray, Webb-Johnson, & Bridgest, 2003). Further, behaviors that are acceptable and normative in Black students' homes and communities may be pathologized by teachers who lack training in cultural competence or familiarity with Black culture (Graves & Howes, 2011; Irvine, 1990; Monroe & Obidah, 2004). Within the context of school discipline, this lack of cultural synchrony between students and teachers may result in more harsh and reactive punishments than are required to manage Black students' behavior (Downey & Pribesh, 2004; Ho, Gol-Guven, & Bagnato, 2012; Takei & Shouse, 2008).

Evidence Supporting the Cultural Synchrony Hypothesis

Ratings of academic success. There is some evidence to support the cultural synchrony hypothesis in terms of the academic perceptions of students of color when considering student–teacher race/ethnicity congruence (Bates & Glick, 2013; Downey & Pribesh, 2004; Driessen, 2015; Ho et al., 2012; McGrady & Reynolds, 2013; Saft & Pianta, 2001). Students of color tend to receive more negative academic ratings with White teachers than with teachers of the same race/ethnicity (Dee, 2005; Downey & Pribesh, 2004). Academically, Black students show the least benefit when they have a White teacher as compared to students of other races/ethnicities (McGrady & Reynolds, 2013), but show increases in reading and math achievement when they have Black teachers (Dee, 2004; Egalite, Kisida, & Winters, 2015). Importantly, the positive effects of having same-race teachers are especially prominent among low-performing students (Egalite et al., 2015).

Behavior ratings. Similar patterns are observed when considering teacher ratings of student behavior by race/ethnicity. Black students receive more negative ratings of externalizing behaviors from White teachers than Black teachers (Bates & Glick, 2013), even when controlling for various individual and school-level characteristics associated with externalizing behavior problems. Additionally, White English and social studies teachers tend to rate their Black students lower than their White students on measures of citizenship, participation, and engagement within school and classwork activities (Takei & Shouse, 2008). Interestingly, differences in student ratings by race/ethnicity are not evident in vignette-based studies, perhaps due to the analogue nature of the design (Noltemeyer, Kunesh, Hostutler, Frato, & Sarr-Kerman, 2012). Together, most research suggests there are fewer perceptions of behavioral and social problems and perceptions of higher academic achievement when Black students are taught by Black instructors.

White teachers' negative evaluations of Black students may be rooted in the quality of student–teacher relationships. Teachers rate their relationships with students more positively when they are of the same race (Saft & Pianta, 2001). Same-race teacher–child interactions tend to be warmer than racially incongruent teacher–child interactions, which are characterized by more conflict (Ho et al., 2012). Similarly, when Black students have supportive teacher relationships, they have been reported to be less aggressive (Meehan, Hughes, & Cavell, 2003).

Purpose

Collectively, these results suggest student–teacher racial/ethnic congruence may play a significant role in the educational outcomes of Black students, providing some support for the cultural synchrony hypothesis. However, only two studies have examined the effect of racial/ethnic congruence on students' discipline risk directly. Bradshaw, Mitchell, O'Brennan, and Leaf (2010) investigated whether student–teacher racial/ethnic congruence influenced Black students' risk for Office Discipline Referrals (ODRs) after controlling for students' classroom behavior and school demographic characteristics. Interestingly, they found no empirical support for the cultural synchrony hypothesis, in that Black students were as likely as White students to receive an ODR from a White or a Black teacher. In contrast, Roch, Pitts, and Navarro (2010) reported that greater student–teacher racial/ethnic congruence was associated with lower risk for in- and out-of-school suspension in public schools in Georgia. Given these contradictory findings, additional research is needed to determine the extent student–teacher racial/ethnic congruence influences disproportionate discipline practices.

The current study examines whether student–teacher racial/ethnic congruence can account for secondary students' risk for exclusionary discipline sanctions when controlling for demographic and school contextual characteristics. Expanding this work into the secondary school years is important since all students, especially Black students, are at elevated risk for discipline in these years (Losen & Skiba, 2010). This study also extends the literature in two important ways. First, we investigate disproportionality beyond urban school settings by using a statewide dataset to examine discipline risk, providing a more robust test of factors contributing to discipline risk in secondary schools. Second, we assess the effect of student–teacher racial/ethnic congruence on school discipline risk after controlling for other potentially influential factors.

METHODS

Data

The data for this study was drawn from a statewide dataset consisting of annual information for all students in the state of Texas in three 7th grade public school cohorts from the 2000–2001, 2001–2002, and 2002–2003 school years, each tracked for five years, beginning in the 7th grade (Fabelo et al., 2011). Because the data was available each of the five years the students were in secondary school, the panel dataset tracked 928,940 individual students from 7th grade through at least their expected graduation date. As such, students appeared in our dataset up to eight years (7th through 12th grade plus two years of follow-up for the 2000–2001 cohort and one year of follow-up for the 2001–2002 cohort for those who were held back in grade during their academic career). We analyzed the data for each child every year they were represented in the dataset (student-years), providing over 5.1 million student-year records. For example, a student who is in the dataset for 7th through 9th grades would have three student-years in the dataset.

The database contained an extensive set of variables[1] concerning students' academic performance, demographics, and information on each reported discipline event (including in-school suspensions, out-of-school suspensions, placement in disciplinary alternative education campuses, assignment to juvenile justice alternative education campuses, and/or expulsion). The overall sample was roughly equal in regard to gender (51% male), with 39% identified as Hispanic, 14% as Black, 43% White, and the remaining 4% representing students from multi-racial/ethnic, Asian, or Native American backgrounds.

Variables

Dependent Variable

Whether a student was disciplined at least once during his/her secondary school career served as the dependent variable. A student was considered disciplined if s/he received any type of school sanction, in- or out-of-school suspension, disciplinary alternative education placement, juvenile justice alternative education placement, or expulsion.

Independent Variables

The congruence between the racial/ethnic composition of the faculty and students, a school-level measure, served as the key independent variable. We modified slightly the student–teacher racial/ethnic congruence index developed by Fabelo et al. (2011) as a measure of the similarity of the racial compositions of the faculty and student bodies:

$$\left[\begin{array}{l} \left(\% \text{Faculty}_{\text{Black}} - \% \text{Students}_{\text{Black}}\right)^2 + \left(\% \text{Faculty}_{\text{Hispanic}} - \% \text{Students}_{\text{Hispanic}}\right)^2 + \\ \left(\% \text{Faculty}_{\text{White}} - \% \text{Students}_{\text{White}}\right)^2 + \left(\% \text{Faculty}_{\text{Other Race}} - \% \text{Students}_{\text{Other Race}}\right)^2 \end{array} \right]$$

$$(1)$$

In order to ensure a more normal distribution, we utilized a square root transformation (Osborne, 2010). After the square root transformation, a campus with a perfect congruence between its student and faculty racial/ethnic makeup resulted in a value of 0. With perfect incongruence (e.g., 100% White faculty teaching a student body that was 100% Hispanic), the maximum value was 141.4, a value which was in fact observed in the data. To facilitate a more intuitive interpretation, this value was standardized to have a mean of zero and standard deviation one. With this approach, a school with an average level of congruence has a value of zero, while a high-congruence school that is one standard deviation below the mean would have a value of negative one and a low-congruence school that is one standard deviation above the mean would have a value of one.

Other individual-level independent variables included in the model were student race/ethnicity (individual-level); student gender (individual-level); an interaction effect measuring student race/ethnicity by gender; an interaction of the congruence index with race/ethnicity and with gender; and a three-way interaction of the congruence index, race/ethnicity, and gender.

At the school level, we included a measure of the campus diversity using the Greenberg diversity measure:

$$\left[\begin{array}{c} 1-\left(\%\,\text{Students}_{\text{Black}}\,/\,100\right)^2 - \left(\%\,\text{Students}_{\text{Hispanic}}\,/\,100\right)^2 \\ -\left(\text{Students}_{\text{White}}\,/\,100\right)^2 - \left(\%\,\text{Students}_{\text{Other Race}}\,/\,100\right)^2 \end{array}\right] \tag{2}$$

A perfectly homogenous school (e.g., 100% White) would result in a score of 0 and a perfectly diverse school (i.e., 25% of each race/ethnicity including other) would score 0.75 (maximum diversity in our dataset was 0.749, and perfect homogeneity was observed in other cases).

Control Variables

As a control for academic performance, we accounted for whether the student had been retained the previous school year (individual-level). To control for student maturation, we also included a variable representing the number of years the student had been in the data (individual-level). Additionally, we controlled for individual-level poverty by including the student's free- or reduced-price lunch status.

In terms of the campus environment, we included the school's Title I status, student/teacher ratio, and school size as campus-level control variables. To account for county-level characteristics, we controlled for the county urbanicity and income per-capita.

Analytic Approach

Data was available on an annual basis; as such, the student-year served as the unit of analysis. Once a student was disciplined in a given year, he/she was ineligible to have a first discipline sanction in following years. Thus, students were only included in the model in a year if they had not been disciplined in previous years. For instance, a student disciplined in 2003 was included in the dataset from 2001 to 2003, but not in following years. In all, 2,915,617 student-years were modeled utilizing binary logistic regression.

Given the nested structure of the data (e.g., students nested within schools), it is likely that the probability of student discipline risk is partially attributed to variation in school-level discipline policies as well as students' movement between school campuses, due either to academic progression or a physical move. Failure to account for data dependency resultant of nested data tends to produce artificially small standard errors, leading to an increased probability of a Type I error (Primo, Jacobsmeier, & Milyo, 2007). To correct for this, we utilized binomial logistic regression with standard errors clustered by students and campus year for data analyses as computational constraints, as our sample size prevented us from implementing multilevel modeling (Bryk & Raudenbush, 1992). Robust clustered standard errors allow for the variance to differ by the clustering variable and performs similarly to mixed-level modeling in estimation of standard errors, but takes less time to converge (Franzese, 2005; Kam & Franzese, 2007; Primo et al., 2007). We utilized clustered standard errors to account for the variance related to clustering by students and by campus year in our logistic regression analyses. Table 5.1 reflects the relationship between each independent/control variable and the probability of discipline within a student-year.

RESULTS

Student–Teacher Racial/Ethnic Congruence

Overall, 59.6% of the sample had been disciplined between 7th and 12th grades. Table 5.1 details the results from the binary logistic regression analyses. The key variable of interest, student–teacher racial/ethnic congruence, showed that as a school's faculty and students became less similar in terms of their race/ethnicity, the likelihood of discipline increased. While significant, the base effect was small. A standard deviation decrease in student–teacher racial/ethnic congruence leads to a 3% increase in the odds of being disciplined. However, the effect of this congruence varied greatly by race and gender. For females, the odds of discipline increased by an additional 5% when in less congruent schools (for a total 8% increase after adding the 3% main effect and 5% female-specific effect). Black students saw an additional 10% increase in the odds of discipline when educated in a less congruent school relative to a more congruent school (for a total of 13% [10% Black plus 3% main effect]), while Hispanic students saw an additional 8% increase in the same situation (for a total of 12%, [8% Hispanics plus 3% main effect plus rounding differences]). For Black girls, the effect was less pronounced, with a 6% reduction in the odds of discipline relative to Black males (for a total of 12% [3% main effect plus 10% Black effect plus 5% female effect minus 6% Black female effect]) when moving to a school with less congruence. The interaction

Table 5.1 Predictors of first time school discipline within a year

	Coefficient[a]	Std. error	Odds ratio
Congruence			
Student/teacher congruence	0.003**	0.011	1.03
Congruence × Black	0.093***	0.018	1.10
Congruence × Hispanic	0.081***	0.011	1.08
Congruence × other race	0.077***	0.023	1.08
Congruence × female	0.048***	0.009	1.05
Congruence × Black female	−0.062***	0.015	0.94
Congruence × Hispanic female	−0.020	0.011	0.98
Congruence × other race female	0.001	0.032	1.00
Individual level			
Black	0.498***	0.016	1.64
Hispanic	0.192***	0.010	1.21
Other race	−0.492***	0.021	0.61
Female	−0.524***	0.008	0.59
Black female	0.149***	0.014	1.16
Hispanic female	0.162***	0.010	1.18
Other race female	−0.073*	0.029	0.93
Years in cohort	−0.147***	0.004	0.86
Free/reduced-price lunch	0.488***	0.007	1.63
Retained last year	0.936***	0.016	2.55
School level			
Title 1 school	−0.046**	0.016	0.96
Campus size	−0.000***	0.000	1.00
Student teacher ratio	0.010***	0.003	1.01
Greenberg student diversity measure	0.444***	0.045	1.56
Campus size	−0.000***	0.000	1.00
Title 1 school	−0.046**	0.016	0.96
Student teacher ratio	0.010***	0.003	1.01
Greenberg student diversity measure	0.444***	0.045	1.56
County-level			
County income per-capita income	−0.000***	0.000	1.00
Campus in suburban county	−0.041*	0.016	0.96
Campus in non-metro adjacent county	−0.010	0.020	0.99
Campus in rural county	−0.253***	0.037	0.78
Constant	−1.764***	0.055	–
			n = 2,915,618

[a]Coefficients reflect the results of a binary logistic regression
***$p < 0.001$, **$p < 0.01$, *$p < 0.05$

for Hispanic girls was not significant, indicating that the effect of being female did not differ for Hispanic students relative to White students.

Figure 5.1 depicts the effect of congruence after accounting for the accumulating effect of aggregating across the six years of 7th to 12th grades. As illustrated, the effect of attending a high-congruence (one standard deviation below the mean) campus relative to a low-congruence (one standard deviation above the mean) campus on students' discipline risk was substantial for females and students of color.[2] As the figure shows, the effect of being in a high-congruence school was especially pronounced for students of color, with an odds ratio of 1.44 for Black males. In other words, Black males who attended a low student–teacher racial/ethnic congruence school had 44% higher odds of being disciplined between 7th and 12th grade than similar students who attended a high-congruence school.

Demographic, Academic, and School-Level Predictors

In regard to other independent variables, the racial/ethnic diversity of students at schools (measured by the Greenberg diversity index) was a strong predictor of discipline risk. Attending a perfectly diverse school rather than a perfectly racially/ethnically homogenous school, leads to a 40% increase in the likelihood of discipline in a given year.[3] This finding warrants further investigation to examine the root cause of such a result.

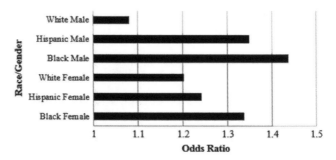

Fig. 5.1 Odds ratio of discipline when moving from a high- to low-congruence school over a six-year secondary school career

While not the theoretical thrust of this chapter, even after controlling for a myriad of factors, race/ethnicity and gender both remained strong predictors of discipline involvement.[4] After accounting for student and campus characteristics, Black male students had discipline odds 1.64 times higher than that of White male students, the base category (the odds ratio associated with Black students yields appropriate results for Black males). Hispanic male students had a smaller, but substantial, 1.21 times increase in the odds of being disciplined relative to White males (for the males, the odds ratio associated with Hispanics yields appropriate results for Hispanic males).

Additionally, being female appeared to be a significant protective factor, with White females having an odds ratio of 0.59 relative to White males (for White students, the female odds ratio provides appropriate results for White females). However, the protective nature of being female was not as strong for Hispanic or Black girls; their female-specific odds ratios were 0.69 and 0.70, respectively.[5] Relative to White males, the net result of being a Hispanic female was 16% lower odds of being disciplined in a given year. For Black females, the net result was actually 13% higher odds of discipline in a year than for White males.[6]

In regard to the control variables, the analyses showed that academic failure (i.e., a history of grade retention) was the strongest predictor of discipline risk. Those students who were retained the previous year had odds of current year discipline that were 2.55 times higher than students who were not retained. Further, individual-level poverty (i.e., free- or reduced-price lunch status) was associated with 63% higher odds of discipline in a year than for students who did not qualify for these programs. Even after controlling for congruence, the racial-ethnic composition of the student body, race/ethnicity and gender, academic performance, and socioeconomic status remained powerful predictors of school discipline involvement.

DISCUSSION

Racial/ethnic disparities in school discipline have been identified as a national crisis (Losen & Gillespie, 2012). The cultural synchrony hypothesis suggests that these educational disparities among others are associated with a lack of cultural synchrony between Black students and their teachers, who do not share their same cultural and racial/ethnic background (Irvine, 1990). This chapter contributes to the school discipline literature by using the cultural synchrony hypothesis as a theoretical framework to understand how the racial/ethnic congruence between students and teachers affects students of colors' discipline risk.

We found that student–teacher racial/ethnic congruence was a significant predictor of discipline risk. Attending a school where the faculty mirrors the student body appears beneficial for all students, but especially students of color, who have repeatedly been shown to be overrepresented in the school discipline system (Fabelo et al., 2011). It is both interesting and troubling that the difference in discipline risk changes based on the level of student–teacher racial/ethnic congruence in a given school, with less discipline risk associated with higher representation of teachers that match the race/ethnicity of the student body. For Black students, the odds of being suspended during 7th through 12th grade are nearly 44% higher for Black males, and 34% for Black females, than students of other races/ethnicities when which the teaching faculty is less representative of its student body's racial/ethnic background. A similar, but less elevated, pattern of risk is found for Hispanic students, with higher odds of being suspended in their secondary career for males (34%) and females (24%) than like peers when they attend a school where the teaching faculty's race/ethnicity differs from their own.

Drawing from a large statewide dataset of secondary school students, we found evidence for the disparate impact of school discipline on Black and Hispanic students and partial support for the cultural synchrony hypothesis. Consistent with prior research, students' individual-level SES, history of academic failure, and the racial composition of the student body, as represented by the Greenberg diversity measure, emerged as highly significant predictors of discipline risk (Gregory, Skiba, & Noguera, 2010; Hoffman, Erickson, & Spence, 2013; Welch & Payne, 2011). However, when accounting for these and other factors, Black and Hispanic students remained at significant risk for being suspended compared to White students. That is, racial/ethnic differences in school discipline sanctions persisted even when controlling for individual- and school-level poverty and academic failure, three important contributors to discipline risk. This finding was also true of gender: when controlling for a number of individual and school-level variables, Black males and Hispanic males were at the greatest risk of school suspension, followed by Black females.

Limitations

Collectively, these findings suggest partial support for the cultural synchrony hypothesis. However, this study tested only the degree of cultural incongruence between students and teachers in a school, that is, the extent to which the makeup of a school's faculty is representative of the diversity of the student body. The data did not allow us to examine the daily teacher interactions that are the foundation of the theory of cultural synchrony in American schools. In order to fully understand the impact of student–teacher relationships on behavioral outcomes and racial/ethnic differences on student–teacher relationship quality, more nuanced tests of the cultural synchrony hypothesis are necessary. Such tests will allow us to understand exactly how cultural missteps and misunderstandings in classrooms might fuel inequitable discipline practices. To that end, future studies testing this hypothesis should employ mixed-method techniques, drawing from qualitative, observational, and advanced statistical methodology traditions to provide a more complete picture of the interactive effect of student–teacher racial/ethnic congruence on students' discipline risk. Future research should also investigate the role student racial composition plays in moderating the relationship between student–teacher racial/ethnic congruence and student discipline risk.

Policy Implications

In light of our findings, we recommend the following:

- Higher education institutions with teacher preparation programs should increase the diversity of students majoring in education, and should receive funding for recruitment services dedicated to this purpose. For decades, educational scholars have called for the diversification of the teaching workforce (Villegas & Irvine, 2010). The recognition that efforts should be made to ensure that teacher composition reflects student composition in terms of their racial/ethnic background is rooted in part in cultural synchrony theory (Rosenberg, 1979) and consistent with findings from the literature on representative bureaucracy, which states that social groups benefit when leadership is demographically similar to the body it represents or serves (Meier, Wrinkle, & Polinard, 1999). Racially/ethnically diverse students have been found to benefit behaviorally and academically when the race/ethnicity of the teaching and administration workforces are similar to the student body (Grissom, Kern, & Rodriguez, 2015; Roch et al., 2010; Rocha & Hawes, 2009). The argument for diversifying the teaching workforce is based on the notion that teachers who share the cultural and racial/ethnic heritage of their students have the background and experiences needed to understand culturally centered and ambiguous behaviors, reducing the likelihood of misunderstanding and mislabeling these behaviors as "deviant" (Blake et al., 2011; Blake et al., 2015). As the demographics of the USA continue to evolve, the need to diversify the teaching staff becomes more pressing. By 2024, students who have been racial/ethnic minorities will comprise the numerical majority in American schools (Kena et al., 2014). Because students of color may face educational adversity by attending schools where the teaching staff does not share their racial/ethnic background, our findings provide additional justification for universities to make concerted efforts to diversify the teaching workforce.

- Given the difficulty in achieving a representative faculty in the near term, efforts to improve the cultural competency of current teachers should be an immediate priority. A call has been issued for schools to integrate implicit racial bias training into their professional development programs (Rudd, 2014), in order to support teachers who struggle with equitably disciplining their students.

- Increased funding for teachers' professional development based on a tiered-support model to address inequitable school discipline should be made available to public schools. This model for professional development would involve providing all teachers with classroom behavior management and implicit bias training as part of their regular professional development activities. For teachers who exceed discipline thresholds for the number of discipline referrals or racial/ethnic disparities in discipline referrals made, focused support services would be made available. These support services may take the form of teachers being paired with more experienced peers who are successful at managing their classroom to serve as coaches. Coaching might include modeling and mentoring teachers who over-refer students in the delivery of effective classroom management practices. Additionally, teachers could complete in-depth training covering implicit bias and cultural competency (see e.g., *My Teaching Partner*, Center for Advanced Study of Teaching and Learning, 2015; see also

Gregory, Bell & Pollock, this volume). For teachers who are unsuccessful with these added support services, individual assistance may be provided, such as participation in culturally informed behavioral consultation with school psychologists (Ingraham, 2008; Newell, 2010; Newell, in 2016).

- Each of these recommendations is not without its own costs. However, to achieve the goals set out by various levels of government, such as the Supportive School Discipline Initiative of the US Departments of Education and Justice (2014), steps such as these are likely necessary.

CONCLUSION

Using a panel dataset of more than 900,000 students across several years, we have found that the extent to which the racial/ethnic diversity of a school's student population matches its faculty, the less likely students are to experience discipline. These findings are most robust for students of color—the individuals who are most plagued by disproportionate discipline. Given these findings, the creation of programs to recruit faculty of color in K-12 settings have promise. While such recruitment is taking place, we recommend that professional development programs be implemented to ensure that teachers are fully prepared to deal with classroom behavior in a culturally competent manner.

NOTES

1. See Appendix A of Fabelo et al. (2011) for a more detailed list of variables within the dataset and the main text for various demographics of the study cohort.
2. Because of the complicated and interactive nature of the graphic, the overall probabilities for each scenario were calculated and the odds ratios calculated from these probabilities. Both procedures follow Long (1997, 79–81). In particular, for each bar, the coefficient for grade, race, gender, congruence, race × congruence, gender × congruence, and race × gender × congruence were accounted for while leaving other values at their means, and follows a student from 7th to 12th grade calculating the overall odds of discipline over a six-year academic career.

3. Because odds ratios are non-linear, simply adding together the separate odds ratios or multiplying an odds ratio by a factor will often yield improper values. When properly interpreting logistic regression, odds ratios are calculated by $e^{(x)}$ where x is equal to the coefficient in question, the total value of combined coefficients, or the appropriate value of the independent variable multiplied by the corresponding coefficient (Long, 1997). In this case, with a maximum change in diversity of 0.75, the resulting odds ratio is calculated by $e^{(0.75 \times 0.444)}$.

4. When discussing race/ethnicity, gender, and the interactions of the two, an average congruence campus is assumed to eliminate any compounding effects from the student–teacher racial/ethnic congruence interactions.

5. Interactive odds ratio calculated as $e^{(0.162-0.524)}$ for Hispanics and $e^{(0.149-0.524)}$ for Black girls.

6. When compared to White males, the odds ratios are calculated as $e^{(0.162-0.524+0.192)}$ for Hispanic females and $e^{(0.149-0.524+0.0498)}$ for Black girls.

References

Aud, S., Wilkinson-Flicker, S., Kristapovich, P., Rathbun, A., Wang, X., & Zhang, J. (2013). *The condition of education 2013 (NCES 2013-037)*. Washington, DC: U.S. Department of Education, National Center for Education Statistics.

Bates, L. A., & Glick, J. E. (2013). Does it matter if teachers and schools match the student? Racial and ethnic disparities in problem behaviors. *Social Science Research, 42*, 1180–1190.

Blake, J. J., Butler, B. A., Lewis, C. L., & Darensbourg, A. (2011). Unmasking the inequitable discipline experiences of urban Black girls: Implications for urban stakeholders. *Urban Review, 43*, 90–106.

Blake, J. J., Butler, B. A., & Smith, D. (2015). Challenging middle class notions of femininity: The cause for Black females' disproportionate suspension rates. In D. J. Losen (Ed.), *Closing the school discipline gap: Equitable remedies for excessive exclusion* (pp. 75–88). New York: Teachers College Press.

Bradshaw, C. P., Mitchell, M. M., O'Brennan, L. M., & Leaf, P. J. (2010). Multilevel exploration of factors contributing to the overrepresentation of Black students in office disciplinary referrals. *Journal of Educational Psychology, 102*, 502–520. doi:10.1037/a0018450.

Bryk, S. W., & Raudenbush, A. S. (1992). *Hierarchical linear models: Applications and data analysis methods*. Thousand Oaks, CA: Sage.

Center for Advanced Study of Teaching and Learning. (2015). *MyTeachingPartner*. Retrieved October 8, 2015, from http://curry.virginia.edu/research/centers/castl/mtp

Children's Defense Fund (1975). *School suspensions: Are they helping children?* Cambridge, MA: Washington Research Project.

Cullinan, D., & Kauffman, J. M. (2005). Do race of student and race of teacher influence ratings of emotional and behavioral problem characteristics of students with emotional disturbance? *Behavioral Disorders, 30*, 393–402.

Dee, T. S. (2004). Teachers, race, and student achievement in a randomized experiment. *Review of Economics and Statistics, 86*, 195–210.

Dee, T. S. (2005). A teacher like me: Does race, ethnicity, or gender matter? *American Economic Review, 95*(2), 158–165. doi:10.1257/000282805774670446.

Downey, D. B., & Pribesh, S. (2004). When race matters: Teachers' evaluations of students' classroom behavior. *Sociology of Education, 77*, 267–282. doi:10.1177/003804070407700401.

Driessen, G. (2015). Teacher ethnicity, student ethnicity, and student outcomes. *Intercultural Education, 26*, 179–191.

Egalite, A. J., Kisida, B., & Winters, M. A. (2015). Representation in the classroom: The effect of own-race teachers on student achievement. *Economics of Education Review, 45*, 44–52. doi:10.1016/j.econedurev.2015.01.007.

Fabelo, T., Thompson, M. D., Plotkin, M., Carmichael, D., Marchbanks, M. P., & Booth, E. A. (2011). *Breaking schools' rules: A statewide study of how school discipline relates to student's success and juvenile justice involvement.* New York: Council of State Governments Justice Center, and College Station, TX: A&M University: Public Policy Research Institute. Retrieved from http://knowledgecenter.csg.org/kc/system/files/Breaking_School_Rules.pdf

Francis, D. V. (2012). Sugar and spice and everything nice? Teacher perceptions of Black girls in the classroom. *The Review of Black Political Economy, 39*, 311–320.

Franzese, R. J. (2005). Empirical strategies for various manifestations of multilevel data. *Political Analysis, 13*, 430–446. doi:10.1093/pan/mpi024.

Goldring, R., Gray, L., & Bitterman, A. (2013). *Characteristics of public and private elementary and secondary school teachers in the United States: Results from the 2011–12 schools and staffing survey (NCES 2013-314).* Washington, DC: U.S. Department of Education, National Center for Education Statistics.

Graves Jr., S. L., & Howes, C. (2011). Ethnic differences in social-emotional development in preschool: The impact of teacher child relationships and classroom quality. *School Psychology Quarterly, 26*, 202–214. doi:10.1037/a0024117.

Gregory, A., Skiba, R. J., & Noguera, P. A. (2010). The achievement gap and the discipline gap: Two sides of the same coin? *Education Researcher, 39*, 59–68. doi:10.3102/0013189X09357621.

Grissom, J. A., Kern, E. C., & Rodriguez, L. A. (2015). The "representative bureaucracy" in education: Educator workforce diversity, policy outputs, and outcomes for disadvantaged students. *Educational Researcher, 44*, 185–192.

Ho, H., Gol-Guven, M., & Bagnato, S. J. (2012). Classroom observations of teacher-child relationships among racially symmetrical and racially asymmetrical teacher-child dyads. *European Early Childhood Education Research Journal, 20*, 329–349.

Hoffman, J. P., Erickson, L. D., & Spence, K. R. (2013). Modeling the association between academic achievement and delinquency: An application of interactional theory. *Criminology, 51*, 629–660. doi:10.1111/1745-9125.12014.

Ingraham, C. L. (2008). Studying multiracial aspects of consultation. In W. P. Erchul & S. M. Sheridan (Eds.), *Handbook of research in school consultation* (pp. 323–348). New York: Lawrence Erlbaum Associates.

Irvine, J. J. (1990). *Black students and school failure: Policies, practices, and prescriptions.* New York: Greenwood Press.

Kam, C. D., & Franzese, R. J. (2007). *Modeling and interpreting interactive hypotheses in regression analysis.* Ann Arbor, MI: University of Michigan Press.

Kena, G., Aud, S., Johnson, F., Wang, X., Zhang, J., Rathbun, A., Kristopovich, P. (2014). *The condition of education 2014* (NCES 2014-083). Washington, DC: U.S. Department of Education, National Center for Education Statistics.

Landsman, J., & Lewis, C. (Eds.) (2011). *White teachers/diverse classrooms: Creating inclusive schools, building on students' diversity and providing true educational equity* (2nd ed.). Sterling, VA: Stylus.

Long, J. S. (1997). *Regression models for categorical and limited dependent variables.* Thousand Oaks, CA: Sage Publications.

Losen, D. J., & Gillespie, J. (2012). *Opportunities suspended: The disparate impact of disciplinary exclusion from school.* Los Angeles, CA: The Center for Civil Rights Remedies at The Civil Rights Project/Proyecto Derechos Civiles.

Losen, D. L., & Skiba, R. J. (2010). *Suspended education: Urban middle schools in crisis.* Los Angeles, CA: The Center for Civil Rights Remedies at The Civil Rights Project/ Proyecto Derechos Civiles, and Montgomery, AL: Southern Poverty Law Center.

McGrady, P. B., & Reynolds, J. R. (2013). Racial mismatch in the classroom: Beyond Black-White differences. *Sociology of Education, 86*, 3–17.

Meehan, B. T., Hughes, J. N., & Cavell, T. A. (2003). Teacher-student relationships as compensatory resources for aggressive children. *Child Development, 74*, 1145–1157. doi:10.1111/1467-8624.00598.

Meier, K. J., Wrinkle, R. D., & Polinard, J. L. (1999). Representative bureaucracy and distributional equity: Addressing the hard question. *Journal of Politics, 61*, 1025–1039.

Monroe, C. R., & Obidah, J. E. (2004). The influence of cultural synchronization on a teacher's perceptions of disruption: A case study of an African American middle-school classroom. *Journal of Teacher Education, 55*, 256–268. doi:10.1177/0022487104263977.

Neal, L. I., McCray, A. D., Webb-Johnson, G., & Bridgest, S. T. (2003). The effects of African American movement styles on teachers' perceptions and reactions. *Journal of Special Education, 37*, 49–57.

Newell, M. (2010). The implementation of problem-solving consultation: An analysis of problem conceptualization in a multiracial context. *Journal of Educational and Psychological Consultation, 20*, 83–105. doi:10.1080/ 10474-411003785529.

Newell, M. (2016). Consultation-based intervention services for racial minority students. In S. L. Graves & J. Blake (Eds.), *Psychoeducational assessment and intervention for ethnic minority children: Evidence-based approaches* (pp. 197–212). Washington, DC: American Psychological Association.

Noltemeyer, A., Kunesh, C., Hostutler, C., Frato, P., & Sarr-Kerman, B. J. (2012). Effects of student and teacher characteristics on teacher impressions of–and responses to–student behaviors. *International Education Studies, 5*, 96–111. doi:10.5539/ies.v5n4p96.

Oates, G. (2009). An empirical test of five prominent explanations for the black–white academic performance gap. *Social Psychology of Education, 12*, 415–441.

Osborne, J. W. (2010). Improving your data transformations: Applying the Box-Cox transformation. *Practical Assessment, Research & Evaluation, 15*, 1–9.

Primo, D. M., Jacobsmeier, M. L., & Milyo, J. (2007). Estimating the impact of state policies and institutions with mixed-level data. *State Politics and Policy Quarterly, 7*, 446–459. doi:10.1177/153244000700700405.

Roch, C. H., Pitts, D. W., & Navarro, I. (2010). Representative bureaucracy and policy tools: Ethnicity, student discipline, and representation in public schools. *Administration & Society, 42*, 38–65.

Rocha, R. R., & Hawes, D. P. (2009). Racial diversity, representative bureaucracy, and equity in multiracial school districts. *Social Science Quarterly, 90*, 326–344. doi:10.1111/j.1540-6237.2009.00620.x.

Rome, D. (2004). *Black demons: Mass media's depiction of the Black male criminal stereotype*. Westport, CT: Preager.

Rosenberg, M. (1979). *Conceiving the self*. New York: Basic Books, Inc.

Rudd, T. (2014). *Racial disproportionality in school discipline: Implicit bias is heavily implicated*. Columbus, OH: Kirwan Institute for the Study of Race and Ethnicity.

Saft, E. W., & Pianta, R. C. (2001). Teachers' perceptions of their relationships with students: Effects of child age, gender, and ethnicity of teachers and children. *School Psychology Quarterly, 16*, 125–141.

Skiba, R. J., Michael, R. S., Nardo, A. C., & Peterson, R. L. (2002). The color of discipline: Sources of racial and gender disproportionality in school punishment. *The Urban Review, 34*, 317–342. doi:10.1023/A:1021320817372.

Skiba, R. J., Poloni-Staudinger, L., Gallini, S., Simmons, A., & Feggins-Aziz, R. (2006). Disparate access: The disproportionality of African American students with disabilities across educational environments. *Exceptional Children, 72*, 411–424. doi:10.1023/A:1021320817372.

Takei, Y., & Shouse, R. (2008). Ratings in Black and White: Does racial symmetry or asymmetry influence teacher assessment of a pupil's work habits? *Social Psychology of Education, 11*, 267–387.

Tenenbaum, H. R., & Ruck, M. D. (2007). Are teachers' expectations different for racial minority than for European American students? A meta-analysis. *Journal of Educational Psychology, 99*, 253–273.

U.S. Department of Education. (2014). *Civil rights data collection: School discipline snapshot* (Issue Brief No. 1). Retrieved from http://ocrdata.ed.gov/Downloads/CRDC-School-Discipline-Snapshot.pdf

U.S. Department of Education, U.S. Department of Justice. (2014). *U.S. Departments of Education and Justice release school discipline guidance package to enhance school climate and improve school discipline policies/practices.* Washington, DC: Author. Retrieved from http://www.ed.gov/news/press-releases/us-departments-education-and-justice-release-school-discipline-guidance-package-

Villegas, A. M., & Irvine, J. J. (2010). Diversifying the teaching force: An examination of major arguments. *The Urban Review, 42*, 175–192.

Wallace Jr., J. M., Goodkind, S., Wallace, C. M., & Bachman, J. G. (2008). Racial, ethnic, and gender differences in school discipline among U.S. high school students: 1991–2005. *The Negro Educational Review, 59*, 47–62.

Welch, K., & Payne, J. J. (2011). Exclusionary school punishment: The effect of racial threat on expulsion and suspension. *Youth Violence and Juvenile Justice, 10*, 155–171.

West, C. M. (1995). Mammy, Sapphire, and Jezebel: Historical images of Black women and their implications for psychotherapy. *Psychotherapy: Theory, Research, Practice, Training, 32*, 458–466.

CHAPTER 6

Reducing Racial Disparities in School Discipline: Structured Decision-Making in the Classroom

Aishatu R. Yusuf, Angela Irvine, and James Bell

Over the past ten years, the juvenile justice system has experienced a 41% reduction in the number of incarcerated youth, and yet a growing proportion of those who remain are youth of color (Davis, Irvine, & Ziedenberg, 2014). Eighty percent of youth on probation, in out-of-home placements and secure facilities in 2012 were youth of color, compared to 67% in 2002 (Davis et al., 2014). Research and advocacy by a wide range of stakeholders has linked racial and ethnic disparities in court-involved youth to school disciplinary practices (Skiba, Arredondo, & Williams, 2014). Notably, 90% of youth who are detained by probation departments have at one time been suspended or expelled by their school (Irvine & Yusuf, 2015).

The intersection between youth justice and school discipline can be traced to the explosion of zero-tolerance policies that began in the late 1980s. One of the first manifestations of the school-based tough-on-crime philosophy in federal legislation was intended to prevent gun violence in school: the Gun

A.R. Yusuf (✉)
Oakland, CA, USA

A. Irvine
Impact Justice, Oakland, CA, USA

J. Bell
W. Haywood Burns Institute, Oakland, CA, USA

© The Author(s) 2016
R.J. Skiba et al. (eds.), *Inequality in School Discipline*,
DOI 10.1057/978-1-137-51257-4_6

Free School Act (GFSA), passed by Congress in 1994, required schools to expel a student who possessed a gun while on school grounds (Skiba & Peterson, 2000). Despite the fact that youth crime declined beginning in the 1990s (Puzzanchera & Adams, 2011), the idea that certain young people were dangerous stuck in the public mind. This idea was exacerbated by political scientist John DiIulio, who warned in 1995 that the USA faced an imminent threat from a coming wave of young "super-predators" (DiIuio, 1995). The combination of federal law, fears about youth violence, and a small number of high profile school shootings led to an increase in school districts across the country instituting on-campus law enforcement, security guards, and metal detectors to create safer schools.

In concert with the increase in zero-tolerance discipline in schools, the number of out-of-school suspensions and expulsions issued to students began to rise across the USA, with dramatic increases in some places. Nationally, the number of secondary school students suspended or expelled over the course of a school year increased roughly 40%, from 1 in 13 in 1972–1973 to 1 in 9 in 2009–2010 (Losen & Martinez, 2013). The expansion of these policies has led to disproportionately high numbers of suspensions and expulsions for students of color and students with disabilities. In school districts like Palm Beach County, Florida, and Milwaukee, Wisconsin, for example, the district-wide middle school suspension rate in 2006 for Black male students exceeded 50% (Losen & Skiba, 2010). Recent research suggests that students who identify as lesbian, gay, bisexual, questioning, gender nonconforming, and transgender (LGBT) also experience more severe disciplinary responses and disproportionate suspensions and expulsions (Anyon et al., 2014; Burdge, Hyemingway, & Licona, 2015; Irvine & Yusuf, 2015).

Sadly, many of these suspensions and expulsions are not required by federal or state law. In the study *Breaking Schools' Rules*, researchers at the Council of State Governments and Public Policy Research Institute at Texas A&M University found that only 3% of suspensions and expulsions were for conduct for which federal or state law mandates punitive disciplinary action (Fabelo et al., 2011). The majority of punitive disciplinary actions were issued in response to relatively minor violations of local schools' conduct codes in which other, non-punitive measures could have been issued.

These inequitable school responses appear to have a series of long-term consequences for young people, including increased exposure to the juvenile justice system. Research by John Hopkins University found that 49% of students who entered high school with three suspensions on their record eventually dropped out of school (Balfanz, Byrnes, & Fox, 2014; Losen, Hodson, Keith, Morrison, & Belway, 2015). Similarly, more than one third of males suspended for ten or more days had been confined in a secure justice facility (Losen et al., 2015; Shollenberger, 2015). Youth of color are disproportionately affected by this crossover between school discipline and justice involvement. National data collected by the US Department of Education documents racial disparities in school-based referrals to law enforcement: while Black students represented 19% of American public school students, they made up 27% of students referred to law enforcement by schools and 31% of students subjected to a school-related arrest in 2006 (National Center on Education Statistics, 2014).

In this chapter, we describe an effort to help educators change the policy and practices that marginalize children of color and other vulnerable populations by developing a decision-making matrix, or response grid, to guide teachers' decisions on discipline in the classroom. Through a process of discussion and reflection, we helped teachers at one middle school in Oakland, California, consider the consequences of their disciplinary choices and to collaboratively identify other, less punitive options for responding to students' behavior. The response grid developed by teachers, as well as the process used to create it, offers a potentially powerful strategy that schools can use to establish more consistency in responses to behavior while increasing teachers' voices and commitment to changing school discipline policy and practice.

Tools such as a response grid for structured decision-making have been used in government sectors, particularly the juvenile justice system, to reduce punitive responses to youth behavior as well as to reduce racial and ethnic disparities. More than 15 years ago, youth justice experts identified that subjective decisions by probation officers lead to unnecessary detentions and high rates of disparities for youth of color (Hoyt, Schiraldi, Smith, & Ziedenberg, 2001; Mendel, 2009; Short & Sharp, 2005). In response, the justice field began implementing decision-making tools that establish agreed-upon objective criteria to limit individual discretion of polices, practices, and interpretation of youth behavior, thus creating tools for responding to youth behavior within agreed-upon parameters (Steinhardt, 2006). The results in the justice field have been drastic, with a substantial decrease in overall detention numbers and positive results in decreasing racial disparities (Mendel, 2009).

BACKGROUND ON THE OAKLAND UNIFIED SCHOOL DISTRICT

The Oakland Unified School District (OUSD) was selected as a site for this work because of a growing effort in the district to address disparities in suspensions. The 2012 Urban Strategies Council's (USC) study,

A Deeper Look at African American Males in the Oakland Unified School District, documented that young African American males languish behind their peers in key areas such as academic achievement, graduation rates, literacy, and attendance, while outpacing them in suspensions and juvenile detention rates (Brown et al., 2012). In 2010–2011, for example, 18% of African American males were suspended at least once, compared to just 3% of White males. Almost half (44%) of Oakland students were suspended for "willful defiance or disruption," a category for which there is often substantial variation in interpretation of student behavior (Brown et al., 2012).

OUSD implemented multiple reforms to address these disparities, including restorative justice disciplinary practices and the development of the Office of African American Male Achievement, which promotes positive growth in the academic achievement of Black boys and young men. The district also implemented Positive Behavior Intervention and Supports (PBIS), a school-based reform intervention to help school personnel identify, adopt, and organize evidence-based behavioral interventions into an integrated continuum of supports that enhances academic and behavioral outcomes for all students (see www.pbis.org). Additionally, OUSD entered into a Voluntary Resolution Plan (VRP) with the US Department of Education's Office of Civil Rights to address the disproportionality in discipline. As part of its agreement in the VRP, OUSD created a work group to update and make the district's discipline handbook more accessible, standardize discipline procedures for all district teachers, help parents and guardians become aware of expectations and policies, and reduce discretion in discipline.

Methods

Data reported in this chapter were collected from a professional development session with middle school teachers in 2013. This session was part of a larger project that explored the feasibility of developing tools for teachers and administrators that might help to disrupt patterns of disproportionate suspensions and expulsions for students of color. The larger project was guided by a project leadership advisory committee called the Suspension and Expulsion Reduction Collaborative (SERC) that included a cross-section of government and community stakeholders.[1] As part of that larger project, the research team observed five OUSD VRP discipline workgroup meetings focused on revising the district's school discipline handbook,[2] as well as a community meeting facilitated by the school district's director of the Office of African American Achievement.

PARTICIPANTS

The teacher professional development session was held in an Oakland middle school in a neighborhood with high rates of violence and poverty and a strong police presence. Teachers were recruited for the professional development session by the school principal and their peers. Participation was voluntary, and nine teachers took part. The teachers varied in length of teaching experience, age, race, and gender. The group was multi-racial: four were Black, three Latina/os, and two White. Five teachers were male and four female. Teaching experience ranged from one to 16 years. The majority of participants had more than five years of teaching experience.

PROCEDURES

The session format and protocol were created by juvenile justice researchers, including a former educator. Facilitation of the session was done by a juvenile justice researcher. The session format was developed primarily to maximize teacher engagement and emphasize peer learning and conversations through interaction and prompts. Participants were asked two sets of questions. The first set of questions were about the school's overall approach to school discipline. They centered on understanding how teachers were involved in the implementation of reforms such as PBIS, the extent of teacher buy-in to those reforms, and their perception of the results. The second set of questions focused on teachers' personal approaches to discipline, examining the rules they established in their classrooms, the behaviors they saw as infractions, their responses when students did not adhere to their rules, and their reasons for referring students to the school administration for disciplinary issues.

The professional development session lasted approximately two hours and was facilitated using a structured question-based protocol. The facilitator asked questions that initiated teacher conversation about school discipline in their classrooms and current school discipline reforms. The facilitator primarily listened to the teacher discussion. However, during periods of disagreement on how to respond to student behavior, the facilitator encouraged teachers to challenge each other and share their ideas and frustration regarding these topics. The facilitator also encouraged teachers to share frequent classroom challenges, protocols, and school norms. The session ended with a group activity in which teachers were asked to categorize different behaviors as minor or major infractions, brainstorm responses to each type of infraction, and construct a response grid (also referred to as a graduated response protocol) to guide other teachers in responding to student misbehavior in the classroom. The facilitator took notes throughout the session, which was also recorded and later transcribed, summarized, and reviewed in order to identify common themes within the discussion.

Results

We begin our discussion of results with a description of the response grid and then explore the teachers' perspective on school discipline. To set the stage for the tool-development exercise, the facilitator opened the discussion with an overview of national and local school discipline patterns and what is known from research on the long-term impacts of suspensions and expulsions. Participants were then engaged in reflecting on discipline in their own school and classrooms.

While the initial purpose of this exercise was to generate an in-classroom teacher response grid, the process of creating it proved to be a powerful form of professional learning. It expanded teachers' understanding of the choices they have when managing their classrooms, how their decisions could be aligned more consistently with a vision of positive discipline, and how that greater consistency might reduce the number of suspensions and expulsions issued by principals. This process also provided an avenue for input from teachers about changes in policy and practice that are being implemented in their district as well as nationwide.

Developing a Response Grid

The ultimate goal of a response grid is to provide teachers with discipline alternatives when responding to student behavior in the classroom. The response grid enables teachers to quickly assess student behavior, decide if it represents an emerging pattern or is a one-time action, and consider a wider range of discipline options than simply sending a young person out of the classroom to the principals' office.

In the exercise, teachers were first asked to write down student behaviors they encounter most often in their classrooms. They were directed not to list those for which suspension or expulsion is suggested or required by the California education code. Those excluded behaviors include: possessing a firearm/weapon, selling a controlled substance, and sexual harassment/assault. In an effort to be consistent with the PBIS reforms being utilized by the school, participants identified behavioral infractions based on the level of severity—minor or major—as shown below in Table 6.1. Teachers were then given sticky notes and asked to jot down their typical responses to these behaviors and distinguish their responses depending on how often the student exhibited it. Using a large board visible to all participating teachers, the facilitator placed these sticky notes next to the relevant behavior, creating a grid as shown in Table 6.2.

With their attention directed to the board, teachers were asked to reflect on the results among themselves. The facilitator then reminded them of the data on discipline disparities and asked them to consider whether those same patterns were evident in their classrooms. The teachers noted that their heavy reliance on detention and office referrals for student behaviors may be a contributing factor to excessive suspension.

For the next portion of the professional development session, the facilitator asked the teachers if they agreed with the discipline responses represented on the board. The question produced much conversation and debate. Participants challenged each other about how they would respond to different behaviors. For example, one teacher asked, "Why would you [a participating teacher] send a student to detention for a first time minor behavior?. I don't agree with that." During the conversation, teachers examined their responses to the student behaviors and indicated whether they agreed with their choices, felt another teacher's choices were more appropriate, or if an entirely different alternative not present on the list was needed.

Table 6.1 Common behavior infractions identified by teachers

Minor	Major
• Tardy	• Inappropriate minor sexual behaviors or gestures
• Cutting class	• Bullying (including cyber bullying)
• Inappropriate language	• Marijuana consumption (suspected)
• Hats/cell phone/gum chewing	• Fighting
• Defiance	• Minor aggression (rough play)
• Being unprepared	• Cheating
• Inappropriate hallway behavior	• Harassment/discrimination
• Teasing/joking	• Theft
• Property damage	• Vandalism

Table 6.2   How individual OUSD teachers respond to student behavior

	Minor behavior response	Major behavior response
First time	• Verbal warning • Separation of students • Detention • Send to hall	• Referral to administration • Conference with student • Send to hall • Buddy room • Automatic failing of an assignment (particularly for cheating)
Repeated	• Referral to administration • Loss of class privilege or reward • Detention • Conference with student • Time-out • Buddy room • Parent/guardian call	• Referral to administration • Detention • Send student to hall • Parent/guardian call • Parent/guardian–teacher conference
Constant	• Detention • Parent/guardian call • Long-term loss of privilege • Permanent seat change • Parent/guardian–teacher conference • Referral to administration	• Referral to administration • Detention
Chronic	• Parent/guardian–teacher conference • Office referral	• Office referral

[a]Buddy room refers to a temporary holding classroom where the student will spend the remainder of the class period from which they were removed. It is not required that a student enter with classroom homework, and it is usually supervised by a teacher.

After allowing time for unstructured conversation between teachers, during which the facilitator did not participate or interfere, the latter brought teachers' attention back to the table listing student behaviors and discipline choices. Given the data previously provided and the agreed-upon goal to have less punitive discipline choices, the facilitator asked teachers to choose alternative disciplinary responses for each behavior listed. One by one, the teachers selected alternatives they felt were most appropriate for each type of behavior. This process asked teachers not just to place a disciplinary response next to a behavior, but also to consider the potential implications of each response for the child. One teacher stated, "Instead of detention for a minor repeated behavior, I can move the student or assign more homework … at least that doesn't kick them out of the classroom."

Although most teachers agreed on the final discipline choices for behaviors, some did not, and full consensus was not reached on all items. For example, one teacher felt that too much leniency in discipline lent itself to a reduction in classroom control. Nonetheless, the discussion resulted in a response grid with a wider set of options for teacher responses to disciplinary problems that were less punitive than the responses originally identified. Table 6.3 shows the response grid created collaboratively with the group. Key changes to the list of teachers' disciplinary responses include:

- removing detention entirely as a response to minor behaviors;
- delaying referrals to the administration, referrals to the buddy room, and parent/guardian calls for repeated minor behaviors;
- adding responses such as giving students demerit points, verbal warnings, new tasks and assignments for minor behaviors, and loss of class privileges, a time out, and permanent seat change for major behaviors; and removing automatic failing of an assignment for a first-time major behavior.

Table 6.3 Collaborative classroom matrix

	Minor behavior response	Major behavior response
First time	• Verbal warning • Student conduct demerit point (particularly for students that are late) • Separation of students	• Conference with student • Loss of class privileges or reward • Time out
Repeated	• Verbal warning with threat of consequence • Temporary separation of students • Loss of class privileges or reward • Conference with student • Time out • Assign additional task	• Buddy room • Detention • Send to hall • Parent/guardian call • Permanent seat change • Referral to administration (only for fighting or bullying)
Constant	• Buddy room • Assign additional task/assignment • Conference with student • Parent/guardian call • Long-term loss of privilege or reward • Permanent seat change	• Parent/guardian–teacher conference • Referral to administration • Detention
Chronic	• Parent/guardian teacher conference • Referral to administration	• Referral to administration

TEACHER VIEWS OF CLASSROOM MANAGEMENT
AND SCHOOL DISCIPLINE

Despite a significant district-wide effort to engage all stakeholders in reducing disproportionate suspensions and expulsions for Black students, teachers generally felt they lacked input in district-wide changes and were underappreciated for their daily struggle to respond to the mental health and behavioral needs of their students. At the same time, they acknowledged their role in the disproportionate suspension of Black students, and believed that better tools and greater consistency in the application of classroom management strategies would help to reduce this.

In the course of the professional development process that produced the grid, the facilitator engaged teachers in a structured conversation and reflection on the discipline practices used in their school. This discussion proved to be both challenging and insightful, and offered a perspective often missing from the literature and discourse on how to improve school discipline in the classroom. A number of themes that emerged are summarized below.

Insufficient teacher input in district-wide reforms. Teachers in the professional development session felt that, in general, OUSD teachers had not played a central role in most of the district-wide reforms being implemented. While teachers had heard about the district's Voluntary Resolution Plan (VRP) and knew about PBIS and the African American Male Achievement Initiative, they knew very little about these efforts, and felt they had little say in how these strategies would be implemented. For example, although from the district view, PBIS was envisioned as a collaborative process, teachers in the professional development session felt they had not been consulted in creating their schools' PBIS materials or in advising on the implementation process. As one teacher recounted, "I came into the school, had a staff meeting and was told I was now going to be doing PBIS [and] needed to read the materials and use this referral form if I wanted to send a kid to the office." Similarly, although administrators, staff, and former teachers participated in district meetings to revise the discipline handbook, the absence of current OUSD teachers in the process limited the flow of information on the reforms.

The challenges of disciplining traumatized students. In the context of the district-wide shifts in discipline, the teachers grappled with how to meet the mental health and behavioral needs of students. "Sometimes I'm more like a parent or a counselor in my classroom," observed one teacher.

When dealing with negative student behavior, teachers believed that too often students are victims and witnesses of crime and that their mental health needs need to be taken into account. Several noted that students' exposure to traumatic events in their neighborhoods, as well as the normal developmental process for adolescents, creates the need for additional social-emotional support in the classroom.

Effective and consistent classroom management. Strong and consistent classroom management was viewed by participants as essential to a successful learning environment. One teacher remarked, "If I had better classroom management skills earlier on in my career, I would have been able to handle kids misbehaving a lot better." Another teacher explained:

> You have to set standards at the start of the year because some kids do not know when or how to switch how they act at home from how they need to act in the classroom, we need to remind them. If we set standards, and reinforce those standards with all the students, the students are more likely to follow.

Creating boundaries and expectations early was viewed by the teachers as necessary in establishing a healthy learning environment. Effective classroom management, they explained, is when the teacher does not have to stop the learning of other students to talk with or discipline an individual student(s). Teachers shared their strategies for building a sense of collective ownership over classroom behavior. One teacher said,

> I manage my classroom by getting the whole class involved. I don't have individual demerits, the class has demerits. So if someone keeps disrupting the class, the students will say, 'Hey, stop talking. We want our movie day.' This allows fellow students to check each other; it makes them responsible for each other.

In addition to managing their own classrooms effectively, teachers identified the need for more consistency across classrooms and between teachers and administrators in responding to student behavior. A teacher explained:

> Wearing a hat or using inappropriate language is OK in some classrooms, and it is not OK in others. This makes it difficult for students to follow guidelines. We need to have the same rules in every classroom.

Without sufficient guidelines for teachers on how to address the variety of behaviors that students present, student behaviors are handled inconsistently across different classrooms. Participating teachers reported very different ways of managing their classroom. Some stated that they manage by sending or threatening to send students out when they misbehave. Others managed their classrooms by having a check mark system; five check marks meant loss of privileges.

Although the school had established standards for behavior that were well-known by the students, some teachers were more lenient than others in upholding these standards. One participant noted, "We need consistency. We need to create a school culture so that no matter what class you are in the same rules apply." The teachers felt that administrator responses were similarly inconsistent, with disciplinary outcomes determined largely by whom the student encountered in the office. As one teacher explained, "Some administrators are more punitive than others."

Recognizing their role in disproportionate suspensions. While teachers recognized the need for consistency, they did not immediately see the link between their decisions and those of administrators. Instead, teachers believed that the final arbiters of disciplinary consequences are administrators and did not recognize the part they play in suspensions and expulsions. As one teacher summed up, "We have no control over who is suspended and who is not." In fact, a number of participants reported feeling unfairly targeted for blame in the school. "Everything gets pushed to teachers and not administration," observed one teacher. "It's our fault too many kids are being suspended, it's our fault kids aren't learning, it's our fault kids lose too much class time. It is always our fault, yet we can only do what the administration allows us."

Nonetheless, a few participants recognized that they play a role in punitive discipline, especially in the choice to send a student to the office with a referral and whether they recommend suspension or expulsion. When the facilitator asked the group, "What happens after a teacher sends a student to the office?" one teacher explained, "There are only a few options when they get kicked out of a classroom: in-school suspension or out-of-school suspension. Depending on what administrator the student gets, they [the student] may get sent back to class."

This question shifted the focus of the conversation to help teachers reflect on their role in disproportionate Black suspensions. The facilitator's prompt directed teachers' attention to the connection between their actions and those of the administrators in their school. Taking it one step further, one teacher said, "If my choice to send students to the office is the first step (aside from the student behavior) in getting them suspended, I need to come up with some other options."

This discussion brought teachers full circle to see the need for opportunities to sit with their peers to establish agreement on how to manage behavior and create tools that can provide guidance on how to respond to different behaviors. As one teacher explained, "Sometimes, in the heat of a moment, all you want to do is remove a child from the class. But having a guide or a check [would] allow me to take a second look at my choice and perhaps make a better decision."

Conclusions

IMPLICATIONS FOR REDUCING DISCIPLINARY DISPARITIES WITHIN SCHOOLS

The teacher response grid provides an additional tool that OUSD and other school districts can use to help reduce the number of office referrals and subsequently the number of suspensions and expulsions. Through the participatory engagement of teachers in creating it, and their use of the tool in their classrooms, we hope that schools will be able to make decisions by individual teachers and administrators more consistent.

Most of the teachers in the professional development session saw their role extending beyond teaching curricula to facilitating an environment that promotes positive youth development. Yet they also observed how challenging it can be to teach in the face of constant student misbehavior and disruption, and were very open to tools and strategies that would allow them to manage their classrooms more effectively. The conversation among teachers deepened their understanding of the consequences of their choices, and helped them to agree on responses to common classroom misbehaviors. This process also created a sense of community that, teachers felt, allowed them the space to identify problems and learn about effective practices from peers.

The professional development session also helped teachers understand that they share responsibility for school discipline with administrators. Faced with the day-to-day challenges of the classroom, teachers rarely have time to think about how routine decisions shape larger trends of disproportionate suspensions and expulsions of youth of color. However, as the discussion developed, they began to recognize that, just as administrators have the choice to send a student back to class or create in-school alternatives, teachers have the choice to make a different disciplinary decision in the classroom. The response grid was welcomed by teachers in part because they saw how it could generate consistency and common practice. With high levels of buy-in from teachers, such grids have the potential to reduce out-of-classroom referrals, making all responses less punitive and improving outcomes for students—particularly students of color. The teachers' openness to rethinking their disciplinary approach suggests that if more opportunities were created for them to engage in discussions like these, schools might be able to see faster and more successful transformation in their classrooms. In addition, it also reveals how teachers' decision-making about discipline can be improved without eliminating their total discretion in the classroom. Efforts to replicate this approach in other schools and school districts should consider ways to involve school and district administrators, in addition to teachers.

Untying the Link Between School Discipline and the Juvenile Justice System

Stemming the tide of suspended and expelled youth of color into the juvenile justice system will require educators to gain a deeper understanding of the unintended consequences of some disciplinary decisions. Those decisions can inadvertently place youth on a trajectory of justice involvement. Given that the vast majority of youth in the justice system have also come in contact with a school discipline officer, schools play a key role in slowing down the flow of youth into the justice system. This chapter shows how educators can be engaged to do so.

If teachers do not have the information or time to share and understand how suspension and expulsion can lead to justice involvement and other negative lifelong effects, it is unlikely that they will make alternative choices in their classrooms. Our work speaks to the need for and potential of more intensive efforts to engage teachers in a process of learning and action. If we want teachers to take an active role in dismantling the systemic and unjust pathways that our youth often fall victim to, we must ensure they are aware of how removal from the classroom may be a significant first step toward the school-to-prison pipeline.

NOTES

1. These stakeholders included the probation chief, middle school teachers, the director of the OUSD African American Male Achievement program, education and juvenile justice policy advocates and researchers, a middle school principal, a representative from the OUSD Positive Behavior Interventions and Supports (PBIS) office, local clergy, a director of a restorative justice program used in OUSD schools, direct service providers, a program officer from a California foundation, and a representative from the OUSD attendance and discipline support services department
2. The work group comprised representatives from OUSD, restorative justice programs, school resources officers (SRO), Community Schools and Student Services Behavioral Health Initiatives, school administration, and legal counsel.

REFERENCES

Anyon, Y., Jenson, J. M., Altschul, I., Farrar, J., McQueen, J., Greer, E., Simmons, J. (2014). The persistent effect of race and the promise of alternatives to suspension in school discipline outcomes. *Children & Youth Services Review, 44*, 379–386. doi:10.1016/j.childyouth.2014.06.025.

Balfanz, R., Byrnes, V., & Fox, J. (2014). Sent Home and Put Off-Track: The Antecedents, Disproportionalities, and Consequences of Being Suspended in the Ninth Grade. *Journal of Applied Research on Children: Informing Policy for Children at Risk, 5*(2), Article 13. Available at: http://digitalcommons.library.tmc.edu/childrenatrisk/vol5/iss2/13

Brown, R., Williams, J., Marxer, S., Spiker, S., Chang, A., Feldman, A., Budi, E. (2012). *African American male achievement initiative: A closer look at suspensions of African American males in OUSD.* Oakland, CA: Urban Strategies Council.

Burdge, H., Hyemingway, Z. T., & Licona, A. C. (2015). *LGBTQ Youth and School Pushout.* Oakland, CA: Gay Straight Alliance (GSA) Network. Retrieved from http://www.gsanetwork.org/pushout-report

Davis, A., Irvine, A., & Ziedenberg J. (2014). Stakeholders' views of the movement to reduce youth incarceration. (Working Paper). *National Council on Crime and Delinquency.*

DiIuio, J. (1995). The coming of the super-predators. *The Weekly Standard, 1*(11). Retrieved from http://www.weeklystandard.com/Content/Protected/Articles/000/000/007/011vsbrv.asp

Fabelo, T., Thompson, M. D., Plotkin, M., Carmichael, D., Marchbanks, M. P., & Booth, E. A. (2011). *Breaking schools' rules: A statewide study of how school discipline relates to student's success and juvenile justice involvement.* New York: Council of State Governments Justice Center, and College Station, Texas A&M

University: Public Policy Research Institute. Retrieved from http://knowledgecenter.csg.org/kc/system/files/Breaking_School_Rules.pdf

Hoyt, E. H., Schiraldi, V., Smith, B. V., & Ziedenberg, J. (2001). Reducing racial disparities in juvenile detention. In *Pathways to juvenile detention Reform #8*. Baltimore, MD: Annie E. Casey Foundation.

Irvine, A., & Yusuf, A. (2015). *Nine in ten juvenile-justice involved youth have been disciplined in school: Groundbreaking findings from national study of youth in detention*. (Working Paper) Oakland, CA: Impact Justice.

Losen, D. J., Hodson, C., Keith, M. A., Morrison, K., & Belway, S. (2015). *Are we closing the school discipline gap?* Los Angeles, CA: The UCLA Center for Civil Rights Remedies at The Civil Rights Project.

Losen, D. J., & Martinez, T. E. (2013). *Out of school & off track: The overuse of suspensions in American middle and high schools*. Los Angeles, CA: The Center for Civil Rights Remedies at The Civil Right Project/Proyecto Derechos Civiles. Retrieved from http://civilrightsproject.ucla.edu/

Losen, D. J., & Skiba, R. J. (2010). *Suspended education: Urban middle schools in crisis*. Montgomery, AL: Southern Poverty Law Center.

Mendel, R. (2009). *Two decades of JDAI: From demonstration project to national standard*. Baltimore, MD: Report to the Annie. E. Casey Foundation.

National Center on Education Statistics. (2014). Digest of education statistics. Washington, DC: U.S. Department of Education, Institute of Education Sciences, National Center for Education Statistics. Retrieved from http://nces.ed.gov/programs/digest/d10/tables/dt10_169.asp

Puzzanchera, C., & Adams, B. (2011). *Juvenile offenders and victims: National report series: Juvenile arrests 2009*. Washington, DC: U.S. Department of Justice, Office of Justice Programs, Office of Juvenile Justice and Delinquency Prevention.

Shollenberger, T. L. (2015). Racial disparities in school suspension and subsequent outcomes: Evidence from the National Longitudinal Survey of Youth 1997. In D. J. Losen (Ed.), *Closing the school discipline gap: Equitable remedies for excessive exclusion* (pp. 31–43). New York: Teachers College Press.

Short, J., & Sharp, C. (2005). *Disproportionate minority contact in the juvenile justice system*. Washington DC: Child Welfare League of America.

Skiba, R. J., Arredondo, M. I., & Williams, N. (2014). More than a metaphor: The contributions of exclusionary discipline to a school-to-prison pipeline. Special Issue: Breaking the pipeline: Understanding, examining, and dismantling the school-to-prison pipeline. *Equity and Excellence in Education, 47*(4), 546–564.

Skiba, R. J., & Peterson, R. L. (2000). School discipline at a crossroads: From zero tolerance to early response. *Exceptional Children, 66*(3), 335–346.

Steinhardt, D. (2006). *Juvenile detention risk assessment: A practice guide to juvenile detention reform*. Baltimore, MD: Report to the Annie. E. Casey Foundation.

CHAPTER 7

School-wide Positive and Restorative Discipline (SWPRD): Integrating School-wide Positive Behavior Interventions and Supports and Restorative Discipline

Claudia G. Vincent, John Inglish, Erik J. Girvan, Jeffrey R. Sprague, and Timothy M. McCabe

Students from vulnerable groups (e.g., Black, Latino, American Indian, and non-heterosexual students) are experiencing disproportionately frequent and severe discipline compared to their White, heterosexual peers. Disciplinary disparities across racial/ethnic groups are well documented (Losen, 2014; Skiba, Horner, Chung, Rausch, May, & Tobin, 2011), and evidence documenting disparities for non-heterosexual students is growing (Himmelstein & Brückner, 2011). Inequitable discipline has

This project was funded by the Open Society Foundation through the Research-to-Practice Collaborative on Discipline Disparities (grant # 4402C1) and the University of Oregon Office of Research, Innovation, and Graduate Education (grant # CRVSIC). The opinions expressed are those of the authors and not necessarily of the funding agencies.

C.G. Vincent (✉) • J. Inglish • E.J. Girvan • J.R. Sprague
College of Education, University of Oregon, Eugene, OR, USA

T.M. McCabe
Center for Dialogue and Resolution, Eugene, OR, USA

R.J. Skiba et al. (eds.), *Inequality in School Discipline*,
DOI 10.1057/978-1-137-51257-4_7

115

far-reaching consequences for vulnerable students' educational outcomes and long-term health and wellbeing (Noguera & Wing, 2006). To decrease persistent discrepancies, many policymakers, researchers, and practitioners are using school-wide positive behavioral interventions and supports (SWPBIS) (U.S. Department of Education, 2014). Recognizing the strengths and limitations of SWPBIS, we focus on increasing schools' capacity to reduce disciplinary inequities by blending SWPBIS with restorative discipline, an approach that might improve equity in student discipline outcomes (Simson, 2012).

SCHOOL-WIDE POSITIVE BEHAVIOR INTERVENTIONS AND SUPPORTS (SWPBIS)

SWPBIS is a widely implemented systemic approach to reducing inappropriate student behavior (Horner, Sugai, & Anderson, 2010). Its key components are (a) defining school-wide positive behavioral expectations (e.g., be safe, be responsible, be respectful), (b) proactively teaching what expected behaviors look like in various school settings, (c) consistently rewarding students who comply with behavioral expectations, (d) consistently assigning a continuum of consequences to students who do not comply, and (e) collecting office discipline referral (ODR) data to assess students' responsiveness to the supports provided and offer feedback to implementers (Sugai & Horner, 2002). SWPBIS interventions are organized around a three-tiered continuum, with universal support provided to all students at all times, secondary support to groups of students insufficiently responsive to universal support, and tertiary support to individual students with significant behavioral challenges (Sugai et al., 2010). Implementation of SWPBIS occurs through a school-based team consisting of administrators, general and special education teachers, and other school personnel (Sugai & Horner, 2002).

When implemented with fidelity, SWPBIS has consistently been associated with positive outcomes (Sugai & Horner, 2002). Office discipline referral (ODR) reduction is the most common metric used to measure those outcomes (Sugai, Sprague, Horner, & Walker, 2000). At the whole-school level, SWPBIS is associated with reductions in ODRs (Muscott, Mann, & LeBrun, 2008; Taylor-Greene, et al., 1997). Randomized control trials conducted with elementary schools have experimentally linked SWPBIS implementation to whole-school reductions in ODRs (Bradshaw, Mitchell, O'Brennan, & Leaf, 2010), as well as improved staff perceptions of school safety (Horner et al., 2009). These outcomes clearly document the benefits of a systemic approach to establishing a positive school climate. In a school where students know what is expected of them and teachers consistently reward expected behavior, students are more likely to comply with school rules.

To date, SWPBIS has not been consistently linked to disciplinary equity, with students from vulnerable groups often being disproportionately represented in ODR data. Researchers have found that, in schools implementing SWPBIS, African American elementary students had significantly greater odds of receiving an ODR than White students (Bradshaw et al., 2010; Kaufman et al., 2010); African American middle-school students with multiple ODRs were less likely to receive secondary support than their peers (Vincent, Tobin, Hawken, & Frank, 2012); Native American and Latino middle-school students had higher truancy rates than their peers (Vincent, Sprague, CHiXapkaid, Tobin, & Gau, 2015); and students with a disability were excluded from the classroom for longer durations than their non-disabled peers (Vincent & Tobin, 2011). The effectiveness of SWPBIS on non-heterosexual students' discipline rates has yet to be explored.

SWPBIS is clearly highly effective in (a) organizing adult behavior to facilitate disciplinary consistency across classrooms and (b) reducing overall ODR rates. Its limited effectiveness in reliably reducing disciplinary inequities affecting vulnerable students might be due to its limited focus on (a) proactively building teacher–student and peer relationships, (b) promoting students' perceptions of discipline as fair and procedurally just, and (c) restoring relationships after a discipline incident has occurred. Research has found that positive student–teacher and peer relationships tend to be more commonly experienced by White students than those from vulnerable groups (Gregory & Ripsky, 2008). Research has also shown that students are socially and academically more successful if they perceive their classroom environments as fair and procedurally just (Gouveia-Pereira, Vala, Palmonari, & Rubini, 2003; Sanches, Gouveia-Pereira, & Carugati, 2011). Specific practices to promote social capital (i.e., relationship building and restoring) as well as student perceptions of fairness and procedural justice have been outlined in the literature on restorative discipline.

RESTORATIVE DISCIPLINE

Positive teacher–student and peer relationships, disciplinary fairness and procedural justice, as well as communal problem solving to prevent exclusion of students from the classroom, are the essence of restorative discipline (RD), derived from the concepts and practices of restorative justice (Amstutz & Mullet, 2005). RD practices include (a) affective statements to increase students' awareness of how their behavior makes others feel; (b) affective questions to encourage students to reflect on the motivation and consequences of their behavior; (c) active listening to improve mutual understanding of behavioral incidents; (d) reframing to encourage students (and teachers) to change their perspectives; (e) conducting proactive circles to promote students' sense of classroom community and emotional safety; and (f) conducting restorative circles to repair harm, prevent disciplinary exclusion, and reintegrate students who have been suspended or expelled (Costello, Wachtel, & Wachtel, 2009; Costello, Wachtel, & Wachtel, 2010).

The evidence base supporting RD implementation in schools is limited to small-scale investigations and case studies. These studies associate RD implementation with improved student perceptions of the classroom as a safe place in which to share problems (Morrison & Martinez, 2001), improved teacher–student relationships (DeWitt & DeWitt, 2012), and improved peer relationships (McCarthy, 2009). Some evidence tentatively links RD implementation to greater disciplinary equity across students from various racial/ethnic backgrounds (Dravery & Winslade, 2006; Gregory, Clawson, Davis, & Gerewitz, 2014; Simson, 2012; see also Gregory et al., this volume). Such results suggest that relationship building/restoring may be a conduit for disciplinary equity.

Implementing RD as a school-wide intervention could present a number of challenges in a school setting. Some RD practices, such as using affective questions and conducting proactive circles, tend to be time-consuming. Restorative circles following disciplinary incidents could require expertise in mediation that school personnel might not routinely have. The success of RD practices, such as proactive circles, also likely depends on student buy-in, which may take time to build. Teachers trained to be in control of their classrooms through managing student behavior may also find it challenging to engage in practices requiring openness, trust, and sharing control of the classroom with students (Lasky, 2005). Without systemic support from a school-based team, these challenges might be difficult to overcome.

School-wide Positive and Restorative Discipline (SWPRD)

Based on this review, it appears that the capacity of the SWPBIS systems' approach to promote disciplinary equity could be enhanced with RD practices, and the implementation of RD practices in schools might be facilitated with systems put in place by SWPBIS. This blended approach,

School-wide Positive and Restorative Discipline (SWPRD), conceptualizes RD along a three-tiered continuum. At the universal tier, proactive circles can be used to define behavioral agreements and teach why they are important. Students who practice the agreements could be frequently acknowledged by teacher-delivered, behavior-specific affective statements. Both teachers and students can use active listening to gain greater awareness of each other's support needs and motivations. Alternatives to low-level inappropriate behavior can be encouraged through reframing the student's experience that might have triggered the behavioral violation in the first place. At the secondary and tertiary tier, disciplinary incidents can be addressed through restorative circles involving the entire class, or smaller restorative circles involving key stakeholders, including students, teachers, parents, and administrators. Figure 7.1 provides an overview of how RD practices map onto the three-tiered support continuum of SWPBIS. Data to assess the effectiveness of this blended approach and make decisions regarding students' support needs might include student perceptions of relationships, fair-

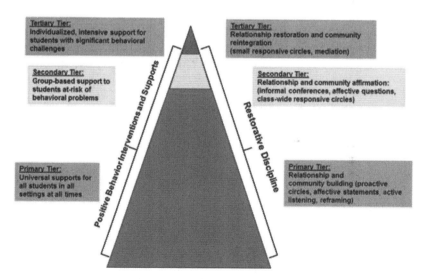

Fig. 7.1 Three-tiered continuum of SWPRD blending restorative discipline practices with SWPBIS support tiers

ness, and procedural justice in addition to ODR reflecting teacher perceptions of student behavior.

To examine if we could encourage teacher use of RD practices in a school implementing SWPBIS in order to promote disciplinary equity, we designed a study driven by the following research questions:

1. Do teachers familiar with SWPBIS implement restorative discipline following SWPRD training?
2. Does membership in groups defined by race/ethnicity and sexual orientation predict student perceptions of fairness, procedural justice, and social capital before and after teachers implement restorative discipline?
3. Is teacher use of restorative discipline associated with greater equity in office discipline referrals?

METHODOLOGY

We developed a curriculum designed to train school personnel implementing SWPBIS in RD practices. Module 1 introduced school personnel to the key concepts of RD (e.g., social capital, procedural justice, relationship building, and relationship restoring). Module 2 focused on Tier 1 preventative practices, including conducting proactive circles to establish behavioral expectations by classroom consensus, delivering behavior-specific affective statements as positive reinforcement of appropriate behavior, using active listening to promote positive relationships, and using reframing to help students become aware of alternatives to problematic behavior. Module 3 focused on responsive RD practices (Tier 2 and 3), including conducting impromptu conferences with students following reoccurring minor behavioral violations, and restorative circles following more severe behavioral violations. We also developed staff and student surveys to assess the feasibility and acceptability of the curriculum and student perceptions of fairness, procedural justice, and social capital.

We partnered with one high school that had implemented SWPBIS since the 2009–2010 school year to field-test SWPRD training during the 2013–2014 school year and assess its impact on teacher practices, equity in student perceptions of fairness, procedural justice and social capital, and equity in ODR through a one-sample pre- and post-design.

Sample

The high school's overall enrollment in grades 9 through 12 was n = 1025 students from racially and ethnically diverse backgrounds: 70.5% of students were White, 17.5% Latino, 6.7% Multiracial, 2.1% Asian/Pacific Islander, and 1.6% each American Indian/Alaska Native and Black. To assess its SWPBIS implementation status, the school-based team completed the *Benchmarks of Quality* (BoQ) annually. The BoQ has been found to have acceptable validity; a score of 70 and above indicates SWPBIS implementation with fidelity (Cohen, Kincaid, & Childs, 2007). In May 2013, the school scored 89 on the BoQ, and in May 2014, it scored 79, providing evidence that the school was implementing SWPBIS with fidelity during the study years. In the year prior to our study, the school experienced racial/ethnic disparities in discipline: 22.22% of Black, 19.30% of Latino, 25.00% of Asian, 3.60% of multiracial, and 12.50% of American Indian students received at least one ODR, compared to 16.62% of White students.

Procedure

We delivered SWPRD training to the entire school staff through a flipped classroom approach (e.g., training was delivered after school personnel familiarized themselves with the training materials made available on a shared secure website). Training materials in the form of narrated PowerPoint presentations, Word documents, and exercises were made available to all staff members prior to the face-to-face training sessions. Face-to-face training occurred in one 30-minute and one 60-minute session. Session 1 focused on Module 1 of the SWPRD curriculum and Session 2 focused on Module 2. Because of the small scale of the project, we were unable to field-test Module 3 or conduct follow-up coaching on any training content with individual teachers.

Measures

To assess the extent to which staff implemented RD practices, as well as the acceptability of the SWPRD approach, we developed a staff survey. The survey consisted of six sections: (1) the extent to which bullying and harassment occurred in the school, (2) the discipline process currently used, (3) the extent to which the teacher implemented Positive Behavior Interventions and Supports (PBIS) in his/her classroom, (4) the extent to which he/she was familiar with and used RD in the classroom, (5) the potential benefits and challenges of blending PBIS and RD into SWPRD, and (6) his/her understanding of SWPRD. Section 6 was administered post-intervention only. All items were scored on a 5-point scale ranging from 1 = strongly disagree/not at all/never to 5 = strongly agree/very much/always. Prior to the SWPRD training, 40 staff members completed the survey and 32 completed it after training. A total of 27 staff completed the survey both pre- and post-intervention.

Although we were unable to interact with students directly, we assessed student perceptions of bullying and harassment, disciplinary fairness, social capital, and procedural justice across groups defined by race/ethnicity and sexual orientation before and after the introduction of SWPRD. To assess student perceptions of these constructs, we developed a student survey which blended items from the school climate survey routinely used by the school district with items from the Sense of Community Scale (Perkins, Florin, Rich, Wandersman, & Chavis, 1990), and the Perceptions of Justice in the School Context measure used by Gouveia-Pereira and colleagues (Gouveia-Pereira et al., 2003).

Items were scored on a 5-point scale ranging from 1 = strongly disagree/not at all/never to 5 = strongly agree/very much/always, or on a 7-point scale ranging from 1 = strongly disagree to 7 = strongly agree. Table 7.1 provides an overview of the demographic characteristics of the student respondents before and after the introduction of SWPRD. The

Table 7.1 Demographic characteristics for student survey respondents at pre- and post-intervention

Demographic characteristic		Pre (n = 672)	Post (n = 516)
Race/ethnicity	White	403 (60%)	306 (59.3%)
	Latino	63 (9.4%)	51 (9.9%)
	Black	11 (1.6%)	0 (0%)
	American Indian/Alaska native	11 (1.6%)	10 (1.9%)
	Asian/Pacific Islander	8 (1.2%)	11 (2.1%)
	Multiracial	125 (18.6%)	86 (16.7%)
	Omitted	42 (6.3%)	31 (6%)
Sexual orientation	Heterosexual	551 (82%)	416 (80.6%)
	Lesbian, gay, bisexual, transgender	44 (6.5%)	34 (6.6%)
	Questioning	17 (2.5%)	18 (3.5%)
	Omitted	60 (8.9%)	48 (9.3%)

post-intervention survey was administered during the last week of the school year, when competing activities might have interfered with students' survey completion. Because the school had a very small population of Black students, none of whom completed the survey post-intervention, we focused our analyses on differences in the perceptions of White, Latino, and multiracial students, the school's largest racial/ethnic groups.

The school used the School-wide Information System (May et al., 2003) to collect ODR data. The district's school psychologist made the school's data on ODRs available to us for the year prior to our project as well as the project year.

Data Analysis

Staff surveys were individually coded to allow linking pre- and post-intervention responses. We conducted repeated measures analysis of variance to assess changes in self-reported teacher use of the four RD practices trained in Module 2 (affective statements and questions, active listening, reframing, and conducting proactive circles). We examined descriptive outcomes to assess the acceptability of SWPRD with post-intervention data only. To account for multiple tests, we adjusted the significance level to $\alpha = 0.05/4 = 0.0125$ (Tabachnick & Fidell, 2001). Student surveys were not individually coded and therefore pre- and post-intervention responses could not be linked. We conducted multiple sets of analysis of variance for each measurement occasion with race/ethnicity and sexual orientation as independent variables and the primary constructs of interest (student perceptions of bullying and harassment, social capital, racial fairness, sexual orientation fairness, and procedural justice) as dependent variables to assess if race/ethnicity and sexual orientation were statistically significant predictors in how students perceived the constructs of interest. To account for multiple tests, we adjusted the significance level to $\alpha = 0.05/5 = 0.01$. Due to the unequal number of survey respondents in each racial/ethnic and sexual orientation group, our ANOVA model was highly unbalanced. Because we were primarily interested in the main effects of race and sexual orientation, and one-way ANOVA is generally robust to unequal cell sizes (Tabachnick & Fidell, 2001), we did not weight responses to achieve a balanced design. To answer research question three, we conducted descriptive analyses to compare disciplinary equity across student race/ethnicity both before and after SWPRD was introduced.

FINDINGS

We first examined if our training resulted in changes in self-reported teacher use of the classroom RD practices presented in Module 2. We then examined the impact of students' race/ethnicity and sexual orientation on their perceptions of their classroom experiences. Finally, we reviewed ODR patterns across race/ethnicity.

Teacher Survey

Outcomes from the repeated measures analysis of teacher survey data are presented in Table 7.2. Based on teacher self-reports, use of all four RD practices increased from pre-intervention to post-intervention. The increase in using affective statements and questions and active listening did not reach statistical significance; the increase in using reframing and proactive circles was statistically significant. At post-intervention, teachers rated the acceptability of SWPRD above the scale midpoint, meaning that they were marginally enthusiastic about the intervention.

The Impact of Race/Ethnicity on Student Perceptions

Table 7.3 summarizes the impact of membership in a racial/ethnic group on students' perceptions of bullying and harassment, racial fairness, procedural justice, and social capital before and after the intervention, and

Table 7.2   Changes in self-reported teacher use of RD practices

RD practice/social validity	Pre mean (SD)	Post mean (SD)	F-value	p-value
Use of affective questions & statements	2.95 (0.96)	3.41 (0.88)	6.084	0.021
Use of active listening	3.61 (0.80)	3.78 (0.71)	0.464	0.502
Use of reframing	2.9 (0.97)	3.22 (0.71)	21.024	<0.0005
Use of proactive circles	2.12 (0.87)	2.44 (0.91)	10.947	0.003
SWPRD acceptability		3.30 (0.48)		
SWPRD contextual Fit		3.40 (0.85)		
SWPRD effectiveness		3.30 (0.76)		

Note: All F-values are based on $df(1, 26)$. Family-wise α was set to 0.0125

Table 7.3 The impact of race/ethnicity on student perceptions of the constructs of interest, and means and standard deviations for the largest non-white student groups at pre- and post-intervention

Construct of interest (number of items)	Pre				Post			
	Impact of race/ ethnicity p-value	White M (SD)	Latino M (SD)	Multiracial M (SD)	Impact of race/ ethnicity p-value	White M (SD)	Latino M (SD)	Multiracial M (SD)
Racial fairness (1)	0.0005	4.05 (1.22)	3.64 (1.39)	5-point scale 3.52 (1.32)	0.060	3.80 (1.29)	3.68 (1.27)	3.39 (1.38)
Absence of bullying and harassment (6)	0.043	4.04 (0.67)	4.25 (0.62)	4.00 (0.80)	0.167	3.96 (0.66)	4.20 (0.69)	3.92 (0.73)
Procedural justice (12)	0.613	3.30 (1.36)	2.93 (1.51)	7-point scale 3.30 (1.37)	0.001	5.06 (1.11)	5.45 (0.98)	4.61 (1.51)
Social capital (10)	0.023	3.95 (0.85)	3.81 (0.76)	3.75 (0.84)	0.019	3.85 (0.73)	4.06 (0.61)	3.71 (0.73)

Note: Family-wise α was set to 0.01

provides means and standard deviations for White, Latino, and multiracial students' perceptions of these constructs before and after the intervention. Prior to the intervention, race/ethnicity was a statistically significant predictor of student perceptions of racial fairness at the $\alpha = 0.01$ significance level ($p = 0.0005$). White students rated their school environment as largely fair across racial groups, while Latino and multiracial students rated their school environment as less so. At post-intervention, race/ethnicity was no longer a statistically significant predictor of student perceptions of racial fairness ($p = 0.060$). Latino students' ratings of the school environment's racial fairness improved slightly, while White and multiracial students' ratings of the school environment's fairness decreased. Race/ethnicity did not predict student perceptions of bullying/harassment before or after the intervention. Prior to the intervention, race/ethnicity did not predict student perceptions of procedural justice. After the intervention, race/ethnicity was a statistically significant predictor of procedural justice at the $\alpha = 0.01$ significance level ($p = 0.001$). While all students rated procedural justice higher after the intervention, Latino students rated it highest, followed by White and multiracial students. Race/ethnicity did not predict student perceptions of social capital before or after the intervention. Latino students' rating of social capital increased, while White and multiracial student's ratings decreased from pre- to post-intervention.

The Impact of Sexual Orientation on Student Perceptions

Table 7.4 summarizes the impact of membership in a group defined by sexual orientation on students' perceptions of similar constructs at pre-intervention and post-intervention, and provides means and standard deviations for heterosexual and gay, lesbian, bisexual, and transgender (LGBT) students' perceptions of these constructs. We omitted students who identified as Questioning due to their low numbers. Prior to the intervention, sexual orientation was a statistically significant predictor of students' perceptions of bullying and harassment at the $\alpha = 0.01$ significance level ($p = 0.007$). Heterosexual students reported higher absence of bullying and harassment than LGBT students. At post-intervention, sexual orientation was no longer a statistically significant predictor of bullying and harassment ($p = 0.018$). LGBT students' rating of the absence of bullying and harassment increased from pre- to post-intervention, while het-

Table 7.4 The impact of sexual orientation on student perceptions of the constructs of interest, and means and standard deviations for heterosexual and LGBT students at pre- and post-intervention

Construct of interest (number of items)	Pre			Post		
	Impact of sexual orientation p-value	Hetero M (SD)	LGBT M (SD)	Impact of sexual orientation p-value	Hetero M (SD)	LGBT M (SD)
			5-point scale			
Absence of bullying and harassment (6)	0.007	4.06 (0.70)	3.69 (0.76)	0.018	4.00 (0.68)	3.81 (0.88)
Sexual orientation fairness (1)	0.080	4.06 (1.14)	3.80 (1.17)	0.893	3.86 (1.22)	3.88 (1.19)

Note: Family-wise α was set to 0.01

erosexual students' ratings decreased slightly. Sexual orientation did not predict students' perceptions of their school environment's fairness across groups with different sexual orientations before or after the intervention.

Office Discipline Referrals

Finally, we examined changes in ODR rates across students' race/ethnicity from the year prior to our SWPRD training (2012–2013) to the year when we conducted the SWPRD training (2013–2014). Because the School-wide Information System (SWIS) does not collect data on students' sexual orientation, we were unable to examine ODR rates by student sexual orientation. Table 7.5 summarizes the outcomes of our comparison. Overall, the number of students who received an ODR decreased substantially, even though there was a slight increase in enrollment. This decrease appeared consistent across all racial/ethnic groups. After the introduction of SWPRD, Asian, multiracial, and Black students did not receive any ODRs. Prior to the introduction of SWPRD, the difference between the percentage of Latino students referred to the office and the percentage of White

Table 7.5 Students enrolled, students with ODR, and referral rates by student race/ethnicity across academic years and discipline approaches

Racial/ethnic group	2012–2013 (SWPBIS)			2013–2014 (SWPRD)		
	Students enrolled	Students with ODR	Percent of students with ODR	Students enrolled	Students with ODR	Percent of students with ODR
Pacific Islanders	2	0	0	3	1	33.33[1]
Native American	16	2	12.50	16	1	6.25
Asian	16	4	25.00	19	0	0
Multiracial	82	3	3.66	69	0	0
Black	16	4	22.22	16	0	0
Latino	171	33	19.30	179	9	5.03
White	692	115	16.62	723	33	4.56
Total	997	161		1025	44	

[1]Percentages based on low enrollment numbers can be misleading. In this case, the percentage of Pacific Islander students with ODR represents one of three students enrolled

students referred to the office was 2.68 percentage points. After the introduction of SWPRD, this difference was reduced to 0.47 percentage points.

SUMMARY, LIMITATIONS, IMPLICATIONS, AND RECOMMENDATIONS

The outcomes of our study are promising. In our experience, school staff familiar with SWPBIS appear aware of its limited attention to positive relationship building and do not commonly measure students' perceptions of fairness and procedural justice. In this implementation of SWPRD, staff reported increased efforts to engage in RD classroom practices designed to promote positive relationship building and thereby students' perceptions of the classroom as fair and the discipline process as just. Even with the relatively brief training time we had with school staff, there were substantial changes in student perceptions. We were able to document progress in reducing the impact of race/ethnicity on students' perceptions of their school environment's fairness and of sexual orientation on students' perceptions of bullying and harassment. We were also able to document students' increased perceptions of their school environment as procedurally just after the SWPRD intervention, with Latino students reporting the highest gains. At post-intervention, all students, especially White students, rated their school environment as less fair than at pre-intervention. Perhaps teachers' heightened emphasis on promoting fairness across racial groups made students more aware of a lack of fairness in their environment. Greater awareness in both students and teachers might be a first step toward achieving greater equity in discipline outcomes.

The changes in ODR data seem to substantiate that claim. The school implemented SWPBIS with fidelity in the years prior to our study and during our study, and ODR data improved. This improvement in the form of a substantial drop in overall ODR and reduction in racial disparities of ODR rates might have been due to the introduction of SWPRD. These results suggest that introducing restorative teacher practices into a school that implements SWPBIS may be able to improve student behavior overall as well as reduce disciplinary disparities.

Limitations

The outcomes of our study need to be interpreted in the context of a number of limitations. Most importantly, our study design was a one-sample pre-intervention to post-intervention comparison and as such did not contain a control group. Therefore, we were unable to control for internal threats to validity. These threats need to be addressed in larger follow-up studies with rigorous experimental designs. The relatively small scope of our study resulted in very limited training time with school staff. Since the initial field-testing, our SWPRD training materials have been revised to comprise multiple days of training and a total of six training modules targeting administrators, teachers, students, and parents. Delivery of all training modules is likely to produce stronger effects. Because we conducted our study in a school with a predominantly White and heterosexual student population, our ANOVA model was highly unbalanced and analytical results must therefore be interpreted as purely exploratory. Despite these limitations, our study allows us to define a number of implications for future practice.

Implications

In general, our findings imply that SWPRD, a blend of traditional positive behavior support approaches and restorative discipline practices focused on relationship building, may be one way to strengthen the capacity of school-wide discipline systems to reduce disparities in discipline outcomes across students from vulnerable groups defined by race/ethnicity and sexual orientation. Within current, primarily adult-driven, implementations of SWPBIS, whose success is measured by reductions in ODRs reflecting adult perceptions of student behavior, approaches to reducing these disparities necessarily focus primarily on adult behavior (McIntosh, Girvan, Horner, Smolkowski, & Sugai, 2014). Our study suggests that shifting the focus to teachers *and* students, implementing practices that promote positive relationships between teachers and students, and measuring student perceptions of the classroom environments as well as ODR might contribute to decreasing disciplinary disparities affecting vulnerable students.

Actively engaging students in shaping their learning environments, especially at the high-school level, where adolescent students value autonomy (Yeager, Fong, Lee, & Espelage, 2015), might promote shared responsibility for an equitable school climate. Practices promoted by RD emphasize this sharing of responsibility by giving students a voice through proactive and responsive circles, raising awareness of their perspectives through reframing, and emphasizing the impact of their behavior on others through affective statements.

Sharing responsibility means building positive and trusting relationships that facilitate dialogue. Dialogue appears critical in raising awareness of underlying assumptions, stereotypes, or implicit biases (McIntosh et al., 2014). Teachers as well as students bring their own culturally conditioned expectations and past experiences into the classroom, and this cultural conditioning likely affects how they perceive their environment as well as each other (Sanches et al., 2011). Dialogue built on mutual trust might result in better understanding of expectations and past experiences which, in turn, might lead to fewer discipline decisions driven by assumptions or implicit biases (Costello et al., 2009; Costello et al., 2010).

Recommendations

Research supports the need for systemic and consistent discipline delivery (Sugai et al., 2010). This approach to discipline is at the core of SWPBIS. In a primarily adult-driven approach to discipline, however, students tend to be passive recipients of behavioral lessons, acknowledgements, and consequences. Based on the literature supporting RD (Costello et al., 2009; Costello et al., 2010; Morrison & Martinez, 2001) and our own study, we recommend shifting the focus of discipline implementation to adults *and* students. When students become active participants in implementing discipline policies by which they are affected, they are more likely to perceive them as fair (Gouveia-Pereira et al., 2003). Implementing proactive circles where all students can voice their perspective on how school rules relate to their individual situations is likely to promote a sense of ownership that—in turn—is likely to promote rule compliance.

Specific relationship-building strategies like active listening, affective statements, and affective questions (Costello et al., 2009, 2010) can promote students' cognitive engagement with behavioral incidents and allow them to problem-solve. Through this communicative problem-solving process, many discipline incidents might be sustainably resolved without referrals to the office.

Finally, the ultimate goal of school-wide behavioral support is students' social and academic success (Sugai et al., 2000). Students' perceptions of fairness, procedural justice, and social capital might be predictors of social success (Gouveia-Pereira et al., 2003; Sanches et al., 2011). A focus on those constructs might create school environments where students from vulnerable backgrounds can have an equitable voice and an equitable opportunity to succeed.

References

Amstutz, L. S., & Mullet, J. H. (2005). *The little book of restorative discipline for schools: Teaching responsibility: Creating caring climates.* Intercourse, PA: GoodBooks.

Bradshaw, C. P., Mitchell, M. M., O'Brennan, L. M., & Leaf, P. J. (2010). Multilevel exploration of factors contributing to the overrepresentation of black students in office disciplinary referrals. *Journal of Educational Psychology, 102*(2), 508–520. doi:10.1037/a0018450.

Cohen, R., Kincaid, D., & Childs, K. E. (2007). Measuring school-wide positive behavior support implementation development and validation of the benchmarks of quality. *Journal of Positive Behavior Interventions, 9*, 203–213.

Costello, B., Wachtel, J., & Wachtel, T. (2009). *The restorative practices handbook for teachers, disciplinarians, and administrators.* Bethlehem, PA: International Institute for Restorative Practices.

Costello, B., Wachtel, J., & Wachtel, T. (2010). *Restorative circles in schools: Building community and enhancing learning.* Bethlehem, PA: International Institute for Restorative Practices.

DeWitt, D. M., & DeWitt, L. J. (2012). A case of high school hazing: Applying restorative justice to promote organizational learning. *NASSP Bulletin, 96*(3), 228–242. doi:10.1177/0192636512452338.

Dravery, W., & Winslade, J. (2006). *Developing restorative practices in schools: Flavour of the month or saviour of the system?* Waikato, NZ: University of Waikato, School of Education. Retrieved from www.aare.edu.au/03pap/dre03675.pdf

Gouveia-Pereira, M., Vala, J., Palmonari, A., & Rubini, M. (2003). School experience, relational justice and legitimation of institutional. *European Journal of Psychology of Education, 18*, 309–325.

Gregory A., Clawson, K., Davis, A., & Gerewitz, J. (2014). The promise of restorative practices to transform teacher–student relationships and achieve equity in school discipline. For a special issue on restorative justice in the *Journal of Educational and Psychological Consultation.* doi:10.1080/10474412.2014.929950

Gregory, A., & Ripsky, M. B. (2008). Adolescent trust in teachers: Implication for behavior in the high school classroom. *School Psychology Review, 37*, 337–353.

Himmelstein, K. E., & Brückner, H. (2011). Criminal-justice and school sanctions against nonheterosexual youth: A national longitudinal study. *Pediatrics, 127*(1), 49–57. doi:10.1542/peds.2009-2306.

Horner, R. H., Sugai, G., & Anderson, C. M. (2010). Examining the evidence base for school-wide positive behavior support. *Focus on Exceptional Children, 42*(8), 1–14.

Horner, R. H., Sugai, G., Smolkowski, K., Eber, L., Nakasato, J., Todd, A., et al. (2009). A randomized, waitlist-controlled effectiveness trial assessing school-wide positive behavior support in elementary schools. *Journal of Positive Behavior Interventions, 11*, 133–144. doi:10.1177/1098300709332067.

Kaufman, J. S., Jaser, S. S., Vaughan, E. L., Reynolds, J. S., Di Donato, J., Bernard, S. N., & Hernandez-Brereton, M. (2010). Patterns in office discipline referral data by grade, race/ethnicity, and gender. *Journal of Positive Behavior Interventions, 12*, 44–54.

Lasky, S. (2005). A sociocultural approach to understanding teacher identity, agency and professional vulnerability in a context of secondary school reform. *Teaching and Teacher Education, 21*, 899–916.

Losen, D. J. (2014). *Closing the school discipline gap: Equitable remedies for excessive exclusion.* New York: Teachers College Press.

May, S., Ard III, W., Todd, A. W., Horner, R. H., Glasgow, A., Sugai, G., et al. (2003). *School-wide Information System.* Eugene, OR: Oregon Educational and Community Supports University.

McCarthy, F. (2009). *Circle time solutions: Creating caring school communities.* (Report for the NSW Department of Education. Sydney, NSW): Department of Education.

McIntosh, K., Girvan, E., Horner, R., Smolkowski, K., & Sugai, G. (2014). *Recommendations for addressing discipline disproportionality in education.* Eugene, OR: OSEP Technical Assistance Center on Positive Behavioral Interventions and Supports.

Morrison, B. E., & Martinez, M. (2001). *Restorative justice through social and emotional skills training: An evaluation of primary school students.* Unpublished honours thesis. Australian National University, Canberra.

Muscott, H., Mann, E., & LeBrun, M. (2008). Positive behavioral interventions and supports in New Hampshire: Effects of large-scale implementation of schoolwide positive behavior support on student discipline and academic achievement. *Journal of Positive Behavior Interventions, 10,* 190–205.

Noguera, P., & Wing, J. Y. (2006). *Unfinished business: Closing the racial achievement gap in our schools.* San Francisco, CA: Jossey-Bass.

Perkins, D. D., Florin, P., Rich, R. C., Wandersman, A., & Chavis, D. M. (1990). Participation and the social and physical environment of residential blocks: Crime and community context. *American Journal of Community Psychology, 18,* 83–115.

Sanches, C., Gouveia-Pereira, M., & Carugati, F. (2011). Justice judgements, school failure, and adolescent deviant behaviour. *British Journal of Educational Psychology, 82,* 606–621. doi:10.1111/j.2044-8279.2011.02048.x.

Simson, D. (2012, May). Restorative justice and its effects on (racially disparate) punitive school discipline. Paper presented at the *7th Annual Conference on Empirical Legal Studies Paper,* Stanford, CA: Stanford University.

Skiba, R. J., Horner, R. H., Chung, C. G, Rausch, M. K., May, S. & Tobin, T. (2011). Race is not neutral: A national investigation of African American and Latino disproportionality in school discipline. *School Psychology Review, 40,* 85–107.

Sugai, G., & Horner, R. H. (2002). The evolution of discipline practices: School-wide positive behavior supports. In J. K. Luiselli & C. Diament (Eds.), *Behavior psychology in the schools: Innovations in evaluation, support, and consultation* (pp. 23–50). New York: Haworth.

Sugai, G., Horner, R. H., Algozzine, R., Barrett, S., Lewis, T., Anderson, C., et al. (2010). *School-wide Positive Behavior Support: Implementers' blueprint and self-assessment.* Eugene, OR: University of Oregon.

Sugai, G., Sprague, J. R., Horner, R. H., & Walker, H. M. (2000). Preventing school violence: The use of office discipline referrals to assess and monitor school-wide discipline interventions. *Journal of Emotional and Behavioral Disorders, 8,* 94–101.

Tabachnick, B. G., & Fidell, L. S. (2001). *Using multivariate statistics.* Boston, MA: Allyn and Bacon.

Taylor-Greene, S., Brown, D., Nelson, L., Longton, J., Gassman, T., Cohen, J., Hall, S. (1997). School-wide behavioral support: Starting the year off right. *Journal of Behavioral Education, 7,* 99–112.

U.S. Department of Education. (2014). *Guiding principles: A resource guide for improving school climate and discipline.* Washington, DC: Author. Retrieved from http://www2.ed.gov/policy/gen/guid/school-discipline/guiding-principles.pdf

Vincent, C. G., Sprague, J. R., CHiXapkaid, Tobin, T., & Gau, J. (2015). Effectiveness of School-wide Positive Behavior Interventions and Supports in reducing racially inequitable disciplinary exclusions. In D. Losen (Ed.), *Closing the school discipline gap: Equitable remedies for excessive exclusion* (pp. 207–221). New York: Teachers College Press.

Vincent, C. G., & Tobin, T. J. (2011). An examination of the relationship between implementation of School-wide Positive Behavior Support (SWPBS) and exclusion of students from various ethnic backgrounds with and without disabilities. *Journal of Emotional and Behavioral Disorders, 19,* 217–232.

Vincent, C. G., Tobin, T. J., Hawken, L., & Frank, J. (2012). Disciplinary referrals and access to secondary interventions: Patterns across students across African-American, Hispanic-American, and White backgrounds. *Education and Treatment of Children, 35,* 431–445.

Yeager, D. S., Fong, C. J., Lee, H. Y., & Espelage, D. L. (2015). Declines in efficacy of anti-bullying programs among older adolescents: Theory and a three-level meta-analysis. *Journal of Applied Developmental Psychology, 37,* 36–51.

CHAPTER 8

Ecologies of School Discipline for Queer Youth: What Listening to Queer Youth Teaches Us About Transforming School Discipline

L. Boyd Bellinger, Nicole Darcangelo, Stacey S. Horn,
Erica R. Meiners, and Sarah Schriber

One dean just had it out for me, I don't know why. I don't [know] if he didn't like the way I dressed or he didn't understand me. I feel like he didn't know how to communicate to someone like me. So like he would like never take the time to just talk to me or ask me a certain question. He would just be like 'oh you're f---ng up again.

—Study Participant

While an emerging body of literature has begun to document discipline disparities for queer youth,[1] very little research has been done to investigate the reasons behind these disparities (Skiba, Arredondo, & Rausch,

L.B. Bellinger (✉) • N. Darcangelo • S.S. Horn
College of Education, University of Illinois at Chicago, Chicago, IL, USA

E.R. Meiners
College of Education, Northeastern Illinois University, Chicago, IL, USA

S. Schriber
Prevent School Violence Illinois, Chicago, IL, USA

© The Author(s) 2016
R.J. Skiba et al. (eds.), *Inequality in School Discipline,*
DOI 10.1057/978-1-137-51257-4_8

135

2014). In this study we examined two critical, yet under-explored, questions. First, how do queer young people's experiences with school discipline relate to their other intersecting identities (e.g., race, ethnicity, class)? Second, in what ways are queer young people's experiences with school discipline connected to and/or shaped by their experiences with bullying and harassment?

Previous Research

Research demonstrates that queer young people experience higher rates of interaction with punitive systems and more severe forms of punishment than gender-conforming and heterosexual youth (Himmelstein & Bruckner, 2011; Irvine, 2010; Skiba et al., 2014). Queer youth report rates of harsh and exclusionary discipline that are three times that of their heterosexual and gender-conforming peers (Poteat & Russell, 2013). Exclusionary school discipline places queer and other marginalized students at risk for serious educational consequences such as academic disengagement, failure, push-out, and involvement with the juvenile justice system (Skiba et al., 2014; Snapp, Hoenig, Fields, & Russell, 2015). A majority of suspensions and expulsions experienced by young people in school, including queer young people, are the result of minor violations of a school's code of conduct (e.g., tardiness, cell phone use, dress code) (Morgan, Salomon, Plotkin, & Cohen, 2014) and other informal school norm/gender norm violations (e.g., dress, speech, mannerisms) (Snapp et al., 2015), rather than acts that have the potential to cause serious harm to others within the school community.

Although research on discipline disparities among queer youth is nascent, a robust body of literature exists on the higher rates of bullying and harassment students experience in school as a result of sexual orientation and/or gender identity. Research provides evidence that queer young people report high rates of multiple types of victimization in school—ranging from verbal teasing to sexual harassment and physical assault (Kosciw, Greytak, Palmer, & Boesen, 2014). Due to the ways schools reinforce and promote normative constructs of heterosexuality and cisgender identity,[2] queer youth who do not adhere to these normative constructs are at heightened risk for negative treatment at the hands of both peers and adults in school (Palmer, Kosciw, & Boesen, 2016). A recent study notes that queer young people are frequently punished for retaliating against ongoing harassment that has been ignored by school personnel (Snapp et al., 2015), but the interaction between bullying and discipline is generally less well understood.

There is a fairly extensive body of research on disproportionate discipline related to race/ethnicity (especially for African American and Latino males) and students with disabilities, but until recently, this research has not investigated the ways in which sexual orientation and gender identity/expression contribute to these experiences. This study expands the literature on the salience of intersections of sexuality, gender, and gender identity with other social categories such as race/ethnicity (Crenshaw, 2015; Snapp et al., 2015).

METHODOLOGY AND PROJECT OVERVIEW

Research Team

We convened our five-person research team based on our shared and ongoing commitments to educational research that informs the development of just school practices for queer students and staff. Our team includes two doctoral students, two university faculty members, and the director of a statewide school climate transformation and bullying prevention coalition. All members of the research team identify as White and queer. We research, teach, organize, and advocate in a state that has some existing systemic support for queer students, but also contains school districts with some of the highest suspension and expulsion rates for youth of color in the country (Losen & Martinez, 2013).

Participants and Procedures

We conducted in-depth, one-on-one interviews in private or semi-private settings with 20 young people who met our age criterion (ages 16–21) and who identified their sexual orientations and gender identities in a variety of ways (e.g., queer, gender queer, transgender, androgynous, gay, lesbian, omnisexual; Latino, Black, Colored, European American). We recruited participants from two queer youth advocacy organizations in the Chicago area and interviewed, on a first come, first-served basis, a group of young people who volunteered to participate and share their experiences with school discipline, school bullying, and the criminal legal system. Interviews lasted approximately 20–50 minutes each and all participants provided assent/consent prior to the interviews.[3]

Interview Protocol and Coding

We developed our interview protocol using an existing, semi-structured protocol (Irvine, 2010), which we piloted and refined. The protocol included questions in the following areas: self-identification of demographics, family structure, living/housing situation, employment/sources of income, school history, school context, experiences with bullying, experiences with school discipline, experiences with the juvenile justice system, and recommendations for educators.

All the interviews were audio recorded and transcribed, after which each team member reviewed the recordings and transcripts. Throughout the process, we met regularly to discuss impressions, generate and refine codes, and create consensus around our readings of the transcripts. Once we determined our coding structure and themes had emerged, we created visual maps of the disciplinary pathways for each of the participants, highlighting the real or perceived transgressions and the formal and informal disciplinary sanctions related to each. We also highlighted any precipitating or contextual factors that contributed to each transgression[4] and sanction, and identified the ways each participant perceived these to be directly related to their sexual orientation, gender identity, and/or gender presentation.

RESULTS

Our project sought to better understand how queer youth experience school discipline, and how their intersecting identities and any bullying and harassment they face might be related to their disciplinary experiences. Our participants described school climates that, at best, were antagonistic to queer youth and, at worst, replete with institutionalized heterosexism and racism that contributed to and supported interpersonal acts of homophobic, racist, and/or transphobic aggression. No single pathway surfaced to explain the disproportionate discipline of queer youth. While all our participants offered complex, and often painful, examples of their experiences with school discipline, we selected Kiki, Casey, and Joaquin[5] to highlight in this chapter. We chose these three young people because they represent diverse identities, school contexts, experiences with formal and informal sanctions, and experiences with bullying and harassment.

Kiki, a 16-year-old straight female who was assigned male at birth, self-identifies as "colored," and is an out and proud student in her public high school. Her presence as an urban, transgender Black woman in a suburban, predominantly White high school marks her as non-normative in multiple and ultimately inseparable ways. Casey is a White, Jewish 16-year-old "genderqueer" youth who identifies as "omnisexual" and "androgynous." Preferring the gender pronoun *they*, Casey attends a desegregated school in a suburban district. Joaquin is a 21-year-old gay Hispanic male who attended a large, urban, public high school from ninth to twelfth grades, but left high school just a half credit short of graduation. After leaving his public school, Joaquin briefly attended an alternative high school and then a technical high school, where he earned his General Education Diploma (GED).

Individually and collectively, Kiki, Joaquin, and Casey illustrate the three central findings from this research project. First, queer youth's experiences of disproportionate discipline frequently stem from schools being sites of gender normativity and gender regulation that deem certain identities and expressions as normal and appropriate while others must be sanctioned, regulated, and controlled. Second, queer students' experiences with school discipline do not follow a simple, linear transgression-to-sanction format. Rather, their experiences of discipline are connected to multiple relationships, interactions, and behaviors that at first seem like disparate events but are actually part of complex ecologies of school discipline. Third, young people's experiences of school discipline include acts of resistance and self-advocacy that help them navigate and survive oppressive school cultures but, at times, also lead to additional sanctions (see also Poteat et al. chapter in this book). These themes are elucidated below.

Schools as Sites of Enforced Gender Normativity

Participants frequently described school contexts rife with the policing of clothing, embodiment, and affect perceived to be outside the boundaries of "appropriate" binary gender scripts. While not all of the interactions participants reported involved formal disciplinary actions, experiences of harassment by various school personnel shaped their life pathways in numerous ways.

Kiki recounted that school administrators expressed that her clothing and gender expression justified the harassment she experienced at the hands of her peers:

> The head principal actually said that if I wasn't dressing so much as a drag queen I wouldn't be getting bullied so much … [S]he said she used to teach LGBT students…to not be so openly gay.

Despite the existence of a policy prohibiting the precise type of verbal and physical harassment to which she was subjected, Kiki knew from experience that reporting harassment would not lead to sanctions of the perpetrators and might actually have encouraged additional harassment:

> I was getting, you know, bullied very bad. Like people were throwing things at me, you know; they were calling me names. It came to a point where I didn't know who was doing it anymore. I couldn't really point out. I became mute about telling people because of retaliation, the fear of retaliation. And, you know, nobody would really do anything about it and then. I ended up in the hospital, a mental hospital because I was having suicidal thoughts and I was cutting again.

Kiki reported that, with support from a school social worker, she was able to take classes online at an alternative school and only had to spend her mornings at the mainstream high school. While sympathetic, the social worker opted to ensure Kiki's safety by pushing her into an alternative educational environment. However, despite spending less time at her mainstream school, Kiki continued to experience bullying during her mornings there.

Kiki was aware that, rather than addressing those who bullied her or the impact of the institutional oppression at the school, the school determined that her presence as a transgender woman in a gender normative environment was the problem. By moving Kiki out of her mainstream school and into an alternative setting, the school effectively sanctioned her for the harassment she had experienced.

Like Kiki, Joaquin was repeatedly and openly harassed by school security guards for his clothing and also how he walked or stood "a certain way." He stated that at least "twice a week" the "way I chose to express myself, I guess, in school [was] what got me in trouble." Joaquin identified that the students whose appearance deviated from binary norms were perceived to be queer and targeted for verbal harassment by the guards:

> They would clearly say fag or queer. They'd make it known that they were talking to a LGBTQ person. You know? Like if it was a girl, they'd call her a dyke. If it was a guy they would call him a faggot.

As a result of the harassment he received related to his non-normative gender presentation, Joaquin acknowledged experiencing serious depression throughout his school years. When asked how he dealt with the harassment and sanctions, Joaquin replied:

I would either not go to school, or ditch class, or I'd rebel for no reason. Just be upset. I was always upset. Or at least I hadn't ... I used to cut [myself]... So that's how I would deal with it. But eventually I ended up leaving.

Although Joaquin organized within the school in response to targeted harassment, in the end, the failure of school staff to support him effectively sanctioned him by pushing him out altogether.

Casey, too, revealed that appearance—particularly clothing—was deeply linked to institutionalized gender norms and being heavily, yet differentially, policed and monitored in their school. Although Casey suggested that clothing was policed less often in high school than in middle school, gendered and heterosexist norms were still regulated. For example, while the school required Casey to remove a t-shirt printed with "Vagina Expert" they received while volunteering at Planned Parenthood, Casey recalled a cisgender (White) male student repeatedly wearing a shirt that stated, "I'd hit that!"

While many of our participants reported negative experiences in school based on their gender identities, the data also demonstrated that gender non-normativity and queerness were inseparable from their other social identities when it came to being surveilled in school and experiencing disproportionate formal and informal sanctions. Their experiences of school discipline suggest an indivisibility of race, gender, and sexuality, as well as ability and socioeconomic status.

Casey, who is White, reported that a transgender woman of color in the same school district was suspended for using the "wrong bathroom." While discussing this incident, Casey said, "I know I'm not allowed to use the men's bathroom." Yet when asked "what would happen if you did," Casey stated:

Casey: I'd like to think I would be suspended. I don't think I would be.

Interviewer: Why do you think that?

C: 'Cause I am White and I am not seen as a threat.

I: Hm, say more about that.

C: So, when my friend at the other school did it she was perceived as a Black man going into the women's restroom and she would have been perceived as a threat. Um, me being perceived as a petite White girl doesn't seem to put as much of a threat.

Casey was acutely aware that race, in relation to gender and sexuality, affects students' experiences with disciplinary consequences.

Our participants' experiences with gender-related harassment and resulting sanctions affected their lives both within and outside of school. Joaquin talked about leaving school just one-half credit shy of graduating because he couldn't handle all of the "nonsense" anymore. In addition, Kiki, Joaquin, and Casey all discussed dealing with significant mental health issues that resulted from the ongoing harassment and bullying they experienced at school, as well as the lack of any effective interventions regarding this harassment.

Ecologies of School Discipline

The mapping of our participants' disciplinary pathways highlighted complex relationships among their daily experiences of harassment, bullying, and school discipline. In schools, queer youth experience a wide range of institutional and interpersonal forms of interrelated racism, homophobia, misogyny, and transphobia enacted by both adults and their peers. Queer youth often do not report these forms of harassment and when they do, school personnel frequently do not take meaningful action, blame or do not believe the victim, or potentially respond in ways that increase the victim's vulnerability (Snapp et al., 2015). Additionally, it is often the case that, upon reaching their limits, queer youth finally resist by fighting back, disobeying authority, or skipping school (Diaz & Kosciw, 2009; Snapp et al., 2015). As demonstrated by the experiences described by the young people we interviewed, youth may also resist by engaging in self-harm. In response to their resistance, queer youth often receive formal or informal sanctions (see Poteat et al., this volume). Multi-directional and concurrent, these layered pathways are apparent throughout our participants' experiences with school discipline.

Participants reported that while they could identify some individual teachers and staff who were supportive of queer youth, they explained that others—sometimes key school administrators—were not supportive and actively participated in creating homophobic, misogynistic, or racist school climates. For example, Joaquin, continuing to recount his experiences with a dean who "had it out for me," stated:

> He would say stuff like, 'typical fag-like complaining...,' like a bunch of random crap that, yeah. That and the security guards that would make comments about how tight my pants were if they were tight. Or how I would walk a certain or stand a certain way. It was really stupid s—.

When queer students reported their experiences of harassment or bullying, they were frequently ignored. More than once, Kiki, a trans woman of color, noted that the reports she made after being harassed by peers were insufficient to lead to any meaningful intervention from school leaders: "And [the assistant principal] was like, 'well are there any witnesses?' and I was like, 'no.' And she was like, 'well I can't really do anything.'" Yet when other students (described by Kiki as male and White) reported Kiki as the perpetrator, their claims seemed to be sufficient to warrant Kiki's resulting discipline although they were each other's only witnesses. Kiki was also more harshly sanctioned for actions that, for others, went unpunished. Kiki described singing a song with the word "d–k" in it, in response to which another student, with support from the assistant principal, reported her for sexual harassment:

That's one that really pissed me off because I said a word, and how does that offend you? You know? And I was kind of telling [the assistant principal], you know, [the other student is] telling girls to do sexual acts on him and everything, you know, and it kind of bothers me a little bit that he's doing it and that's sexual harassment towards [the girls], but you know I am sitting here trying to tell you like, "okay...I didn't tell you because I knew you wouldn't do anything." And she [the assistant principal] was like, "well if he did we would need to have witnesses."

Although Kiki was closely monitored by the predominantly White staff at her school, the systemic harassment against her (and, as she notes, other female students) perpetrated by a male peer was ignored.

Given the persistence of homophobia in schools, even the threat of a formal or informal school sanction that might disclose information related to sexual or gender identity or behaviors can augment queer students' vulnerability (Snapp et al., 2015). For example, when Casey was 13 years old, their flirting with another girl triggered a series of homophobic interpersonal and institutional responses:

We would say sexually explicit things, and one day her very conservative, very Catholic parents found out and took it to the school saying I was sexually harassing her and saying they were going to charge me with sexual harassment. Which they never did, but 13-year-old me didn't know that. ... Every time I passed her in the hallways I would start having a panic attack. ... I had very intense depression, I was self-harming, cutting myself, and [sighs] eventually the school counselor that told me I wouldn't have any problems if I was straight said that she needed to tell my mom about what happened with the girl that I was texting and if I didn't come out to my mom, she would have to. So at that point I had to come out to my mom. I was already out to my dad, but now it's my mom. So I came out to my mom and she was fine with it.

Despite being threatened with a criminal charge by the parents of her peer, and with the threat of disclosure of her sexuality to her mother by her school counselor, Casey was never formally sanctioned in any way. Still, Casey identified that the panic attacks and forced outing were part and parcel of the punitive, disciplinary climate of the school.

As the experiences of Joaquin, Kiki, and Casey demonstrate, queer students traverse complex ecologies of school discipline. Disproportionately harassed in schools by peers and school personnel and often ignored by staff when they attempt to lodge a complaint, queer students resist in ways that increase the likelihood that they will become targets of formal and informal school disciplinary sanctions.

Youth Resistance and Self-advocacy

Pathways of formal and informal sanctions mark many queer youth's school experiences. Nevertheless, our participants were not passive victims in their discipline scenarios. Despite sometimes being punished as a consequence, they repeatedly defended and advocated for themselves against bullying, harassment, and inequitable treatment.

In a school climate rife with racial animosity, homophobia, and gender coercion, Kiki's identity, body, and self-expression marked her as a target for harassment and differential treatment by adults and peers. Unwilling to accept the limitations of her school, Kiki defended herself, organized, and spoke out. She continued to press for recognition of her identity at school and to advocate for other queer students. Additionally, Kiki started her school's Gay Straight Alliance (GSA), which she viewed as something that "took action back" to support other students going through similar experiences.

Despite the failure of Joaquin's school administration to intervene when security guards harassed him for the way he dressed, stood, and walked, he and other students resisted. They alerted the administration and their families that they planned to organize against the harassment perpetrated by the security guards:

The last interaction that I had with [the guards] was when I was actually wearing some skinny jeans and they felt the need to comment and make jokes that I was gay or whatnot and I brought to the attention of my principal and then I had my aunt and my mom working on—their part of the school council, local school council, something like that.

In addition, with support from teachers, Joaquin and his GSA pursued a partnership with a local queer theater company that facilitated a collaborative theatrical production focused specifically on queer violence and bullying.

Despite the negative consequences of their experiences at school, our participants demonstrated a well-developed sense of justice and had concrete ideas about what effective discipline would look like. Many put those ideas into action. Casey told us they were "in the process of starting a policy change group just for ... my school district. And one of the things on my list of things to change is our zero tolerance policy and bringing in restorative justice instead of punitive justice." The youth in our project were able to articulate how to resist punitive discipline and/or harassment from peers or adults, in addition to advocating for both their own rights and the rights of others in the school.

RECOMMENDATIONS

As Kiki, Joaquin, and Casey suggested, some schools have made attempts—including hosting assemblies, supporting student clubs, and creating or strengthening policies—to support queer youth. In isolation, however, none of these efforts has proven to be the key to rectifying the problem of the disproportionately punitive discipline of marginalized youth or the bullying and harassment they experience. To truly transform the disciplinary experiences of queer youth, we recommend that schools commit to an ongoing process that is comprehensive and contextualized.

As a first step, we recommend listening to Kiki, Joaquin, Casey, and similarly situated youth, because they tell us what has not worked—and more importantly, what has—to make them feel safe, respected, and even honored in their school communities. Our participants suggested a range of possibilities to help schools become more supportive places. Their recommendations ranged from increasing the number of mental health counselors at schools to creating sexuality support groups for students to implementing restorative justice practices. Guided by our participants' recommendations, the key efforts we propose address the three themes of our project: schools as sites of gender policing, the complex ecologies of school discipline, and the ways that young people resist the injustices they face.

Engage Students as Active Participants

We present the following recommendation first, as it is in many ways our most important, and is a direct and specific way to put listening to young people into action. Additionally, this recommendation can—and should—be integrated into each of the others that follow, which increases the likelihood of success in creating safer schools. Students like Kiki, Joaquin, and Casey reveal critical insight into the overlapping issues they face in their schools—racial profiling, gender coercion, homophobia—and are tenacious in their efforts to challenge them. As such, students make up a critical stakeholder group, but are often devalued or overlooked (Hughes & Pickeral, 2013; Pittman, Martin, & Williams, 2007). If those typically empowered to make changes in schools collaborate authentically with students by seeking their input and actively engaging with them in the transformation process, students' experiences and insights become assets that contribute to relevant and effective solutions.

As highlighted by Kiki, Joaquin, and Casey, schools' efforts to protect marginalized students, for example by removing them to another setting, frequently compound harm to queer students. Rather than viewing particular queer students as the problem and subsequently targeting or excluding them because they do not conform to school-based norms, schools can engage the experiences and expertise of students to address and transform the systemic biases that make them vulnerable (Palmer et al., 2016; Poteat, 2016). As demonstrated by Kiki, Joaquin, and Casey, when queer young people participate in transforming their schools by naming and breaking down the harms they have experienced, their contributions improve school climates to better support all students, including other queer students.

Yet before engaging young people in collaborative school transformation efforts, school leaders must acknowledge the power relations at play and work to protect young people from potential harm. It can be counterproductive and even dangerous to bring young people who are already vulnerable into school transformation work before the adults in a school are supported to understand the complex ecologies of school discipline. This leads us to our second recommendation, which is aimed at helping adults learn to better support queer youth.

Provide Both Baseline and Targeted Professional Development

It is clear from the experiences of the young people we interviewed that schools are often biased, explicitly and implicitly, against non-normatively gendered and racialized bodies, suggesting the need for baseline professional development on anti-oppressive education, both within pre-professional preparation programs and as a part of a regular cycle of in-service professional development within schools. Even within the larger context of systemic oppression, however, the biases that impact queer students manifest in different ways in different school communities. How youth in our project experienced school discipline was dependent on the situated norms of their schools and the ways systemic biases—including racism, sexism, cis-sexism, homophobia, and classism—were reinforced in the attitudes and actions of people (and policies) in their school contexts.

To transform the disciplinary issues unique to their school communities, schools can provide ongoing professional development tailored to the particular ways in which racism, hetero- and cis-sexism, homophobia, transphobia, and other institutionalized forms of oppression impact formal disciplinary systems, as well as students' informal experiences of school discipline (Espelage, Basile, & Hamburger, 2012; Espelage, Low, Polanin, & Brown, 2015; Schriber, Horn, Peter, Bellinger, & Fischer, 2016; Szalacha, 2003). For example, to address the interplay of gender coercion, harassment, and school discipline reported by Kiki, Joaquin, and Casey, schools could train those school personnel most often charged with enforcing dress codes (and implicitly monitoring gender norms), including security guards, to recognize and respond appropriately to issues of gender and gender non-conformity.

Ongoing professional development that is tailored to address a particular school context can also support all school personnel in understanding the impacts of bias on bullying and harassment and the consequences of failing to take these behaviors seriously (Schriber et al., 2016). Kiki's, Joaquin's, and Casey's experiences demonstrate the serious damage caused when those charged with students' safety and wellbeing ignore, aggravate, or instigate the harassment or disparate treatment of queer youth.

To transform a school climate that is antagonistic to queer youth, schools can rethink and positively develop the ways varied personnel interact with students. Kiki, Joaquin, and Casey each confirmed that the adults at school who knew them well were ultimately the most supportive of their safety and wellbeing. In order to foster these supportive relationships, a school can train all personnel, including those often left out of trainings, such as building leaders, deans of discipline, and security guards, in the basics of queer identities, communities, and terminology. Additionally, targeted training can help these varied personnel to recognize the tremendous power they have in their school setting and how to use this influence to positively and productively interact with queer students. Schools can optimize the impact of professional development on school climate transformation by supporting all personnel to participate and by continuing to follow up with and provide additional support to staff as they work to put their learning into action in effective and productive ways.

Assess School Policies and Their Implementation

A school's educational policies represent the shared values, commitments, and priorities of the school community (Schriber et al., 2016). Strong, school-level policies that state explicitly that students are protected against bullying, discrimination, and inequitable treatment related to queer identities and provide clear guidance to both students and staff about rights, protections, and procedures for intervention (Russell, Kosciw, Horn, & Saewyc, 2010), are crucial to reducing bias-related bullying and harassment, as well as inequitable discipline.

Policies alone, however, cannot sufficiently address disparate discipline or bullying and harassment (Fischer, Bellinger, Horn, & Sullivan, 2016; Lugg & Murphy, 2016; Meyer, 2009). To improve the effectiveness of anti-bullying, non-discrimination, dress codes, discipline, and other school policies intended to maintain schools as safe and supportive for all students, schools can create ongoing initiatives to assess whether policy implementation is equitable and aligns with their intended purposes. For example, while a school may develop a strong anti-bullying policy intended to prevent bullying by sanctioning "bullies," its policy may inadvertently lead to the use of its corresponding discipline policy to sanction students who defend themselves against ongoing harassment. In this way, an anti-bullying policy ends up triggering the punishment of the very students it aims to protect. Casey's effort to convene a district policy work group offers schools an example of one way to address these unintended consequences. Additionally, Kiki, Joaquin, and Casey revealed that their experiences with school discipline or informal sanctions often stemmed from their dress and self-presentation. Schools can examine the ways in which they interpret, implement, and enforce dress codes and whether such policies permit and aggravate implicit and explicit gender policing.

Utilize Data to Uncover How the Intersections of Biases Related to Race, Gender, and Sexuality Impact Queer Students

Our final recommendation is that schools continually engage in attempts to bring to the surface the ways both direct and implicit biases toward queer students impact their experiences with discipline, harassment, and inequitable treatment. One way to do this is through data collection. In Illinois, to better understand the ways in which systemic biases related to such social identities as race, ethnicity, gender, and religion impact students at an institutional level, schools have begun to administer the Bias-Based Bullying Survey (BBBS) (Prevent School Violence Illinois, 2012), an instrument available free of charge. Schools can analyze their BBBS information alongside other data—such as existing discipline records—to discern which groups of students are disciplined, how often, and for what reasons, and to uncover the ways that young people with multiple "marginalized" identities might be at heightened risk for discipline due to discrimination and bias. To ensure the data are most relevant, schools can revise the forms they use to document instances of harassment and discipline to include categories of bias such as race/ethnicity, sexual orientation, and gender identity. Informed by their own unique data, schools can tailor professional development and other interventions that are relevant and impactful.

Data collection can also be informal and student-led. For example, schools could support students in a club or a class to do participatory action research or lead focus groups to gather information around issues important to them (see Chmielewski et al., this volume). Students can then use that information to recommend and implement the interventions they believe would improve the ways in which they experience school.

Conclusion

Our project expands a limited body of research by seeking to understand how and why queer youth experience disproportionately punitive school discipline. It suggests that youth's experiences with school discipline are complex and multifaceted, related to their intersecting identities and the cycles of surveillance and harassment to which they are continuously sub-jected within schools. To rectify the disproportionate discipline of queer youth, schools can commit to a comprehensive approach that coordinates tailored educational, data collection, policy, and student engagement interventions. In this way, schools can become safer, more supportive, more equitable, and, ultimately, more engaging spaces for all.

Notes

1. Throughout this chapter, unless otherwise specified by participants or when citing relevant research, we use the term "queer" as a proxy for LGBTQ (lesbian, gay, bisexual, transgender and/or queer), to represent a wide range of non-norming sexual and gender identities and expressions.
2. Cisgender is a term denoting or relating to a person whose gender identity conforms with the gender that corresponds to their biological sex or sex assigned at birth; not transgender.
3. For the purposes of participant safety, we requested and were granted a waiver of parental permission for the study by the University of Illinois at Chicago Institutional Review Board.
4. Throughout this chapter, *sanction* refers to an actual or threatened institutional response from adult disciplinary actors and/or an informal response from school personnel or peers. We use *transgression* to refer to the actions, as recounted by the young person that precipitated a disciplinary sanction, regardless of whether the action violated any actual school rule or policy.
5. All three are pseudonyms.

References

Crenshaw, K. (2015). *Black girls matter: Pushed out, overpoliced and underpro-tected*. New York: African American Policy Forum, Center for Intersectionality and Social Policy Studies. Retrieved from www.atlanticphilanthropies.org/sites/default/files/uploads/BlackGirlsMatter_Report.pdf

Diaz, E. & Kosciw, J. G. (2009). *Shared differences: The experiences of lesbian, gay, bisexual, and. transgender students of color in our nation's schools*. New York: Gay, Lesbian, Straight Education Network. Retrieved from http://www.umass.edu/stonewall/uploads/listWidget/25157/shared%20diff.pdf

Espelage, D. L., Basile, K. C., & Hamburger, M. E. (2012). Bullying perpetration and subsequent sexual violence perpetration among middle school students. *Journal of Adolescent Health, 50*, 60–65. doi:10.1016/j.jadohealth.2011.07.015.

Espelage, D. L., Low, S., Polanin, J. R., & Brown, E. C. (March–April 2015). Clinical trial of Second Step© middle-school program: Impact on aggression & victimization. *Journal of Applied Developmental Psychology*, *37*, 52–63. doi:10.1016/j.appdev.2014.11.007

Fischer, D., Bellinger, L. B., Horn, S. S., & Sullivan, S. L. (2016). Advocacy to support gender identity development in schools in the face of organized backlash. In S. T. Russell & S. S. Horn (Eds.), *Sexual orientation, gender identity, and schooling: The nexus of research, practice, and policy* (pp. 219–237). New York: Oxford University Press.

Himmelstein, K. E. W., & Bruckner, H. (2011). Criminal-justice and school sanctions against non-heterosexual youth: A national longitudinal study. *Pediatrics*, *127*(1), 49–57. doi:10.1542/peds.2009-2306.

Hughes, W. H., & Pickeral, T. (2013). School climate and shared leadership. In T. Dary & T. Pickeral (Eds.), *School climate practices for implementation and sustainability, A school climate practice brief*, Number 1. New York: National School Climate Center.

Irvine, A. (2010). "We've had three of them": Addressing the invisibility of lesbian, gay, bisexual and gender non-conforming youth in the juvenile justice system. *Columbia Journal of Gender and Law, 19*, 675–701.

Kosciw, J. G., Greytak, E. A., Palmer, N. A., & Boesen, M. J. (2014). *The 2013 National School Climate Survey: The experiences of lesbian, gay, bisexual and transgender Youth in Our nation's Schools*. New York: GLSEN.

Losen, D. J., & Martinez, T. E. (2013). *Out of school and off track: The overuse of suspensions in American middle and high schools*. Los Angeles: The Center for Civil Rights Remedies at The Civil Right Project/Proyecto Derechos Civiles.

Lugg, C., & Murphy, J. (2016). The shifting political winds: LGBTQ students, educational policy and politics, and the dilemmas confronting street level bureaucrats. In S. T. Russell & S. S. Horn (Eds.), *Sexual orientation, gender identity, and schooling: The nexus of research, practice, and policy* (pp. 238–254). New York: Oxford University Press.

Meyer, E. J. (2009). *Gender, bullying, and harassment: Strategies to end sexism and homophobia in schools*. New York: Teacher's College Press.

Morgan, E., Salomon, N., Plotkin, M., & Cohen, R. (2014). *The school discipline consensus report: Strategies from the field to keep students engaged in school and out of the juvenile justice system*. New York: Council of State Governments Justice Center.

Palmer, N. A., Kosciw, J. G., & Boesen, M. J. (2016). Disrupting hetero-gender-normativity: The complex role of LGBT affirmative supports at school. In S. T. Russell & S. S. Horn (Eds.), *Sexual orientation, gender identity, and schooling: The nexus of research, practice, and policy* (pp. 58–74). New York: Oxford University Press.

Pittman, K., Martin, S., & Williams, A. (2007). *Core principles for engaging young people in community change*. Washington, DC: The Forum for Youth Investment.

Poteat, V. P. (2016). Understanding and reducing bias-based harassment and victimization in schools. In S. T. Russell & S. S. Horn (Eds.), *Sexual orientation, gender identity, and schooling: The nexus of research, practice, and policy* (pp. 15–38). New York: Oxford University Press.

Poteat, V. P., & Russell, S. T. (2013). Understanding homophobic behavior and its implications for policy and practice. *Theory into Practice, 52*, 264–271. doi: 10.1080/00405841.2013.829729.

Prevent School Violence Illinois. (2012). *Bias-Based Bullying Survey (BBBS)*. Retrieved from http://psvillinois.org/psvi-s-work/bias-based-bullying.html

Russell, S. T., Kosciw, J., Horn, S., & Saewyc, E. (2010). Safe schools policy for LGBTQ students. *Society for research in child development social policy report, 24*(4), 1–25.

Schriber, S., Horn, S. S., Peter, C. P., Bellinger, L. B., & Fischer, D. (2016). Supporting LGB/T youth: Comprehensive school transformation as effective bullying prevention. In S. T. Russell & S. S. Horn (Eds.), *Sexual orientation, gender identity, and schooling: The nexus of research, practice, and policy* (pp. 75–95). New York: Oxford University Press.

Skiba, R. J., Arredondo, M. I., & Rausch, M. K. (2014). *New and developing research on disparities in discipline*. Bloomington, IN: The Equity Project at Indiana University.

Snapp, S. D., Hoenig, J. M., Fields, A., & Russell, S. T. (2015). Messy, butch, and queer: LGBTQ youth and the school-to-prison pipeline. *Journal of Adolescent Research, 30*, 57–82. doi:10.1177/0743558414557625.

Szalacha, L. A. (2003). Safer sexual diversity climates: Lessons learned from an evaluation of Massachusetts safe schools program for gay and lesbian students. *American Journal of Education, 110*, 58–88.

CHAPTER 9

The Potential of Restorative Approaches to Discipline for Narrowing Racial and Gender Disparities

Anne Gregory and Kathleen Clawson

INTRODUCTION

The US Departments of Education (DOE) and Justice, in their *Guiding Principles: A Resource Guide for Improving School Climate and Discipline* (U.S. DOE, 2014), state that, "Schools should remove students from the classroom as a disciplinary consequence only as a last resort and only for appropriately serious infractions" (p. 3). The recommendation to use exclusionary discipline "as a last resort" follows reports documenting high suspension rates in many districts across the nation (Losen & Martinez, 2013) and research suggesting that suspensions may actually worsen the outcomes of students who are already struggling in school (e.g., Balfanz, Byrnes, & Fox, 2015). Fueling critique of the use of suspensions are the documented racial and ethnic disparities in school discipline sanctions (see Skiba, Arredondo & Rausch, this volume; Losen & Smith-Evans, this volume).

A. Gregory (✉) • K. Clawson
Graduate School of Applied and Professional Pyschology,
Rutgers, The State University of New Jersey, New Brunswick, NY, USA

© The Author(s) 2016
R.J. Skiba et al. (eds.), *Inequality in School Discipline*,
DOI 10.1057/978-1-137-51257-4_9

In light of the negative correlates of exclusionary discipline and racial and gender disparities in school discipline, restorative practices (RP) has been identified as a promising alternative to the current use of punitive measures (e.g., Morgan, Salomon, Plotkin, & Cohen, 2014). Research on RP in American schools is relatively sparse, and empirical examinations of RP implementation and its effect on student outcomes are needed (Hurley, Guckenburg, Persson, Fronius, & Petrosino, 2015). The current chapter builds on prior published analyses (Gregory, Clawson, Davis, & Gerewitz, 2014b) and offers new findings on RP implementation in high school classrooms, with implications for the promise of well-implemented RP in reducing racial and gender disparities in office discipline referrals (ODRs).

Restorative Approaches to Discipline

RP in schools arose out of the restorative justice (RJ) movement, whereby victims, offenders, and other impacted individuals—including families or community members—meet together to resolve conflict and repair relationships (McCluskey et al., 2008; Wachtel, 2013; Zehr, 2002). New Zealand, in the late 1980s, appears to have been the first country to formally incorporate the process of joint problem solving among impacted parties into their handling of juvenile offenses (Doolan, 1999); the underlying values of the New Zealand judicial process are rooted in the indigenous Maori people's emphasis on the role of family and community in addressing wrongdoing. Since then, the use of conferences among disputing parties to resolve and repair harm spread to countries such as Australia and Canada (Wachtel, 2013), and has eventually been integrated into some diversionary programs in the USA (e.g., Jeong, McGarrell, & Hipple, 2012; Swayze & Buskovick, 2012).

Restorative approaches to school discipline include a continuum of practices that range from preventing infractions (Amstutz & Mullet, 2005; Blood & Thorsborne, 2005) to intervention after an infraction (McCluskey et al., 2008; Morrison, 2007). School-based training organizations vary in their menu of practices, but three common practices used in RP include community-building or proactive circles, responsive circles, and restorative conferences (Amstutz & Mullet, 2005). Community-building circles in the classroom are held before conflict occurs to foster trust and sense of community (Restorative Practices Working Group, 2014). Responsive circles are held in reaction to challenges that arise in classrooms to encourage joint accountability and empowerment in setting (or re-setting) positive norms among students and teachers (Mirsky, 2011). Restorative conferences are held after a discipline incident or dispute among school community members (Mirsky, 2011; Restorative Practices Working Group, 2014; Wachtel, O'Connell, & Wachtel, 2010; Zehr & Toews, 2004).

Proactive circles, responsive circles, and restorative conferences share similar procedures. Students typically sit facing each other without barriers, and when students are handed the "talking piece," they have an opportunity to voice their perspective. This gives students an opportunity to learn about one another, and practice social and emotional skills such as active listening and appropriate personal disclosure (Gregory et al., 2014c). The circle or conference facilitator asks participants a series of questions such as, "What happened? What were you thinking about at the time? Who has been affected by what you did? How has this affected you and others? What do you think needs to happen to make things right? What do you think you need to do to make things right?" (O'Connell, Wachtel, & Wachtel, 1999).

Empirical Studies of Restorative Approaches to Discipline

Currently, randomized controlled trials (RCT) of RP are underway in several states (e.g., National Institute of Justice, 2014). Thus, results from rigorous experimental research on school-based RP implementation have not yet been released in the USA. That said, case studies of schools and districts show substantial reductions in the use of ODRs and out-of-school suspensions (for a summary, see Schiff, 2013). This has been replicated in schools around the world, including New Zealand (Buckley & Maxwell, 2007), Scotland, (Kane et al., 2007), and China (Wong & Mok, 2011). Similarly, in the USA, reduced rates of suspension have been found when comparing rates before and after RP implementation in cities such as Denver, Colorado (Anyon et al., 2014), Oakland, California (Jain, Bassey, Brown, & Kalra, 2014), and Minneapolis, Minnesota (Riestenberg, 2013). Studies tracking discipline outcomes over time have shown that students who received a restorative intervention after a discipline infraction have a lower probability of receiving another discipline referral or suspension than peers receiving other sanctions (Anyon et al., 2014; Riestenberg, 2013). Few studies have examined school-wide shifts in achievement, attendance, and graduation rates in response to the implementation of RJ. A noteworthy exception is an evaluation of RJ implementation in the Oakland Unified School District (Jain et al., 2014). Across a three-year period, RJ schools showed greater improvements than non-RJ schools in reading proficiency, graduation rates, and attendance.

It is important to note that interventions may result in benefits for all student groups in general, without substantially narrowing disparities between specific student groups (e.g., Vincent, Sprague, CHIXapkaid, Tobin, & Gau, 2015). As mentioned above, substantial evidence from single case studies of schools and districts in numerous countries suggest RP is associated with reduced use of exclusionary discipline in general (e.g., ODRs and suspensions; Anyon et al., 2014), and in under-resourced schools largely comprising low-income African American and Latino students (Davis, 2014; Lewis, 2009). As of yet, however, only a handful of studies have examined whether RP is associated with reduced racial and gender disparities in discipline (e.g., Anyon et al., 2014; González, 2015; Gregory et al., 2014b; Jain et al., 2014).

Several district-wide evaluations provide insights into the gap-reducing potential of restorative approaches to discipline. Evaluation of RJ in Oakland schools and Denver schools showed that African American students had the greatest decline in suspension rates, relative to other student groups (González, 2015; Jain et al., 2014). In both districts, the gap between the percentage of suspended African American and White students went down by about 6 percentage points. Yet despite the progress in Denver, recent research suggests that student race remained a significant risk factor for discipline sanctions after the introduction of RP. Anyon and colleagues in two different studies (2014; 2016) found that African American students were still significantly more likely to be issued suspensions relative to White students after holding constant school and student characteristics (e.g., low-income status) and the reasons students were referred to the office for misconduct (e.g., tardiness vs. fighting). These findings suggest that, despite the use of restorative approaches to discipline, African American students continued to be issued harsher sanctions relative to White students with similar misconduct and similar characteristics. In sum, the collection of findings from a handful of correlational studies, taken as whole, point to the possibility that restorative approaches have some promise for reducing, but perhaps not yet eradicating, discipline disparities (e.g., Anyon et al., 2014; González, 2015; Gregory et al., 2014b; Jain et al., 2014).

PURPOSE OF THE CURRENT STUDY

This chapter describes a small scale study of RP implementation in two high schools in a mid-sized city in the Northeast. The current research builds upon and extends previous findings (Gregory et al., 2014b) through a focus specifically on the *gender and race* patterns in ODRs for misconduct and defiance. The previous study (Gregory et al., 2014b) did not consider gender and, therefore, the following two central research questions guide the study:

> **Research question 1:** Is RP implementation associated with reduced school-wide gender and racial disparities in misconduct/defiance office discipline referrals?

> **Research question 2:** Is more frequent implementation of RP at the classroom level associated with teachers issuing fewer misconduct/defiance discipline referrals to students of differing gender and race (i.e., White males/females vs. Latino/African American males/females)?

METHODOLOGY

Participating High Schools

Two large and diverse high schools in a small city on the East Coast of the USA participated in the research. Based on school records from 2012, total enrollment across both high schools at the time of the research consisted of 2444 White students (54%), 1428 Latino students (31%), 522 African American students (11%), 149 Asian students (3%), and 9 American Indian students (<1%). The year before the RP program was brought into the schools (2010–2011), referrals related to misconduct/defiance comprised almost 30.3% of all discipline incidents. In the 2010–2011 school year, more than a third of Latino and African American students (34% and 38%, respectively) compared to 5% and 11% of Asian and White students (respectively) were issued referrals for misconduct/defiance.

Restorative Practices at the High Schools

Program. In the 2011–2012 and 2012–2013 school years, the two high schools implemented the International Institute of Restorative Practices'

(IIRP) two-year Safer Saner School program (see Program Overview at http://www.safersanerschools.org/). The program comprised what IIRP describes as the RP Elements, which range from informal (e.g., the use of affective statements to express feelings) to formal restorative interventions (e.g., the use of formal conferences, Wachtel, Costello, & Wachtel, 2009).

Training. During the two RP implementation years in the participating schools, IIRP trainers led full-day workshops with teachers, administrators, and staff. Trainers also provided several days of consultation with teachers and administrators in each school, that included classroom observations, demonstration/modeling of RP Elements, and targeted planning with administrators. Finally, trainers assisted the school in implementing professional learning groups to facilitate teacher support and peer consultation as they implemented RP.

Classroom teachers were trained in the RP Elements most relevant for their everyday interactions with students. Teachers learned about communicating affect (Affective Statements), engaging students in decision-making (Fair Process), acknowledging the emotions of those involved in conflict (Management of Shame) and facilitating daily or weekly community-building circles (Proactive Circles). To address conflict, they were also trained to ask disputants questions such as, "Who has been affected by what you have done?" and "What do you think you need to do to make it right?" (Restorative Questions). Finally, they learned to facilitate circles after moderately serious discipline incidents (Responsive Circles).

Research Procedures

We analyzed de-identified discipline records provided by the district spanning the two years prior to and the two years during RP implementation (2009–2013). During the 2011–2012 school year, the first year in which RP was implemented in both high schools, the team presented the study in faculty meetings and solicited teacher consent to participate. Out of the number of classes across each consented teacher's schedule, we randomly selected one class for study. We presented the study to the students in the selected classes and elicited their assent and caregiver consent to completing a survey.

Survey Respondents

Across the two high schools, 29 teachers consented to participate. The participating teachers had a wide range of experience, with an average of

13 years teaching. Almost three-quarters of the teachers were women and all but one teacher identified as White. On average, 60% of students in each of the 29 classes participated in the surveys. The student sample ($N = 412$) comprised slightly more male (53%) than female students (47%) and was racially and ethnically diverse according to students' own reports: 44% White, 21% Latino, 5% African American, 3% American Indian, 2% Asian, and 25% multiracial.

Measures

School discipline records. The discipline database comprised data on each office discipline referral issued to a student. Referral records included student gender, student race/ethnicity, reason for referral, assigned consequence, and the name of the staff member who issued the referral. Students were issued referrals for 120 different reasons.

Implementation of restorative practices. To examine RP implementation, we administered a student survey developed by IIRP to measure the RP Elements used by teachers in classrooms. Students answered items about their teacher's RP use on a 5-point scale, ranging from not at all to always, rating the frequency with which the teacher engaged in the following RP Elements typically used in classrooms: Affective Statements (alpha = 0.78), Restorative Questions (alpha = 0.87), Proactive Circles (alpha = 0.90), Responsive Circles (alpha = 0.82), Fair Process (alpha = 0.88), and Management of Shame (alpha = 0.80).[1]

Data Analytic Plan

The study focused on a subgroup of reasons for discipline referral related to misconduct and defiance. Out of the 120 reasons for discipline referral, we extracted disrespect, insubordination, profanity/obscenity, misconduct, and disorderly conduct, all of which reflected negative adult-student interactions, and grouped them into a single "misconduct/defiance" category. Previous research has shown that the quality of adult-student interactions, reflected in these types of referrals, may be a substantial driver of the racial discipline gap (Gregory & Weinstein, 2008; Gregory et al., 2014a). We calculated a school's yearly rate of students receiving one or more misconduct/defiance referrals by dividing the number of students who received referrals for that reason by the total school enrollment.

For research question 2, we used multiple regression to analyze the data using SPSS 20. We ran four separate regression models predicting the sum of each teacher's misconduct/defiance referrals from across the entire school year issued to four groups (White males, White females, Latino and African American males, and Latino and African American females). Given the similar rates of disproportionality from the prior school year and the small sample size, we combined school discipline records of Latino and African American students' ODRs.

Findings

Research question 1: Is RP implementation associated with reduced school-wide gender and racial disparities in misconduct/defiance office discipline referrals?

Misconduct/defiance referrals across both high schools. During the RP implementation years (2011–2012, 2012–2013), fewer students were issued misconduct/defiance referrals than in the two previous years.[2] Specifically, compared to 2010–2011, the number of students with one or more misconduct/defiance referrals was reduced by 21% (from 1016 students to 816 students by 2012–2013). From 2010–2011 to 2012–2013, the number of African American and White male referred students reduced by 2%. The number of Latino male referred students reduced by 10%: compared to 2010–2011, about 88 fewer Latino males received at least one misconduct/defiance referral in 2012–2013.

Despite this narrowing of disparities for Latino males, racial and gender gaps in misconduct/defiance referrals were for the most part maintained. During the second year of RP implementation (2012–2013), 11% of White males received one or more misconduct/defiance referrals, while 43% of African American males and 32% of Latino males did so. A similarly large ODR gap occurred among females in the three racial/ethnic groups. In 2012–2013, 6% of White females received one or more misconduct/defiance referrals, yet 32% of African American females and 21% of Latina females did so. Male disproportionality in misconduct/defiance ODRs occurred *within* each racial/ethnic group: even in the second year of RP implementation, a greater percentage of males relative to females received one or more misconduct/defiance referrals within each racial/ethnic group (e.g., 43% of African American males and 32% of African American females; 32% of Latino males and 21% of Latina females).

Research question 2: Is more frequent implementation of RP at the classroom level associated with teachers issuing fewer misconduct/defiance discipline referrals to students of differing gender and race (i.e., White males/females vs. Latino/African American males/females)?

Descriptives. Teacher participants ($N = 29$) issued a total of 54 misconduct/defiance referrals to female students and 167 misconduct/defiance referrals to males. A majority of the referrals for males were issued to African American and Latino students (84%), and a majority of the referrals for females were issued to African American and Latina female students (82%). The participating teachers issued no misconduct/defiance referrals to Asian students.

RP implementation and teachers' misconduct/defiance referrals. Results of the regression analyses predicting rates of misconduct/defiance ODRs are presented in Table 9.1. The regression analyses demonstrate that teacher implementation of one of the six RP Elements scales significantly predicted lower misconduct/defiance ODRs for two subgroups. Teachers perceived by students as higher on the Affective Statement scale issued fewer misconduct/defiance ODRs to African American and Latino males ($\beta = -0.57$, $p < 0.05$) and to African American and Latina females ($\beta = -0.60$, $p < 0.04$), relative to teachers lower on the scale. For these groups, RP scales explained

Table 9.1 Predicting misconduct/defiance referrals by gender and race using ordinary least squares regression

	White male referrals	Af-Amer/Latino male referrals	White female referrals	Af-Amer/Latina female referrals
R^2	0.14	0.37*	0.14	0.26*
Standardized betas				
Affective statements	−0.22	−0.57*	−0.36	−0.60*
Restorative questions	0.43	0.48+	0.42	0.31
Proactive circles	−0.12	−0.26	0.02	0.41
Responsive circles	0.57	0.62	0.27	−0.09
Fair process	−0.70	−0.66	−0.52	−0.11
Management of shame	−0.26	−0.02	−0.22	−0.34

+$p < 0.10$; *$p < 0.05$
Note: Af-Amer = African American

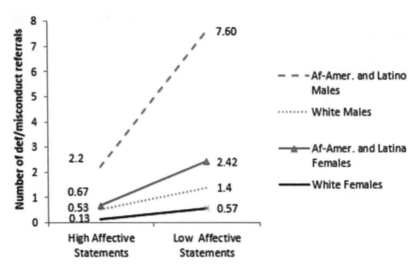

Fig. 9.1 RP implementation and defiance/misconduct referrals by gender and race

a significant percentage of the variance in ODRs (26%–37%, p <0.05). None of the RP scales were significant predictors for misconduct/defiance ODRs issued to White male or White female students.

Figure Fig. 9.1 represents differences in rates of ODRs for misconduct/defiance based on differences in student ratings of teachers on the Affective Statements scale (i.e., how frequently the teacher talked about his or her own feelings, encouraged students to express their feelings, and was respectful when talking about feelings). We split the teachers into groups of those who scored above and those who scored below the mean on the Affective Statement scale. Paired sample t-tests showed that low Affective Statement teachers significantly referred more African American and Latina female students (M = 2.42) compared to White females (M = 0.57; $t(13)$ = 3.42, p = 0.01). In contrast, high Affective Statement teachers did not issue a significantly different number of referrals to African American and Latina female students (M = 0.67) compared to White females (M = 0.13; $t(14)$ = 1.83, p = 0.09). Findings with male students were similar. For male students, high Affective Statement teachers had a small, although significant, difference in number of referrals issued to African American and Latino males (M = 2.2) relative to White males ($M = 0.53$; $t(14) = 2.31$, $p = 0.04$). Low Affective Statement teachers had a larger difference in number of referrals issued to African American and Latino males ($M = 7.6$) compared to White males ($M = 1.4$; $t(13) = 2.73$, $p = 0.02$).

DISCUSSION

The study examined school-wide patterns in misconduct/defiance ODR rates in two diverse high schools during the school years prior to and during RP implementation. Compared to the two years prior, by the end of the second year of RP implementation, 21% fewer students were issued misconduct/defiance ODRs. Despite this overall reduction, racial/ethnic and gender disparities persisted. Specifically, in the second year of RP implementation, African American males were about four times more likely and Latino males were about three times more likely to receive one or more misconduct/defiance ODRs relative to White males. Similarly, African American females were five times more likely and Latina females three and a half times more likely to receive one or more misconduct/defiance ODRs relative to White females. The gender gap also persisted, with males across all groups having higher ODR rates than females.

While such results might be seen as discouraging in general, a closer examination of RP implementation at the classroom level yielded more promising results. The study of 29 classrooms showed that teachers who were perceived by the students as frequently using affective statements tended to issue fewer misconduct/defiance ODRs to African American and Latino males and females, as compared to teachers perceived as less frequently using affective statements. In other words, teachers who communicated or elicited emotions showed smaller gaps between African American/Latino males and White males in their rate of ODRs, and no significant gaps between African American/Latino females and White females. In contrast, teachers who were less communicative about emotions evidenced larger racial/ethnic gaps in ODRs.

RP and African American and Latino Students

The findings linked use of Affective Statements to teachers' discipline referral patterns. Given the small sample size and the correlational research design, it would be premature to draw any definitive conclusions highlighting the effectiveness of this one RP Element over others (e.g., proactive circles, restorative questions). Yet these preliminary results suggest that further exploration of the importance of Affective Statements is warranted. In their professional development workshops, IIRP trainers encourage teachers to offer feedback to students about the impact and scope of intended or unintended harm that can result from negative behaviors. To that end, IIRP trainers help teachers articulate their own emotional experience in the classroom using "I" statements (i.e., "I feel worried when you start roughhousing in the classroom"). IIRP trainers also encourage teachers to assist their students in expressing their own emotional responses to events (see http://www.safersanerschools.org/).

Teachers who systematically express their own feelings in a respectful manner and elicit the feelings of their students (thereby eliciting student perspectives) may be interpersonally skilled in developing trusting relationships with African American and Latino students. Given prior research on emotional competencies, teachers' ability to identify, regulate, and respectfully communicate their own emotions may co-occur with their skills in eliciting and understanding the feelings and perspectives of their students (Jennings & Greenberg, 2009; Zembylas, 2007). Forging deeper connections with their students may thereby reduce potential distrust, implicit bias, and cultural misunderstanding between themselves and students historically over-represented in school discipline (Gregory et al., 2014a; Simson, 2012). In addition, emotionally oriented teachers may be able to skillfully break through postures of toughness (Pollack, 2006; Spencer, Dupree, Cunningham, Harpalani, & Muñoz-Miller, 2003) or adeptly prevent or diffuse negative interactions with students.

Fidelity of Implementation

Programming implemented with varying degrees of fidelity by teachers and administrators may not result in robust effects that shift school-wide discipline patterns. Without a good understanding of differences in implementation, a premature conclusion on the ineffectiveness of the program might be drawn (Durlak & Dupre, 2008). Future research on RP needs to carefully track implementation fidelity to avoid unwarranted conclusions. Using a multi-faceted conceptualization of program fidelity, researchers might consider examining how well RP is implemented in three fidelity domains, including: "delivery" of the program (quality or level of skills with which the treatment is implemented), "treatment receipt" (the degree to which individual students actually comprehend and engage with the program), and "treatment enactment" (the degree to which students demonstrate mastery of skills through the program; Schulte, Easton, & Parker, 2009). Findings from fidelity data could help target where to strengthen implementation supports (Forman, 2015).

Limitations of the Current Research

A number of limitations for the current study should be noted. The most noteworthy limitation is the size of the sample. We examined RP implementation in two schools in one geographic region. Within those schools, we gathered data on the RP Elements in only 29 classrooms. This resulted in low statistical power, limiting our ability to detect relationships between some of the RP Elements (e.g., restorative questions, proactive circles) and ODRs. This may be especially the case for the lack of association between RP Elements and White student ODRs, given the small number of referrals issued to White males ($n = 27$) and White females ($n = 10$) in the sample. Another limitation was that the analyses could not be conducted using a more sophisticated research design (e.g., multilevel modeling) given that the ODR data was not linked to individual student survey respondents. Moreover, the correlational research design limits causal claims—that is, we cannot assert that RP training caused change. The lack of covariates in the analyses means we cannot rule out alternative explanations. For instance, it might be the case that affect-oriented teachers already had low use of ODRs prior to the RP training where they learned about Affective Statements. Given these limitations, conclusions are tentative and suggest the need for larger scale, multilevel, and experimental research on the link between the fidelity of RP implementation in classrooms and discipline practices.

The limitations of student surveys should also be noted. Student responses on the RP implementation surveys may have related to overall perceptions of their teachers and not specifically to what they observed as new disciplinary practices in the classroom (e.g., students may be inclined to report their teachers are doing more RP simply because they want to be positive about teachers with whom they feel connected). Future research would need to corroborate student-reported RP implementation through systematic observations in classrooms.

Summary

The study found that over the two years of RP implementation in two high schools, there were reductions in the use of referrals for misconduct/ defiance. Yet gender and racial disparities in misconduct/defiance ODRs persisted. A closer look into a small sample of the high school classrooms offered a somewhat more nuanced understanding of RP implementation and related outcomes. Teachers rated by their students as engaging more frequently in the RP Element Affective Statements had smaller misconduct/defiance ODR gaps relative to teachers rated by their students as engaging less frequently in the same. The study findings highlight the importance of more closely investigating the fidelity of RP implementation to best capture RP's promise as a civil rights remedy to disproportionality in discipline practices.

Notes

1. Three-item Affective Statements scale ("My teacher is respectful when talking about feelings");
   Four-item Restorative Questions scale ("When someone misbehaves, my teacher responds to negative behaviors by asking students questions about what happened, who has been harmed, and how the harm can be repaired");
   Four-item Proactive Circles scale ("My teacher uses circles to provide opportunities for students to share feelings, ideas, and experiences"); Six-item Responsive Circles scale ("My teacher uses circles to respond to behavior problems"); Four-item Fair Process scale ("My teacher asks students for their thoughts and ideas when decisions need to be made that affect the class"); Three-item Management of Shame scale ("My teacher avoids scolding and lecturing)."
2. The number of students referred for *any* reason also reduced during the RP implementation years. In the two years prior to RP implementation, 3765 students (2009–2010) and 3504 students (2010–2011) were issued one or more discipline referrals. During two years of RP implementation, 2649 students (2011–2012) and 2728 students (2012–2013) were issued one or more discipline referrals.

REFERENCES

Amstutz, L., & Mullet, J. H. (2005). *The little book of restorative discipline for schools*. Intercourse, PA: Good Books.

Anyon, Y., Jenson, J., Altschul, I., Farrar, J., McQueen, J., Greer, E., Simmons, J. (2014). The persistent effect of race and the promise of alternatives to suspension in school discipline outcomes. *Children and Youth Services Review, 44*, 379–386.

Anyon, Y., Gregory, A., Stone, S. I., Farrar, J., Jenson, J. M., McQueen, J., Downing, B., Greer, E. & Simmons, J. (2016). *Restorative Interventions and School Discipline Sanctions in a Large Urban School District*. Manuscript submitted for publication.

Balfanz, J., Byrnes, V., & Fox, J. (2015). Sent home and put off track: The antecedents, disproportionalities, and consequences of being suspended in the 9th grade. In D. J. Losen (Ed.), *Closing the school discipline gap: Equitable remedies for excessive exclusion* (pp. 17–30). New York: Teachers College Press.

Blood, P., & Thorsborne, M. (2005, March). *The challenge of culture change: Embedding restorative practice in schools*. Paper presented at the Sixth International Conference on Conferencing, Circles, and other Restorative Practices, Sydney, Australia.

Buckley, S., & Maxwell, G. (2007). *Respectful schools: Restorative practices in education. A summary report*. Wellington, NZ: Office of the Children's Commissioner and the Institute of Policy Studies, School of Government, Victoria University.

Davis, F. (2014). Discipline with dignity: Oakland classrooms try healing instead of punishment. *Reclaiming Children and Youth, 23*, 38–41.

Doolan, M. (1999, August). *The family group conference: Ten years on*. Paper presented at Building Strong Partnerships for Restorative Practices. Conference, Burlington, VT.

Durlak, J. A., & Dupre, E. P. (2008). Implementation matters: A review of research on the influence of implementation on program outcomes and the factors affecting implementation. *American Journal of Community Psychology, 41*, 327–350. doi:10.1007/s10464-008-9165-0.

Forman, S. G. (2015). *Implementation of mental health programs in schools: A change agent's guide*. Washington, DC: American Psychological Association.

González, T. (2015). Socializing schools: Addressing racial disparities in discipline through restorative justice. In D. J. Losen (Ed.), *Closing the school discipline gap: Equitable remedies for excessive exclusion* (pp. 151–165). New York: Teachers College Press.

Gregory, A., & Weinstein, R. S. (2008). The discipline gap and African Americans: Defiance or cooperation in the high school classroom. *Journal of School Psychology, 46*(4), 455–475. doi:10.1016/j.jsp.2007.09.001.

Gregory, A., Bell, J., & Pollock, M. (2014a). *How educators can eradicate dispari-ties in school discipline: A briefing paper on school-based interventions.* Bloomington, IN: The Equity Project at Indiana University. Retrieved from http://rtpcollaborative.indiana.edu/briefing-papers/

Gregory, A., Clawson, K., Davis, A., & Gerewitz, J. (2014b). The promise of restorative practices to transform teacher–student relationships and achieve equity in school discipline. *Journal of Educational and Psychological Consultation, 25,* 1–29.

Gregory, A., Korth, J., Clawson, K., Davis, A., Gerewitz, J., & Schotland, M. (2014c). *RP-observe manual.* Unpublished manual. New Brunswick, NJ: Rutgers University.

Hurley, N., Guckenburg, S. Persson, H. Fronius, T., & Petrosino, A. (2015). *What further research is needed on restorative justice in schools?* WestEd.org. Retrieved from: https://www.wested.org/research/restorative-justice-schools-more-research-needed-resource/

Jain, S., Bassey, H, Brown, M. A., & Kalra, P. (2014). *Restorative justice in Oakland schools. Implementation and impact: An effective strategy to reduce racially dispro-portionate discipline, suspensions, and improve academic outcomes.* Retrieved from: http://www.ousd.org/cms/lib07/CA01001176/Centricity/Domain/134/OUSD-RJ%20Report%20revised%20Final.pdf

Jennings, P. A., & Greenberg, M. T. (2009). The prosocial classroom: Teacher social and emotional competence in relation to student and classroom out-comes. *Review of Educational Research, 79,* 491–525. doi:10.3102/0034654308325693.

Jeong, S., McGarrell, E. F., & Hipple, N. K. (2012). Long-term impact of family group conferences on re-offending: The Indianapolis restorative justice experi-ment. *Journal of Experimental Criminology, 8,* 369–385. doi:10.1007/s11292-012-9158-8.

Kane, J., Lloyd, G., McCluskey, G., Riddell, S., Stead, J., & Weedon, E. (2007). *Restorative practices in Scottish schools.* Edinburgh: Scottish Executive.

Lewis, S. (2009). *Improving school climate: Findings from schools implementing restorative practices.* Bethlehem, PA: International Institute of Restorative Practices. Retrieved from http://www.iirp.edu/pdf/IIRP-Improving-School-Climate.pdf

Losen, D. J., & Martinez, T. E. (2013). *Out of school and off track: The overuse of suspensions in American middle and high schools.* Los Angeles: The Center for Civil Rights Remedies at The Civil Right Project/Proyecto Derechos Civiles.

McCluskey, G., Lloyd, G., Stead, J., Kane, J., Riddell, S., & Weedon, E. (2008). 'I was dead restorative today': From restorative justice to restorative approaches in school. *Cambridge Journal of Education, 38,* 199–216.

Mirsky, L. (2011). Building safer, saner schools. *Educational Leadership, 69,* 45–49.

Morgan, E., Salomon, N., Plotkin, M., & Cohen, R. (2014). *The school discipline consensus report: Strategies from the field to keep students engaged in school and out of the juvenile justice system*, New York: The Council of State Governments Justice Center. Retrieved from https://csgjusticecenter.org/wp-content/uploads/2014/06/The_School_Discipline_Consensus_Report.pdf

Morrison, B. (2007). Schools and restorative justice. In G. Johnstone & D. Van Ness (Eds.), *The handbook of restorative justice* (pp. 325–350). Devon: William Publishing.

National Institute of Justice. (2014). *Awards related to developing knowledge about what works to make schools safe.* Washington DC: National Institute of Justice. Retrieved from http://www.nij.gov/funding/awards/pages/awards-list.aspx?solicitationid=3878

O'Connell, T., Wachtel, B., & Wachtel, T. (1999). *Conferencing handbook.* Pipersville, PA: The Piper's Press.

Pollack, W. S. (2006). The "war" for boys: Hearing "real boys" voices, healing their pain. *Professional Psychology: Research and Practice, 37*, 190–195. doi:10.1037/0735-7028.37.2.190.

Restorative Practices Working Group. (2014). *Restorative practices: Fostering healthy relationships and promoting positive discipline in schools.* Cambridge, MA: American Federation of Teachers, National Education Association, Advancement Project, and the National Opportunity to Learn Campaign. Retrieved from http://www.otlcampaign.org/sites/default/files/restorative-practices-guide.pdf

Riestenberg, N. (2013). Challenges to education: Restorative approaches as a radical demand on conservative structures of schooling. In H. Cremin, G. McCluskey, & E. Sellman (Eds.), *Restorative approaches to conflict in schools: Interdisciplinary perspectives on whole school approaches to managing relationships* (pp. 207–216). London: Routledge.

Schiff, M. (2013, January). *Dignity, disparity, and desistance: Effective restorative justice strategies to plug the "school-to-prison pipeline."* Paper presented at the Center for Civil Rights Remedies National Conference. Closing the School to Research Gap: Research to Remedies, Washington, DC.

Schulte, A. C., Easton, J. E., & Parker, J. (2009). Advances in treatment integrity research: Multidisciplinary perspectives on the conceptualization, measurement, and enhancement of treatment integrity. *School Psychology Review, 38*, 460–475.

Simson, D. (2012). *Restorative justice and its effects on (racially disparate) punitive school discipline.* Paper presented at the 7th Annual Conference on Empirical Legal Studies. Retrieved from http://ssrn.com/abstract=21072420

Spencer, M. B., Dupree, D., Cunningham, M., Harpalani, V., & Muñoz-Miller, M. (2003). Vulnerability to violence: A contextually-sensitive, developmental perspective on African American adolescents. *Journal of Social Issues, 59*, 33–49.

Swayze, D., & Buskovick, B. (2012). *Minnesota juvenile diversion: A summary of statewide practices and programming*. St. Paul: Minnesota Department of Public Safety. Retrieved from https://dps.mn.gov/divisions/ojp/forms-documents/Documents/Juvenile%20Justice%20Reports/MINNESOTA%20JUV_DIV%20REPORT_Final.pdf

U. S. Department of Education (2014). *Guiding principles: A resource guide for improving school climate and discipline*. Washington, DC: Author Retrieved from http://www2.ed.gov/policy/gen/guid/school-discipline/guiding-principles.pdf

Vincent, C. G., Sprague, J. R., CHIapkaid, M., Tobin, T. J., & Gau, J. M. (2015). Effectiveness of schoolwide positive behavior interventions and supports in reducing racially inequitable discipline exclusion. In D. J. Losen (Ed.), *Closing the school discipline gap: Equitable remedies for excessive exclusion* (pp. 207–221). New York: Teachers College Press.

Wachtel, T. (2013). *Defining restorative*. Bethlehem, PA: International Institute of Restorative Practices.

Wachtel, T., Costello, B., & Wachtel, J. (2009). *The restorative practices handbook for teachers, disciplinarians and administrators*. Bethlehem, PA: International Institute of Restorative Practices.

Wachtel, T., O'Connell, T., & Wachtel, B. (2010). *Restorative justice conferencing: Real justice & the conferencing handbook* (1st ed.). Pipersville: The Piper's Place.

Wong, D. S., & Mok, L. W. (2011). Restorative justice and practices in China. *Journal of Community Justice, 8*, 23–35.

Zehr, H. (2002). *The little book of restorative justice*. Intercourse, PA: Good Books.

Zehr, H., & Toews, B. (2004). *Critical issues in restorative justice*. Monsey, NY: Criminal Justice Press.

Zembylas, M. (2007). Emotional ecology: The intersection of emotional knowledge and pedagogical content knowledge in teaching. *Teaching and Teacher Education, 23*, 355–367.

CHAPTER 10

Intersectional Inquiries with LGBTQ and Gender Nonconforming Youth of Color: Participatory Research on Discipline Disparities at the Race/Sexuality/Gender Nexus

Jennifer F. Chmielewski, Kimberly M. Belmonte, Brett G. Stoudt, and Michelle Fine

This work was supported by a grant from the Discipline Disparities Research-to-Practice Collaborative at Indiana University, Adco Foundation, and Sociological Initiatives.

We would also like to thank our friends, co-researchers, and Advisory Board Members for their work on this project:

FIERCE, Lyons High School, Make the Road New York, Safe Passages Streetwise and Safe, Sylvia Rivera Law Project, The NY Performance Standards Consortium's LGBTQ-inclusive Curriculum Group, The LGBT Community Center, The LGBTQ Juvenile Justice Workgroup (Lambda Legal, The Correctional Association of New York, New York Civil Liberties Union), and Urban Academy Laboratory High School.

J.F. Chmielewski (✉) • K.M. Belmonte • M. Fine
The Graduate Center, City University of New York, New York, NY, USA

B.G. Stoudt
John Jay College of Criminal Justice, City University of New York, New York, IL, USA

© The Author(s) 2016   171
R.J. Skiba et al. (eds.), *Inequality in School Discipline*,
DOI 10.1057/978-1-137-51257-4_10

While a substantial empirical literature documents racial disparities in school discipline, scant attention has been paid to the intersections of race, sexuality, and gender (non)conformity in the field.[1] In this chapter, we examine how school-based surveillance practices affect LGBTQ (lesbian, gay, bisexual, transgender, and queer) students of color in terms of their sense of physical safety, psychological comfort, and academic sense of belonging. We review the psychological and educational impacts for LGBTQ youth as they negotiate, with resilience, humor, and creativity, challenging environments characterized by disproportionately high rates of overt discrimination as well as subtle policing of gender and sexuality by adults and peers. To conclude, we offer critical perspectives from LGBTQ youth of color on the strategic redesign of schools that can ensure student dignity and inclusion, reduction of suspensions, and narrowing of intersectional disparities.

LGBTQ STUDENTS AND SCHOOL DISCIPLINE

Zero-tolerance school discipline policies and practices are increasingly recognized as ineffective and disproportionately targeted against students of color, as they facilitate the movement of youth out of school and into the juvenile justice system (i.e., the "school-to-prison pipeline") (Carter, Fine, & Russell, 2014; Meiners, 2011; New York Civil Liberties Union, 2011; Skiba, Arredondo, & Rausch, 2014). While much attention has been paid to the detrimental impact of school discipline, policing, and criminalization of young Black and Latino men in particular (Rabinowitz, 2006; Skiba et al., 2011), there is a dearth of research on how race intersects with sexuality, gender, and gender (non)conformity.

The research that has been conducted with LGBTQ and gender nonconforming young people related to school discipline has focused on the verbal and physical harassment they experience from adults and peers (Berlan, Corliss, Field, Goodman, & Austin, 2010; Katz-Wise & Hyde, 2012). Findings suggest that LGBTQ students are often harassed based on their actual or perceived sexual orientation and that teachers are often unsure of how to intervene, leaving LGBTQ youth with a lack of support and protection in school (Kosciw, Greytak, Palmer, & Boesen, 2014; Vega, Crawford, & Van Pelt, 2012).

This sexual orientation-based victimization has been associated with a range of negative outcomes for LGBTQ youth. Research has documented a positive relationship between victimization and emotional, psychological, and health issues for LGBTQ youth, including depression, traumatic stress, and substance abuse (for a review see Collier, van Beusekom, Bos, & Sandfort, 2013). Although less research has focused on academic outcomes, school-based victimization has also been linked to decreased feelings of school belonging and safety (Collier et al., 2013; Murdock & Bolch, 2005), increased rates of truancy (Birkett, Russell, & Corliss, 2014; Kosciw et al., 2014), and increases in being pushed out and/or dropping out for LGBTQ students (Bochenek & Brown, 2001). In the absence of effective adult intervention, studies suggest that some LGBTQ students cope by avoiding certain classes, skipping school, and/or fighting back against heterosexist bullying (Snapp, Hoenig, Fields, & Russell, 2015). Such coping behaviors may heighten rates of suspensions, drop-out/pushouts, and may ultimately facilitate LGBTQ students' entry into the juvenile justice system (Mitchum & Moodie-Mills, 2014; Poteat et al., this volume). Trying to cope with hostile school climates, LGBTQ students may be disciplined more frequently, lose educational time and access, and be placed at risk for entering the criminal justice system. Himmelstein and Brückner (2011) conducted a national, longitudinal study and found that lesbian, gay, bisexual, and/or questioning youth were between 1.25 and 3 times more likely to face a range of school and criminal justice sanctions (school expulsion, police stops, juvenile arrest, juvenile conviction, adult arrest, and adult conviction) than heterosexual youth.

AN INTERSECTIONAL LOOK AT LGBTQ STUDENTS NAVIGATING EDUCATION

Research on LGBTQ young people's experiences in schools has tended to focus on individualized experiences of bullying without an intersectional analysis of how gender, sexuality, race, and class combine to affect educational experiences (Payne & Smith, 2012). Yet in order to shift school practices and cultures toward equity for LGBTQ students, it is critical to understand the ways in which cultural systems of power within and outside of school intersect to render LGBTQ young people vulnerable across multiple contexts. To address this gap in the literature, we developed the present project to understand how educational policies and cultures promote hyper- surveillance, policing, and disciplining of sexual minority and gender nonconforming youth of color, and how LGBTQ students respond (Crenshaw, 1991; Hancock, 2007). With a multi-method, participatory project design, we explored the following questions: (1) How do LGBTQ youth of color experience school discipline policies compared to their heterosexual/cisgender peers?[2] (2) To what extent does gender nonconformity, intersecting with sexuality and race, alter patterns of school discipline? (3) What processes within school cultures foster discipline disparities for LGBTQ youth of color?; and (4) What strategies for educational redesign do LGBTQ and gender nonconforming youth recommend for schools to become spaces of academic and social dignity, inclusion and recognition?

METHODOLOGY: A MULTI-PROJECT PARTICIPATORY DESIGN

We designed a participatory multi-method research project with a diverse advisory group of youth, educators, lawyers, and community organizers to explore the rates and consequences of school discipline for LGBTQ youth of color as compared to their heterosexual peers. We collaboratively analyzed two New York City quantitative data sets on youth experiences of school and policing disaggregated by race, sexuality, and gender (non) conformity, to explore educational, criminal justice, and wellbeing outcomes. We then gathered, from schools and community-based organizations, a group of 30 diverse LGBTQ young people and adults, as well as lawyers and activists working on social justice issues related to LGBTQ youth, to work with us as a community advisory board. The young people ranged in age from 16 to 19 and were predominantly Black and Latino/a.[3] Over a series of data-driven dinners, we worked with the advisory board to explore and interpret findings from those quantitative datasets, and generate new questions for stratified, semi-structured focus groups. Members of the advisory board recruited additional LGBTQ youth of color, whom we interviewed in focus groups, to explore their school-based experiences of marginalization and support. We then reconvened our advisory board to help interpret the quantitative and qualitative data and to formulate a list of recommendations on how schools can foster positive educational experiences for students who identify as LGBTQ or gender nonconforming.

A Participatory Quantitative Foundation

This project began with secondary analyses of two large city-wide data sets, *Polling for Justice* (PFJ; Fox et al., 2010; Fox & Fine, 2014) and *Researchers for Fair Policing* (RFP; Stoudt et al., forthcoming). The PFJ database was created by an interdisciplinary research team of faculty and students from the City University of New York (CUNY), youth advocates, public health researchers, lawyers, educators, and youth co-researchers to examine youths' (ages 14–21) experiences with the criminal justice system, education, and health (see Stoudt, Fine, & Fox, 2011). RFP was developed by New York City youth and adult community organizers from the Youth Power Project at Make the Road New York, as well as graduate students, researchers, and professors from the CUNY Graduate Center, John Jay College, and Pratt Institute. RFP was created to understand the intersections of race, gender, and sexuality with particular attention to young people's experiences of police and school discipline. Both surveys used snowball (Browne, 2005) and purposive sampling strategies (Glaser & Strauss, 1967) in public school classrooms and youth-focused community organizations in all five New York City boroughs (N = 1084 for PFJ and N = 1107 for RFP).

In both surveys, respondents were asked to report their race/ethnicity by checking all race/ethnicity categories that applied. Sexual orientation was assessed using a forced choice response in PFJ (gay, lesbian, bisexual, straight, or not sure), and in RFP (gay, lesbian, bisexual, queer, straight, or other). In the RFP survey, respondents also rated how they believed other people perceived their masculinity and femininity on a 7-point Likert scale from (1) *Very Feminine*, (4) *Equally Feminine and Masculine*, to (7) *Very Masculine*, using a 2-item measure of socially assigned gender nonconformity (Wylie, Corliss, Boulanger, Prokop, & Austin, 2010). Participants were categorized as either gender conforming or nonconforming based on their scores.[4]

In order to focus our intersectional analysis, we examined only Black and Latino/a respondents (N = 805 for PFJ and N = 830 for RFP; see Table 10.1). Our final samples included more girls (64% in PFJ; 51% in RFP) than boys (34% in PFJ; 47% in RFP) and a small number of youth who identified as transgender or having a nonbinary gender (approximately 1% in PFJ; 2% in RFP). LGBQ (lesbian, gay, bisexual or queer) youth made up a significant minority of both samples (approximately 11% in PFJ; 19% in RFP).

On both quantitative datasets, we conducted a descriptive, exploratory data analysis (Tukey, 1977) using an iterative, flexible, and graphical approach. Within and across each project, research teams collaborated to analyze and explore the data using a process that resembles some of the inductive quantitative recommendations produced in Glaser and Strauss' (1967) classic grounded theory text (see *stats-n-action* in Stoudt, 2014; Stoudt & Torre, 2014). Our analyses drew largely on percentages and cross tabulations to explore school experiences at the intersections of race/ethnicity, gender, sexual orientation, and gender expression (Hancock,

Table 10.1   Intersectional survey demographics for participants of color

Demographics		PFJ (N = 805)		RFP (N = 830)	
		LGBQ (N = 89)	Straight (N = 712)	LGBQ (N = 143)	Straight (N = 662)
Gender	Male	17.4% (15)	35.8% (252)	21.7% (31)	52.2% (347)
	Female	76.7% (66)	63.7% (448)	71.3% (102)	47% (311)
	Trans/nonbinary	5.8% (5)	0.4% (3)	7% (10)	0.5% (3)
Gender conformity	Gender conforming	NA	NA	45.5% (50)	79.5% (439)
	Gender nonconforming	NA	NA	54.5% (60)	20.5% (113)
Race/ethnicity	Black (African American or Caribbean)	40.4% (36)	46.3% (330)	26.6% (38)	20.8% (138)
	Latino/a	42.7% (38)	42.1% (300)	52.4% (75)	68.7% (455)
	Multiracial	11.5% (15)	16.8% (82)	21% (30)	10.4% (69)

Note: The age range for PFJ participants of color was 14–21 (M = 16.78, SD = 1.17). The age range for RFP participants of color was 14–25 (M = 17.39, SD = 2.30)

2007). This intersectional approach led to small sample sizes, preventing us from conducting statistical tests of significance; thus, our quantitative results should be considered exploratory.

Que(e)rying School Discipline Project

Based on this quantitative foundation, we developed the Que(e)rying School Discipline research project to pursue analyses of RFP and PFJ with our community advisory board. This group helped us unpack, interpret, and re-analyze the survey data. Young people engaged with the data by discussing their own experiences with school safety and how they felt LGBTQ youth were treated by school staff and peers. In small groups, we talked through graphs and tables from our exploratory analyses, which helped us develop new interpretations, new ways to explore the data, and new questions that needed to be asked in order to better understand the discipline disparities for LGBTQ youth of color.

Members of our advisory board then helped connect us with two schools and two community organizations concerned with LGBTQ youth issues in New York City for our subsequent youth focus groups. We conducted four focus groups with participants from these organizations (N = 30), with LGBTQ youth aged 16–21 (87% Black and/or Latino/a; 13% White), lasting approximately two hours each. Interviews focused on LGBTQ identities and issues in school, school discipline, and re-envisioning schools for LGBTQ and gender nonconforming youth. Focus group interviews were audio recorded, transcribed and de-identified using pseudonyms for all participants. Interview transcripts were then analyzed following Braun and Clarke's (2006) guidelines for thematic analysis. First we individually engaged in open coding each transcript, noting our questions and recurrent codes before working collaboratively to develop themes. We repeated this process with each consecutive transcript, iteratively working through previously developed themes and codes as new ideas emerged. The main findings from the grounded codes and themes, like the quantitative data, were once again shared with our advisory board to facilitate discussion, validate key findings, and inform recommendations.

FINDINGS

Survey Findings: LGBTQ Students' Experiences of Discipline and Dispossession

Quantitative survey data revealed a set of important findings on the disciplinary experiences of LGBTQ and gender nonconforming students. In particular, the analysis illustrated that disaggregating the data by multiple sets of intersecting identities provides a more nuanced picture of the disciplinary experiences for students.[5]

Exclusionary discipline and push out. Our participatory analyses support previous research findings, revealing disparities in suspensions as well as drop/push out rates for students of color and LGBTQ youth (Burdge, Licona, & Hyemingway, 2014; Mitchum & Moodie-Mills, 2014). Across both RFP and PFJ surveys, LGBTQ youth of color were almost one-and-a-half times more likely to report having been suspended than straight/cisgender youth of color (see Fig. 10.1). A high percentage of both LGBTQ and straight PFJ respondents reported feeling "pushed out" by their schools, indicating an uneasy relationship between students and school climates for both LGBTQ and straight/cisgender students of color. LGBTQ

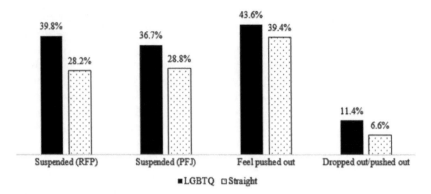

Fig. 10.1 Comparisons of LGBTQ and straight youth of color who have been suspended, feel pushed out of school, or have dropped out or been pushed out. *Note*: Suspension was assessed in RFP by whether students of color reported receiving in-school and/or out-of-school suspensions "at least once since 2010." Reports of in-school and out-of-school suspensions were combined to form an overall rate of suspensions since 2010. Suspension was assessed in PFJ by students' reports of having "ever been suspended or expelled." Feeling pushed out and dropped/pushed out were items from PFJ survey. Feeling pushed out was assessed by whether or not students agreed with the statement, "Sometimes school rules, tests, the way school personnel treat students, and other elements of school make me feel pushed to leave school." Dropped/pushed out was assessed with the question, "Have you ever dropped out or been pushed out of high school?"

respondents of color were almost twice as likely as heterosexuals of color to report that they had actually dropped out or been pushed out of school.

Suspensions by gender and gender nonconformity. Data on suspensions in the RFP survey by sexual orientation, gender, and gender conformity revealed that LGBQ girls of color appear to experience the highest rates of both in- and out-of-school suspensions (34% and 22% respectively). These rates appear to be higher than those reported by straight boys of color (27% and 18% respectively). Furthermore, LGBQ girls who were gender nonconforming reported higher rates of suspension as compared to those who were gender conforming, as well as in comparison to their heterosexual female peers. Gender nonconforming LGBQ girls also reported the highest rates of out-of-school suspension (28.6%). This finding supports recent research documenting disparities in discipline for LGBQ and gender nonconforming girls in particular (Himmelstein & Brückner, 2011; Irvine & Yusuf, 2015).

Intersectionalities and feelings of safety in school. Given the role of school safety agents (SSA) in discipline practices and school climate, we examined students' feelings of safety in schools with school security.[6] LGBTQ youth of color, and gender nonconforming girls in particular, reported lower levels of "feeling safe" with school security. Overall, a higher percentage of LGBTQ (35%) than straight/cisgender students of color (25.8%) disagreed with the statement, "I feel safer because of the school safety agents, school police, or security guards in my school." Those patterns held for LGBQ girls as well as LGBQ boys and transgender/nonbinary gender youth compared to straight boys and girls. While gender conformity did not appear to be related to feelings of safety for LGBQ girls, it did for straight girls. Gender nonconforming straight girls were more likely to report that they did not feel safe with school security (38.8%) compared to gender conforming straight girls (20.9%), an 18 percentage point difference. Gender nonconforming straight girls (22.4%) were less likely than conforming straight girls (31.9%) to report they felt safer with school safety agents. Thus, school safety and security agents may work to produce a sense of relative comfort for gender conforming, heterosexual girls, but a sense of vulnerability for both LGBTQ and gender nonconforming girls of color.

Focus Groups: Exclusion and Vulnerability for LGBTQ Students in Schools

To unpack these disturbing statistical patterns, we turned to our focus groups with young people. Students in those groups identified four social-psychological processes that contribute to their heightened sense of exclusion and vulnerability: sense of invisibility, the ironies of "protection," targeted discipline, and institutional violence.

Feeling invisible. Even those young people who did not describe their school as explicitly homophobic voiced a sense of feeling not seen, not heard, and not acknowledged in schools and in the curriculum. In most schools, history, language arts, and even sex education curricula fail to address diverse gender and sexual identities and histories. Brit, a 16-year-old multi-racial lesbian explained that in her sex education class, "We only learn about straight people and not getting pregnant," while Mariah, a 20-year-old Black lesbian was critical of her social studies courses: "We should learn about our history. We're part of history too!"

Although Gay Straight Alliances (GSAs) have the potential to increase visibility and acceptance for LGBTQ students, most of the young people did not have GSAs in their schools. The few who did have a GSA operating in their school reported being concerned that the GSA functioned separately from the rest of the school. Some students complained that although their GSAs are supportive around sexuality, they fail to recognize significant intersections of sexuality with race, racism, culture, disability, homelessness, undocumented status, or other intersectional identities. Thus, even students who had GSAs in their schools continued to struggle with invisibility.

The ironies of protection from the closet. In addition to invisibility, a second dynamic that contributes to a heightened sense of alienation among LGBTQ students can be found in their relationships with school staff. We heard stories from LGBTQ students about moments of alienation but also connection and care with well-meaning and supportive school staff—most of whom choose to remain in the closet. Tee (19-year-old Black lesbian) told us about the relief she experienced when she finally bonded with a lesbian teacher in her school. Tee described her experience after coming out as "really intense." Students and school staff sexually harassed her and she felt like she had no one in school to turn to until her English teacher came out to her:

> At least I know that she understands me … somebody that's older and has experience would know what I'm going through and I told her like the issues with my mom and her trying to accept it and like how to handle inappropriate questions when it comes up because lesbians get that a lot.

Yet this teacher also confused Tee when she explained that she (the teacher) is not out at school, and asked Tee to "help keep her secret." Carrying a burden of double secrecy, Tee asked: "Now I gotta hold her secret and *mine*?" Tee wished her school could be a place where both she and her teacher could be free to be open about their sexualities in school. Although appreciative of teachers who create extra space in a crowded closet, young people yearn for public advocates, not just silent allies.

Targeted discipline. Although many of our respondents expressed feelings of being invisible and closeted, they also expressed concerns that their sexuality made them highly visible and targeted. Some reported school policies and practices that over-surveil and over-discipline LGBTQ youth who end up feeling hyper-visible and targeted by school policies. Skye, a 21-year-old Black bisexual woman, explained, "I feel like um- the disciplinary code—there are two different standards for students. There is a standard for straight kids and there is a standard for young people who identify as LGBTQ." Relatedly, Amelia, a 17-year-old Latina lesbian, told a story about being outed to her family and excluded from class time after kissing her girlfriend at school:

> At our school, I was kissing some girl in the hallway. And I got sent home. You see straight couples kissing by their locker [and they say] nothing at all. But I got called on the loudspeaker to go home. I didn't get that. And they called my mom and was like, 'your daughter was kissing some girl in the hallway.'

Patricia (17-year-old Black bisexual) agreed: "I was rubbing the nose of a girlfriend of mine and a teacher said, 'Too much PDA' [public displays of affection]. Meanwhile the heterosexual kids are sucking each others' faces off in the hall." There was strong consensus that public displays of same sex sexuality in school receive heightened attention, and often end up in a disciplinary incident.

Institutional acts of structural violence. Finally, and perhaps most dramatically, we heard stories of young people feeling threatened, verbally and/or physically, by the very adults who were supposed to protect them. We heard stories of police, school safety agents, and even educators responding as if the young people were a threat: "A girl in my school is 6'2" and now she came out as a lesbian so the SSA *really* see her as threatening" (Michele, 17-year-old Black bisexual girl). Ell, an 18-year-old Latina lesbian, told us that when she presented herself in more masculine ways she was treated "aggressively" and "with disgust" by teachers and even police. In particular, she told us of a frightening encounter in which she was arrested with classmates right outside of school and sexually harassed by a police officer.

> He like tried to figure out if I was gay and like he asked me, 'did I have a girlfriend?' It was like really like weird. He was like, 'Oh, can I be your boyfriend?' They had me, my hands cuffed on a banister and he was supposed to be watching me. So it was just like him asking me these weird questions in a room with just me and him and it was just really awkward. And I was like, 'What the heck? Why the hell did they put me in here?'

We heard a number of stories of highly charged and aggressive interactions between gender nonconforming youth of color and adults in positions of authority. To the young people, these interactions feel particularly threatening, racialized, and sexualized in precisely those spaces where they most need protection.

BUILDING SCHOOL CULTURES OF VISIBILITY AND INCLUSION FOR LGBTQ STUDENTS

We opened this research with a simple question about how LGBTQ students of color fare under exclusionary discipline policies. But after deliberating with youth and educators who have worked through the sexuality/race/gender intersections, we end by thinking about how to construct school cultures that nurture difference, invite dialogue, and engage a rich sense of community. With the help of LGBTQ youth and educators, we generated a framework for building and sustaining school cultures where *differences*—sexual, racial, gender, (dis)ability, immigration status, criminal justice status—are valued as a resource within strong academic communities, where debate and dissent can flourish, and where power inequities are challenged.

The students we spoke to are looking for spaces where they can belong and flourish, knowing that they are safe to learn about themselves and others. They want a school that is accountable for providing a supportive environment to all students, and one in which queer youth, faculty, and staff are recognized as valuable members of the community. Students in one school spoke about the importance of learning and working across difference in courses on gender and sexuality and LGBTQ history. They discussed their school as one in which students of all sexual and gender identities were accepted. These inclusive practices were evident in: (1) diverse faculty and staff; (2) visibility and comfort of "out" teachers and SSA; (3) curricula that address LGBTQ issues (in history, literature, and sex education); and (d) GSA/restorative justice programs that explore the many layers of oppression, as well as forms of wisdom, that LGBTQ youth of color embody. Young people longed for these schools characterized by warmth, respect, and learning:

> My vision for an ideal school would be one where the students as well as the staff and administration respect everyone. They respect it and really enforce it being a safe space. It would be an ideal environment to learn and where people feel supported and safe. (Blue, Black 17-year-old lesbian)

Our research supports a growing consensus in the field of adolescent development and disciplinary policies: LGBTQ youth are particularly vulnerable to the school-to-prison pipeline, experiencing differential and often discriminatory treatment in schools and a lack of protection after such incidents occur. The cumulative impact of victimization and lack of support can lead to a loss of academic time and learning, and even school push-out (Kosciw et al., 2014; Mitchum & Moodie-Mills, 2014). Our multi-project, multi-method intersectional approach allowed us to document that these dynamics were more extreme for LGBTQ girls of color, particularly those who were gender nonconforming (Himmelstein & Brückner, 2011; Irvine & Yusuf, 2015). Our evidence lifts up a significant new group for policy attention: gender nonconforming young women of color who appear to be disproportionately affected by exclusionary discipline policies and policing in schools. But most fundamentally, our research shifts the focus to examine how the negative outcomes that may accumulate in/on the bodies of LGBTQ youth, gender nonconforming youth, particularly those of color, lie in and are exacerbated by the cumulative institutional betrayals they endure.

Limitations and Future Directions

Our combined use of qualitative and quantitative approaches provides powerful information on young people's experiences of discipline and identity in school at the intersection of race, sexuality, gender, and gender conformity (Crenshaw, 1991; Hancock, 2007). Our commitment to participatory and intersectional approaches led to reduced sample sizes from our non-probability samples, particularly for LGBQ boys and youth with nonbinary genders. Thus we were unable to conduct statistical tests and we cannot claim that our participants or findings are representative of LGBTQ youth of color in NYC. Future research is needed to further examine the intersectional relationships of race/ethnicity with sexuality, gender, and gender conformity in ways that we could not due to small sample sizes. A second limitation rests in our inability to examine the types of discipline that students experience for different infractions in our survey (see e.g., Poteat et al., this volume). Further analyses are warranted to examine discretionary discipline, to link data on discipline and policing disparities in schools, and to determine how school structures, policies, and community habits can widen the zone of moral inclusion and recognition within a school building (Opotow, Gerson, & Woodside, 2005).

CONCLUSION

Across studies and methods, we have documented striking patterns of disciplinary disparities: by race/ethnicity, sexuality, and gender (non)conformity. In these studies, and other recent work (Kosciw et al., 2014), the over-disciplining of gender nonconforming girls of color emerges as a significant area for policy attention. Intersectionality has been useful not only as a methodological approach to the data but for thinking about how to produce more equitable, safe schools. LGBTQ youth and educators across our advisory board and focus groups felt that lower levels of in-school fighting, rates of suspensions, and disciplinary disparities occur when intersectionality is valued in the school. They discussed schools rich in inquiry, dignity, and inclusion; where difference becomes an opportunity to educate and be educated, a chance to grow. We also heard about schools of insufficient resources, high surveillance and low trust—where difference becomes an opportunity for hostility and discrimination. Although LGBTQ youth can be found across all kinds of schools, LGBTQ youth of color with the fewest economic and academic resources are most likely to attend schools of low trust, low dignity, low resources, and high surveillance (Carter et al., 2014; Stoudt et al., 2011). LGBTQ and gender nonconforming youth of color desire and deserve the simple human right to be educated and recognized.

NOTES

1. Gender nonconforming refers to a person who has a gender identity and/or gender expression that does not conform to their biological sex or socially assigned gender roles. Individuals who are transgender or identify as having a nonbinary gender have a gender identity that does not match their biological sex. We use nonbinary gender as an identity label and gender conforming as a description of gender expression.
2. Cisgender refers to individuals whose gender identity matches the gender they were assigned at birth.
3. Our advisory board included youth and adults from FIERCE, Sylvia Rivera Law Project, Streetwise and Safe, Make the Road New York, The LGBT Community Center, Safe Passages, an LGBTQ Juvenile Justice Workgroup (including organizations like Lambda Legal, The Correctional Association of New York, New York Civil Liberties Union), Urban Academy Laboratory High School, Lyons Community School, and the NY Performance Standards Consortium Queer Teachers/Curriculum group.

4. Wylie et al. (2010) do not provide scoring instructions for this measure. We used the scale items as a binary measure of gender conformity or nonconformity. Female participants who scored 4–7 were categorized as gender nonconforming for that item, whereas those who scored 1–3 were categorized as gender conforming. Male participants were categorized as gender nonconforming on items if they scored between 1–4 and gender conforming if they rated themselves 5–7. For the purposes of the present analyses, both items on this measure were used together, where any participant who was categorized as gender nonconforming on one item was considered gender nonconforming, and only participants who were gender conforming in terms of both appearance and mannerisms were considered gender conforming.

5. See the Public Science Project website for complete information regarding these and additional analyses: http://publicscienceproject.org/research/projects/queerying-school-discpline/

6. School Safety Agents handle school discipline and safety, and are employed by the New York City Police Department's School Safety Division. There are currently over 5,000 school safety agents in NYC public schools (see http://www.nyclu.org/content/contract-school-safety).

REFERENCES

Berlan, E. D., Corliss, H. L., Field, A. E., Goodman, E., & Austin, S. B. (2010). Sexual orientation and bullying among adolescents in the Growing Up Today Study. *Journal of Adolescent Health, 46*, 366–371. doi:10.1016/j.jadohealth.2009.10.015.

Birkett, M., Russell, S. T., & Corliss, H. L. (2014). Sexual-orientation disparities in school: The mediational role of indicators of victimization in achievement and truancy because of feeling unsafe. *American Journal of Public Health, 104*, 1124–1128. doi:10.2105/AJPH.2013.301785.

Bochenek, M., & Brown, A. (2001). *Hatred in the hallways: Discrimination and violence against lesbian, gay, bisexual and transgender students in U.S. public schools.* New York: Human Rights Watch. Retrieved from http://www.hrw.org/legacy/reports/2001/uslgbt/toc.htm

Braun, V., & Clarke, V. (2006). Using thematic analysis in psychology. *Qualitative Research in Psychology, 3*, 77–101. doi:10.1191/1478088706qp063oa.

Browne, K. (2005). Snowball sampling: Using social networks to research non-heterosexual women. *International Journal of Social Research Methodology, 8*, 47–60. doi:10.1080/1364557032000081663.

Burdge, H., Licona, A. C., & Hyemingway, Z. T. (2014). *LGBTQ youth of color: Discipline disparities, school push-out, and the school-to-prison pipeline*. San Francisco, CA: Gay-Straight Alliance Network, and Tucson, AZ: Crossroads Collaborative at the University of Arizona.

Carter, P., Fine, M., & Russell, S. T. (2014). *Discipline disparities series: Overview*. Bloomington, IN: The Equity Project at Indiana University. Retrieved from http://rtpcollaborative.indiana.edu/briefing-papers/

Collier, K. L., van Beusekom, G., Bos, H. M. W., & Sandfort, T. G. M. (2013). Sexual orientation and gender identity/expression related to peer victimization in adolescence: A systematic review of associated psychological and health outcomes. *Journal of Sex Research, 50*, 299–317. doi:10.1080/00224499.2012.750639.

Crenshaw, K. (1991). Mapping the margins: Intersectionality, identity politics, and violence against women of color. *Stanford Law Review, 43*(6), 1241–1299.

Fox, M., & Fine, M. (2014). Our troubling *fix* on urban adolescents: A New York story. In P. Kelly & A. Kampe (Eds.), *A critical youth studies for the 21st century* (pp. 379–393). London and New York: Brill Publishers.

Fox, M., Mediratta, K., Stoudt, B., Ruglis, J., Fine, M., & Salah, S. (2010). Critical youth engagement: Participatory action research and organizing. In L. Sherrod, J. Torney-Purta, & C. Flanagan (Eds.), *Handbook of research on civic engagement in youth* (pp. 621–650). Hoboken, NJ: John Wiley & Sons, Publishers. doi:10.1002/9780470767603.ch23.

Glaser, B., & Strauss, A. (1967). *The discovery of grounded theory: Strategies for qualitative inquiry*. London: Wiedenfeld and Nicholson.

Hancock, A. M. (2007). When multiplication doesn't equal quick addition: Examining intersectionality as a research paradigm. *Perspectives on Politics, 5*, 63–79. doi:10.1017/S1537592707070065.

Himmelstein, K. E. W., & Brückner, H. (2011). Criminal-justice and school sanctions against nonheterosexual youth: A national longitudinal study. *Pediatrics, 127*(1), 49–57. doi:10.1542/peds.2009-2306.

Irvine, A., & Yusuf, A. (2015). *NCCD study confirms "school-to-prison pipeline": Nine in 10 juvenile justice-involved youth have been disciplined in school*. Madison, WI: National Council on Crime & Delinquency. Retrieved from http://nccdglobal.org/sites/default/files/publication_pdf/school-to-prison_pipeline.pdf

Katz-Wise, S. L., & Hyde, J. S. (2012). Victimization experiences of lesbian, gay, and bisexual individuals: A meta-analysis. *Journal of Sex Research, 49*, 142–167. doi:10.1080/00224499.2011.637247.

Kosciw, J. G., Greytak, E. A., Palmer, N. A., & Boesen, M. J. (2014). *The 2013 National School Climate Survey: The experiences of lesbian, gay, bisexual and transgender youth in our nation's schools*. New York: GLSEN.

Meiners, E. R. (2011). Ending the school-to-prison pipeline/Building abolition futures. *Urban Review, 43*, 547–565. doi:10.1007/s11256-011-0187-9.

Mitchum, P., & Moodie-Mills, A. C. (2014). *Beyond bullying: How hostile school climate perpetuates the school-to-prison pipeline for LGBT youth.* Washington, DC: Center for American Progress.

Murdock, T. B., & Bolch, M. B. (2005). Risk and protective factors for poor school adjustment in lesbian, gay, and bisexual (LGB) high school youth: Variable and person-centered analyses. *Psychology in the Schools, 42*, 159–172. doi:10.1002/pits.20054.

New York Civil Liberties Union. (2011). *Education interrupted: The growing use of suspensions in New York City's public schools.* New York: New York Civil Liberties Union and Student Safety Coalition. Retrieved from http://www.nyclu.org/publications/report-education-interrupted-growing-use-of-suspensions-new-york-citys-public-schools-

New York Civil Liberties Union. (2012). *School to prison pipeline: A look at New York City school safety.* Retrieved from http://www.nyclu.org/schoolto-prison/lookatsafety

Opotow, S., Gerson, J., & Woodside, S. (2005). From moral exclusion to moral inclusion: Theory for teaching peace. *Theory into Practice, 44*, 303–318. doi:10.1207/s15430421tip4404_4.

Payne, E., & Smith, M. (2012). Rethinking safe schools approaches for LGBTQ students: Changing the questions we ask. *Multicultural Perspectives, 14*, 187–193. doi:10.1080/15210960.2012.725293.

Rabinowitz, J. (2006). Leaving homeroom in handcuffs: Why an over reliance on law enforcement to ensure school safety is detrimental to children. *Cardozo Public Law, Policy, & Ethics Journal, 4*, 153–194.

Skiba, R. J., Arredondo, M. I., & Rausch, M. K. (2014). *New and developing research on disparities in discipline.* Bloomington, IN: The Equity Project at Indiana University. Retrieved from http://rtpcollaborative.indiana.edu/briefing-papers/

Skiba, R. J., Horner, R. H., Chung, C. G., Rausch, M. K., May, S. L., & Tobin, T. (2011). Race is not neutral: A national investigation of African American and Latino disproportionality in school discipline. *School Psychology Review, 40*, 85–107.

Snapp, S. D., Hoenig, J. M., Fields, A., & Russell, S. T. (2015). Messy, butch, and queer: LGBTQ youth and the school-to-prison pipeline. *Journal of Adolescent Research, 30*, 57–82. doi:10.1177/0743558414557625.

Stoudt, B. (2014). Quantitative methods. In D. Coghlan & M. Brydon-Miller (Eds.), *Encyclopedia of action research.* Thousand Oaks, CA: Sage Publications.

Stoudt, B., Fine, M., & Fox, M. (2011). Growing up policed in the age of aggressive policing. *NYLS Law Review, 56*, 1331–1372.

Stoudt, B. G., Cahill, C., Torre, M. E., Lopez, J., Pimentel, A., Belmonte, K., & Harley, K. (forthcoming). *Researchers for fair policing*. Public Science Project.

Stoudt, B. G., & Torre, M. E. (2014). The Morris Justice Project. In P. Brindle's (Ed.), *SAGE cases in methodology*. London: Sage.

Tukey, J. W. (1977). *Exploratory data analysis*. Reading, PA: Addison-Wesley.

Vega, S., Crawford, H. G., & Van Pelt, J. L. (2012). Safe schools for LGBTQI students: How do teachers view their role in promoting safe schools? *Equity & Excellence in Education, 45*, 250–260. doi:10.1080/10665684.2012.671095.

Wylie, S. A., Corliss, H. L., Boulanger, V., Prokop, L. A., & Austin, S. B. (2010). Socially assigned gender nonconformity: A brief measure for use in surveillance and investigation of health disparities. *Sex Roles, 63*, 264–276. doi:10.1007/s11199-010-9798-y.

CHAPTER 11

Research and Training to Mitigate the Effects of Implicit Stereotypes and Masculinity Threat on Authority Figures' Interactions with Adolescents and Non-Whites

Kimberly Barsamian Kahn,
Phillip Atiba Goff, and Jack Glaser

"I said, 'get back or I'm going to shoot you.'
He [Brown] …says,
'You are too much of a pussy to shoot me.'"
—Ferguson Police Officer Darren Wilson,
recounting his fatal shooting of 18 year old
African American Michael Brown
on August 9, 2014, in Ferguson, Missouri

K.B. Kahn (✉)
Department of Psychology, Portland State University, Portland, OR, USA

P.A. Goff
Department of Psychology, University of California, Los Angeles, CA, USA

J. Glaser
Goldman School of Public Policy, University of California, Berkeley, CA, USA

© The Author(s) 2016
R.J. Skiba et al. (eds.), *Inequality in School Discipline*,
DOI 10.1057/978-1-137-51257-4_11

189

The above exchange between Ferguson Police Officer Darren Wilson and 18-year-old African American Michael Brown, Jr. highlights an important aspect of the way authority figures typically interact with adolescents. Officer Wilson, confronting a Black teenager, aims to subdue a perceived threat to his masculinity. His action—fatally shooting Brown—illustrates the potentially deadly outcomes that can result, at least in part, from threats to one's masculine social identity. Implicit racial biases, which operate beneath conscious awareness, may have also played a role in his behavior. How might these identity threats impact interactions between authority figures and youth in schools?

In this chapter, we explore how psychological identity-related threats and subtle forms of racial bias may affect authority figures' interactions with adolescents. Through a related psychological process, we suggest, these same types of identity threats and implicit biases may be evident in the classroom setting (e.g., Van den Bergh, Denessen, Hornstra, Voeten, & Holland, 2010), and may contribute to disciplinary outcomes that disproportionately involve non-White adolescents (e.g., Skiba, Michael, Nardo, & Peterson, 2002). We detail an innovative, empirically based intervention aimed at reducing racial disparities in disciplinary outcomes for adolescents by training authority figures (e.g., law enforcement officers, school administrators, and teachers) who interact with them. The intervention centers on reducing the influence of implicit racial stereotypes and insecure masculinity on authority figures' actions toward adolescents. We discuss the development and content of the intervention. By understanding and intervening in these implicit and identity-related threats that can negatively influence authority–adolescent interactions, we may be able to reduce the potential for these incidents to escalate. We close with implications for schools and police departments.

PREVIOUS FINDINGS: WHAT WE KNOW ABOUT IMPLICIT BIAS AND MASCULINITY THREAT

At a time when explicit racial bigotry appears to be in retreat while racial inequality persists (Bobo, 1988; Goff, Steele, & Davies, 2008), it has become increasingly difficult to address racial discrimination directly. More individuals explicitly report egalitarian attitudes, yet evidence of racial discrimination remains across domains in society (Dovidio, 2001). The emerging fields of implicit bias and social identity threat provide a new landscape for improving racial equity. Below, we provide detailed background on two such processes (masculinity threat and implicit attitudes) and how they may cause problematic behaviors by authorities toward adolescents in schools.

Three categories of authority figures that adolescents interact with in significant ways are school teachers, school administrators, and police officers. Adolescents interact with school teachers and administrators on a daily basis, making these individuals influential authority figures. Further, adolescents are likely to encounter police officers both outside and within school borders, as it is becoming more common for a specific set of police officers to patrol a school campus (Raymond, 2010). Given the frequency of students' interactions with these authority figures, it is essential to understand the ways in which subtle stereotypes and identity threats can influence authority figures' behaviors. Existing research has begun to examine these constructs with police officers, and is extending its focus in schools to include teachers and administrators. We review this literature below.

Implicit Bias

Contemporary forms of racial bias are often subtle in nature, existing at a covert and implicit level (Blair, Dasgupta, & Glaser, 2015; Dovidio, 2001; Dovidio, Kawakami, Johnson, Johnson, & Howard, 1997; Greenwald & Banaji, 1995). Explicit attitudes represent our consciously accessed evaluations and beliefs and are what we traditionally think of in regard to attitudes. However, implicit attitudes are a second, less conscious route through which our attitudes can influence behavior (Olson & Fazio, 2003). Implicit stereotypes are beliefs about traits (e.g., criminal, violent) associated with groups (e.g., Black people, youth) that operate largely outside of conscious awareness and control. Such stereotypes influence real behaviors on the part of those who hold them, leading to discriminatory outcomes (e.g., Glaser & Knowles, 2008; Greenwald, Poehlman, Uhlmann, & Banaji, 2009; Jost et al., 2009). Project Implicit, a compendium of online tests that measures implicit bias, has responses from over 5 million participants across the world, finding that implicit bias is pervasive across groups and cultures (Nosek et al., 2007). A majority of Americans tested hold some form of pro-White, anti-Black bias (Nosek et al., 2007), and the strength of implicit stereotypes at a national level can even predict national differences in achievement (Nosek et al., 2009).

Individuals can hold explicitly egalitarian attitudes, yet still have implicit stereotypes and prejudice (Greenwald & Banaji, 1995), making racial bias harder to both recognize and reduce. One pervasive implicit stereotype is that African Americans, particularly young African American males, are prone to aggression and violence (Devine & Elliot, 1995). The challenge in mitigating this kind of discrimination is that it is *unintentional*, and because the stereotypes are implicit, people may not even realize they hold them, let alone prevent those stereotypes from biasing their behaviors.

Within the criminal justice domain, research has shown that police officers hold these implicit race-crime stereotypes (Eberhardt, Goff, Purdie, & Davies, 2004), which can influence police behavior (Correll et al., 2007). Implicit racial stereotypes impact decisions to shoot in quick decision-making video simulations, such that citizens and police are more likely to mistakenly shoot unarmed Black suspects compared to unarmed White suspects (Correll, Park, Judd, & Wittenbrink, 2002; Kahn & Davies, 2011; Plant & Peruche, 2005). These implicit stereotypes can guide behavior during police interactions with non-Whites, and increase the likelihood that force is applied and incidents escalate.

Within educational contexts, teachers and school administrators may similarly hold these implicit biases that can influence their behavior with non-White or disadvantaged students, despite egalitarian intentions. Teachers, like police officers, hold many of the same cultural biases present in other members of society. Teachers hold gendered stereotypes about their students, for example, stereotyping math as a male domain (Li, 1999). Teachers are aware that stereotypes exist in their classrooms (Gray & Leith, 2004) and also hold their own implicit stereotypes about minority groups (Glock, Kneer, & Kovacs, 2013).

These stereotypes affect important schooling outcomes. For example, teachers' race and gender stereotypes affect their perceptions of students' competence and ability (Parks & Kennedy, 2007; Riegle-Crumb & Humphries, 2012; Tiedemann, 2000, 2002). Stereotypes also influence student learning and educational outcomes across levels of schooling and disciplines. Teachers' gender biases, for example, positively affect boys' achievement while negatively affecting girls' achievement, influencing, for instance, the likelihood of students' enrolling in higher level mathematics courses (Lavy & Sand, 2015).

Some studies have demonstrated the influence of teachers' implicit attitudes on student achievement, finding that teachers' implicit biases predict their students' academic achievement above and beyond explicit or conscious attitudes. To illustrate, it has been shown that teachers' implicit racial stereotypes, but not explicit attitudes, explain some of the racial achievement gap across classrooms, through the route of biased teacher expectations (Van den Bergh et al., 2010). While teachers, police officers, and school administrators may have the best conscious intentions, their behavior may be affected by implicit attitudes, which can disadvantage non-White adolescents.

Masculinity Threat

Another salient identity-related construct that can lead to discriminatory outcomes for adolescents is insecure masculinity. Masculinity threat is a form of social identity threat, which occurs when an individual feels that his or her identity is devalued in a situation. According to the "precarious manhood thesis," masculinity is defined as a tenuous status that must be reinforced and publicly defended (Vandello & Bosson, 2013). Because of this, it compels men to actively assert their manhood in order to maintain it (Vandello & Bosson, 2013; Vandello, Bosson, Cohen, Burnaford, & Weaver, 2008). Masculinity threat often involves males perceiving that they are being associated with femininity, homosexuality, or impotence (Vandello & Bosson, 2013). When males experience a perceived threat to their masculinity, they often enact compensatory behaviors in order to reestablish their manhood (Bosson, Vandello, Burnaford, Weaver, & Wasti, 2009; Goff, Di Leone, & Kahn, 2012). Because toughness and physicality are a central component of the masculine self-concept, these compensatory behaviors often involve physical displays of prowess in order to reestablish dominance (Goff, Di Leone et al., 2012).

The causal role of masculinity threat on men's subsequent aggressive behavior has been experimentally demonstrated across contexts. A typical threat to a man's masculinity in an experimental context may include being forced to complete a stereotypically feminine activity (e.g., braiding hair) or being given feedback that his personality profile is more feminine than masculine. In one experimental demonstration, men given feedback that threatened their masculinity expressed higher support for war, dominance, and hierarchies (Willer, Rogalin, Conlon, & Wojnowicz, 2013). Men are more likely to act aggressively after a masculinity threat (Talley & Bettencourt, 2008), and use physical outlets such as a punching bag or pushups to restore masculinity (Bosson et al., 2009; Goff Di Leone et al., 2012). If men are not allowed to enact these compensatory responses after a masculinity threat, they have higher anxiety and ruminate (Bosson et al., 2009). Similarly, men are more supportive of other men who respond to a masculinity threat with aggression (Weaver, Vandello, Bosson, & Burnaford, 2009).

Importantly, this support of other men's aggression may be moderated by race. For instance, Richardson and Goff (2015) found that threatening White men's manhood influenced how masculine they thought violence was for both Black and White men, but in diverging directions. Specifically, White men participants rated White men who shot and killed a Black teenager as more masculine when the participants' manhood had been threatened than when it was not. Inversely, White men participants rated Black men who shot and killed a White teenager as less masculine after masculinity threatening feedback. This suggests that threats to manhood are met not just with affirmations of masculine-typed behavior, but with racially self-serving affirmations of masculinity.

Masculinity-threatened men also display more negative emotions toward stereotyped group members. In one experiment, men who received feedback that threatened their masculinity reported more negative affect toward effeminate gay men (Glick, Gangl, Gibb, Klumpner, & Weinberg, 2007). Therefore, effeminate gay men may be particularly vulnerable to violence when interacting with masculinity-threatened men. This finding also suggests that these compensatory responses may be disproportionately targeted at stigmatized group members, a theme which we elaborate upon later.

Masculinity threat primarily affects males (Vandello & Bosson, 2013); however, it can also be valuable for females to learn about and consider its potential effects for themselves. First, it is important for female authority figures to recognize masculinity threat in the adolescents they encounter and understand why adolescents may enact compensatory responses. This should aid in authority figures' ability to counteract situations. Secondly, it is possible that female authority figures may experience threat in a given context and respond with a compensatory response in a similar manner to males. For example, schools or police departments often adopt either formal or informal norms of strong discipline in the face of any threat or defiance, taking a hard stance on punishment of infractions to protect the school's authority. Females working in these contexts may adopt these institutional norms and respond in a comparable compensatory manner. Because of these reasons, both female and male authority figures can find value in understanding and learning how to counteract masculinity threat responses.

How does masculinity threat affect the policing context? Masculinity threat has been linked to overly aggressive use of force responses by police officers interacting with non-compliant suspects, including physical restraint, battery, and weapon use (Goff & Martin, 2012; Goff, Martin, & Smiedt, 2012). Police officers higher in trait-level masculinity threat were more likely to experience a threat to their masculinity when interacting with racial non-Whites, and this makes them more likely to shoot non-White compared to White suspects in video simulations (Goff & Martin, 2012; Goff, Martin et al., 2012). Police officers with higher levels of insecure masculinity also significantly deepen their voices (e.g., use more bass in their voice) when interacting with non-Whites compared to Whites as a form of compensatory masculinity when under masculinity threat (Goff & Martin, 2012; Goff, Martin et al., 2012). From the adolescent's perspective, police officers are likely to challenge an adolescent's sense of autonomy, which might be perceived as a threat to the adolescent's manhood. This masculinity threat might lead adolescents to challenge police officers' authority as a compensatory response, which can lead to an escalation of these incidents.

Within schools, threats to masculinity can also have significant effects on adolescents' behaviors and authority figures' responses. The development and negotiation of a masculine identity is a key process affecting boys in school, which can promote disengagement from school, avoidance of authority, and higher levels of disciplinary action in school (Jackson & Dempster, 2009; Kessels & Steinmayr, 2013; Martino, 1995; Renold, 2001). Threats to adolescents' masculinity have been thought to contribute to violence and aggression in schools (Kimmel & Mahler, 2003). Adolescent boys may experience a threat to their masculinity when a teacher directs or demands that they follow instructions or comply with an order. This threat can cause them to defy the authority figure in order to restore their masculinity. Correspondingly, the authority figures (teachers, administrators) themselves may feel that their masculinity is threatened by adolescents' defiance, and enact stronger discipline to restore their threatened status.

Further, due to the long history of racial stereotypes in our society, Black males are perceived to be hyper-masculine (Goff, Thomas, & Jackson, 2008). Because masculinity is stereotypically associated with Black males, threats to masculinity may be differentially perceived when coming from a Black compared to a White adolescent. An authority figure may feel a greater threat to masculinity from non-White adolescents due to these stereotypes, which may contribute to the higher rates of discipline for Black as compared to White boys in schools (Losen, 2011; Mendez, Knoff, & Ferron, 2002; Skiba et al., 2011; Wallace, Goodkind, Wallace, & Bachman, 2008). These acts can lead to the increased perception of aggression associated with non-White youths by authority figures, which could color authority figures' subsequent interactions with them. We suggest that defiance of school police officers may contribute to the relatively high arrest rates of non-White adolescents, while defiance of teachers can contribute to the increase in disciplinary outcomes and suspensions for non-White youth (Gregory & Weinstein, 2008; Skiba et al., 2002).

The Center for Policing Equity (CPE; www.policingequity.org), under the direction of Dr. Phillip Atiba Goff, has conducted investigations into the role of masculinity threat with adolescents and school police officers in schools. Through an ongoing, multi-year, multi-method study, Dr. Goff and CPE researchers examined how school police officers interact with non-White adolescents in schools, and the role that masculinity threat plays in these interactions. The research focuses on junior high and high school locations that contain a dedicated police force assigned to a school district, including a large Southern town with a metropolitan population of over 1 million. Researchers are conducting in-depth qualitative interviews along with structured surveys with students, parents, and school administrators about the role of masculinity threat in schools. The preliminary findings suggest that masculinity threats play a role in adolescent boys' challenge to authority figures and teachers, which then influence how police perceive and treat them. Based on these initial findings, we sought ways to intervene on masculinity threat and implicit bias in schooling and policing contexts.

METHODOLOGY: INTERVENING ON IMPLICIT BIAS AND MASCULINITY THREAT

One approach to addressing the overrepresentation of non-White adolescents in the criminal justice system and within educational discipline systems is to focus on the ways in which authority figures interact with adolescents and non-Whites. Implicit bias is consistently found in both males and females (Greenwald et al., 2009). While insecure masculinity primarily affects males (Vandello & Bosson, 2013), both male and female authority figures should be taught about its effects and how to recognize it in adolescents with whom they interact. By accurately identifying the role that insecure masculinity may be playing, authority figures of both genders can employ strategies to reduce its negative effects. Therefore, females are invited to participate in the training.

To accomplish this goal, we developed an intervention aimed at reducing authority figures' implicit bias and the effects of insecure masculinity during interactions. The intervention helps authority figures recognize masculinity threat in others, and also discusses the ways it might affect their own behavior. For campus police officers, who routinely interact with adolescents, the intervention focuses on common situations in which they encounter youths, for example, in the school parking lot after hours. Within education, we focus on teachers or school administrators as authority figures and use common classroom situations in which they face non-compliant adolescents. Below, we detail the content of the intervention, which can be tailored to focus on implicit bias and masculinity threat together or as separate components based on the group and setting.

Pre-intervention Phase

Before the intervention (2–4 weeks), authority figures (e.g., school police, teachers, administrators) respond to pre-training assessments. These include measures of implicit attitudes and stereotypes about race, such as the Implicit Association Test (IAT; Greenwald, McGhee, & Schwartz, 1998) and the shooter task (Correll et al., 2002). Surveys contain measures of explicit racial attitudes, attitudes about masculine gender norms, and sensitivity to masculinity threat. The surveys also measure potential moderators, such as the extent and quality of participants' experience with non-White adolescents, friends, and associates. This provides a pre-intervention baseline.

Intervention Phase

The intervention phase focuses on mitigating the influence of implicit stereotypes associating non-Whites with crime and compensatory masculine responses. Over a day-long in-person training session, the intervention contains lectures and demonstrations to increase one's understanding of the prevalence and dangers of implicit racial stereotypes and masculinity threat. There are two specific modules included in the program:

Implicit bias training. Counteracting implicit bias begins with teaching and understanding the ways in which implicit attitudes can affect behavior and decision-making. With school police officers, we discuss the ways in which implicit attitudes can influence decision-making and use of force with non-Whites. With teachers and school officials, we detail how implicit bias can influence student expectations, learning support, and disciplinary sanctions.

Next, the intervention contains active simulations that help combat implicit bias. One core implicit bias training component is a computer-based, interactive simulation. In this procedure, authority figures are presented with a series of semi-animated photograph sets of young Black and White individuals who present either with or without a visible, legitimate basis for reasonable suspicion (e.g., dropping or picking up a suspicious object). Participating authority figures are asked to make a quick judgment as to whether the individual warrants additional investigation or potential discipline. Next, authority figures receive training on how to control and counteract implicit bias in these interactions. Training includes cognitive strategies that they can use during these instances to reduce the likelihood that their reactions will be driven by implicit stereotypes, which include cognitive rephrasing, focusing on legitimate indicators of suspicion, and slowing down response times, which have been shown to successfully reduce unintended racially discriminatory behavior (Plant & Peruche, 2005; Plant, Peruche, & Butz, 2005). Participants are given real-time and summary feedback on their performance in terms of the appropriateness of their judgments (whether reasonably suspicious behavior was recognized) and racial disparities. We expect that the improvements they experience in their performance resulting from adopting the new strategies will be reinforcing.

Masculinity threat intervention. The masculinity threat portion of the intervention involves a training session in which the negative effects of insecure masculinity are emphasized for authority figures and adolescents. The first part teaches about masculinity threat and the ways in which it can negatively affect interactions in the given domain. The focus is on recognizing insecure masculinity and its related responses in others, and potentially in oneself. Both males and females participate in this section, as it is beneficial for females to be aware of the concepts and think about the ways in which the concepts might influence their behavior or the behavior of the youth.

After learning about masculinity threat, the male and female authority figures view and participate in interactive scenarios to model responses in the face of masculinity threat. Participants view training videos of authority figures that are either high or low in insecure masculinity and watch how they respond differently to a noncompliant youth (e.g., being verbally and physically aggressive with the non-complaint youth vs. being able to diffuse the situation without aggression). Alternative response behaviors are modeled. The authority figure participants are then able to actively play out and respond in pairs to scenarios involving a masculinity threat by an adolescent. Group discussion coalesces on the problems with the masculinity-threatened response and benefits of alternative responses. Techniques and strategies are shared among the group which can be used to consistently defuse and secure the situation, in spite of potential masculinity threats. Finally, participants are given a summary of strategies to counteract masculinity threat, including broadening the definition of masculinity and behaviors that can be seen as masculine.

Post-intervention Phase

The intervention closes with authority figures responding to post-intervention measures to gauge changes in their masculinity attitudes and racial bias. Measures are compared to the pre-intervention measures to examine change. To the extent possible, long-term follow-up data on the measures given 3–6 months later are also collected. To assess whether the intervention changed behavior in the authority figures' subsequent interactions with non-White adolescents, field measures should also be obtained. For teachers and school administrators, these long-term measures can include data on referrals for discipline and suspensions, while for school police officers, this may entail statistics on school-related arrests, citations, or use of force with adolescents at school.

OVERVIEW OF ONGOING IMPLEMENTATION

We are currently in pilot phases of testing the intervention in police departments and within schools. As part of our ongoing intervention development and testing, we have data from police departments that work with adolescents, school police officers, and teachers in California and Texas. We are currently collecting more data to empirically test the effectiveness of the specific parts of the intervention and the intervention as a whole in reducing insecure masculinity and implicit bias in authority figures. For instance, in testing the efficacy of the intervention material components, our research has demonstrated that shifting conceptions of masculinity from a more narrow to a broad focus through scenario-based learning—which is the core of the intervention—reduces the effects of masculinity threat on compensatory aggressive and disciplinary actions. Preliminary results from pilot tests of the new bias measure in California indicate that we have developed a viable set of stimuli that will serve to effectively assess racial bias in police decisions to stop and search, and offer promise to develop trainings that will reduce the effects of this bias.

Testing the overall efficacy of versions of the intervention itself, preliminary results regarding the intervention have also been encouraging. In one recent implementation in a large police department in Northern California that consistently interacts with youths, we trained over 150 officers through the masculinity threat and implicit bias intervention. Our preliminary analyses suggest that authority figures report less insecure masculinity following the intervention, and long-term follow-up data are being collected to track if these changes hold over time. We also have pilot data on masculinity and implicit bias in schools in Houston, Texas, and are continuing to develop and refine the school-based intervention in light of this new data. We have received inquiries from other schools that are interested in participating in collecting large-scale data regarding the intervention's effectiveness. Finally, a series of presentations to educators in California, Texas, Indiana, Pennsylvania, Alabama, and Minnesota have been met with enthusiasm, with teachers and superintendents reporting they have seen evidence of implicit bias and masculinity threat across their classrooms and disciplinary matrices. We aim to collect longitudinal data on the reach of the trainings' influence in the year to come. More data are needed to firmly establish the effectiveness of the intervention across contexts, but the initial pilot data is promising.

SUMMARY, IMPLICATIONS, AND RECOMMENDATIONS

Training on masculinity threat and implicit bias may provide one route toward reducing inequality in school discipline. Although our specific intervention is still in the pilot phases of implementation and data collection, there are nevertheless important conclusions that can be drawn from this line of research, based on existing evidence and theory. As a first step, we propose that learning that these biases exist and how they can impact behavior has the potential to reduce their negative impacts. We suggest that authority figures in schooling contexts, both male and female, can become more adept at recognizing when students may be acting out and noncompliant as a means to assert masculinity. Authority figures can become more skilled at responding to these threats and reducing the influence of unconscious bias during these interactions.

As more data are collected to test the intervention's efficacy, this type of training could become common practice for authority figures who interact with adolescents. Training on implicit bias and masculinity threat could become a core component in police officer academies and teacher development trainings. For schools that have a particular problem with disproportionate disciplinary actions, these trainings may be more vital. If school-based police officers become better at responding to masculinity threat in a non-forceful manner, schools can hope to see a long-term reduction in disproportionate arrests and aggression by school police officers in their interactions with adolescents and, in particular, non-Whites. Since insecure masculinity has been linked to racial discrimination (Goff, Di Leone et al., 2012), a reduction of bias against non-Whites is a particularly desirable outcome. Effectively improving interactions between authority figures and adolescents has the potential to improve trust and promote more equal treatment and equitable education and opportunity for all youth.

References

Blair, I. V., Dasgupta, N., & Glaser, J. (2015). Implicit attitudes. In M. Mikulincer, P. R. Shaver, E. Borgida, & J. A. Bargh (Eds.), *APA handbook of personality and social psychology, Vol. 1: Attitudes and social cognition* (pp. 665–691). Washington, DC: American Psychological Association. http://dx.doi.org/10.1037/14341-021

Bobo, L. (1988). Group conflict, prejudice, and the paradox of contemporary racial attitudes. In P. A. Katz & D. A. Taylor (Eds.), *Eliminating racism: Profiles in controversy* (pp. 85–116). New York: Plenum Press.

Bosson, J. K., Vandello, J. A., Burnaford, R. M., Weaver, J. R., & Wasti, S. A. (2009). Precarious manhood and displays of physical aggression. *Personality and Social Psychology Bulletin, 35,* 623–634. doi:10.1177/0146167208331161.

Correll, J., Park, B., Judd, C. M., & Wittenbrink, B. (2002). The police officer's dilemma: Using ethnicity to disambiguate potentially threatening individuals. *Journal of Personality and Social Psychology, 83,* 1314–1329. http://dx.doi.org/10.1037/0022-3514.83.6.1314

Correll, J., Park, B., Judd, C. M., Wittenbrink, B., Sadler, M. S., & Keesee, T. (2007). Across the thin blue line: Police officers and racial bias in the decision to shoot. *Journal of Personality and Social Psychology, 92,* 1006–1023. doi:10.1037/0022-3514.92.6.1006.

Devine, P. G., & Elliot, A. J. (1995). Are racial stereotypes really fading? The Princeton trilogy revisited. *Personality and Social Psychology Bulletin, 21,* 1139–1150. doi:10.1177/01461672952111002.

Dovidio, J. F. (2001). On the nature of contemporary prejudice: The third wave. *Journal of Social Issues, 57,* 829–849. doi:10.1111/0022-4537.00244.

Dovidio, J. F., Kawakami, K., Johnson, C., Johnson, B., & Howard, A. (1997). On the nature of prejudice: Automatic and controlled processes. *Journal of Experimental Social Psychology, 33,* 510–540. doi:10.1006/jesp.1997.1331.

Eberhardt, J. L., Goff, P. A., Purdie, V. J., & Davies, P. G. (2004). Seeing black: Race, crime, and visual processing. *Journal of Personality and Social Psychology, 87,* 876–893. doi:10.1037/0022-3514.87.6.876.

Glaser, J., & Knowles, E. D. (2008). Implicit motivation to control prejudice. *Journal of Experimental Social Psychology, 44,* 164–172. doi:10.1016/j.jesp.2007.01.002.

Glick, P., Gangl, C., Gibb, S., Klumpner, S., & Weinberg, E. (2007). Defensive reactions to masculinity threat: More negative affect toward effeminate (but not masculine) gay men. *Sex Roles, 57,* 55–59. doi:10.1007/s11199-007-9195-3.

Glock, S., Kneer, J., & Kovacs, C. (2013). Preservice teachers' implicit attitudes toward students with and without immigration background: A pilot study. *Studies in Educational Evaluation, 39,* 204–210. doi:10.1016/j.stueduc.2013.09.003.

Goff, P. A., & Martin, K. D. (2012). *Unity breeds fairness: The consortium for police leadership in equity report on the Las Vegas Metropolitan Police Department.* University of California, Los Angeles, CA.

Goff, P. A., Martin, K. D., & Smiedt, M. G. (2012). *Protecting equity: The consortium for police leadership in equity report on the San Jose Police Department.* University of California, Los Angeles, CA.

Goff, P. A., Di Leone, B. A. L., & Kahn, K. B. (2012). Racism leads to pushups: How racial discrimination threatens subordinate men's masculinity. *Journal of Experimental Social Psychology, 48,* 1111–1116. doi:10.1016/j.jesp.2012.03.015.

Goff, P. A., Steele, C. M., & Davies, P. G. (2008). The space between us: Stereotype threat and distance in interracial contexts. *Journal of Personality and Social Psychology, 94,* 91–107. doi:10.1037/0022-3514.94.1.91.

Goff, P. A., Thomas, M. A., & Jackson, M. C. (2008). "Ain't I a woman?": Towards an intersectional approach to person perception and group-based harms. *Sex Roles, 59,* 392–403. http://dx.doi.org/10.1007/s11199-008-9505-4

Gray, C., & Leith, H. (2004). Perpetuating gender stereotypes in the classroom: A teacher perspective. *Educational Studies, 30*, 3–17. doi:10.1080/0305569032000159705.

Greenwald, A. G., & Banaji, M. R. (1995). Implicit social cognition: Attitudes, self-esteem, and stereotypes. *Psychological Review, 102*, 4–27. doi:10.1037/0033-295x.102.1.4.

Greenwald, A. G., McGhee, D. E., & Schwartz, J. L. (1998). Measuring individual differences in implicit cognition: The implicit association test. *Journal of Personality and Social Psychology, 74*, 1464–1480. doi:10.1037/0022-3514.74.6.1464.

Greenwald, A. G., Poehlman, T. A., Uhlmann, E. L., & Banaji, M. R. (2009). Understanding and using the Implicit Association Test: III. Meta-analysis of predictive validity. *Journal of Personality and Social Psychology, 97*, 17–41. doi:10.1037/a0015575.

Gregory, A., & Weinstein, R. S. (2008). The discipline gap and African Americans: Defiance or cooperation in the high school classroom. *Journal of School Psychology, 46*(4), 455–475. doi:10.1016/j.jsp.2007.09.001.

Jackson, C., & Dempster, S. (2009). 'I sat back on my computer... with a bottle of whisky next to me': Constructing 'cool' masculinity through 'effortless' achievement in secondary and higher education. *Journal of Gender Studies, 18*, 341–356. doi:10.1080/09589230903260019.

Jost, J. T., Rudman, L. A., Blair, I. V., Carney, D. R., Dasgupta, N., Glaser, J., & Hardin, C. (2009). The existence of implicit bias is beyond reasonable doubt: A refutation of the ideological and methodological objections and executive summary of ten studies that no manager should ignore. *Research in Organizational Behavior, 29*, 39–69. doi:10.1016/j.riob.2009.10.001.

Kahn, K. B., & Davies, P. G. (2011). Differentially dangerous? Phenotypic racial stereotypicality increases implicit bias among ingroup and outgroup members. *Group Processes and Intergroup Relations, 14*, 569–580. doi:10.1177/1368430210374609.

Kessels, U., & Steinmayr, R. (2013). Macho-man in school: Toward the role of gender role self-concepts and help seeking in school performance. *Learning and Individual Differences, 23*, 234–240. doi:10.1016/j.lindif.2012.09.013.

Kimmel, M. S., & Mahler, M. (2003). Adolescent masculinity, homophobia, and violence random school shootings, 1982-2001. *American Behavioral Scientist, 46*(10), 1439–1458. doi:10.1177/0002764203251484.

Lavy, V., & Sand, E. (2015). *On the origins of gender human capital gaps: Short and long term consequences of teachers' stereotypical biases*. Cambridge, MA: National Bureau of Economic Research. doi:10.3386/w20909.

Li, Q. (1999). Teachers' beliefs and gender differences in mathematics: A review. *Educational Research, 41*, 63–76. doi:10.1080/0013188990410106.

Losen, D. J. (2011). *Discipline policies, successful schools, and racial justice*. UCLA: The Civil Rights Project/Proyecto Derechos Civiles. Retrieved from http://escholarship.org/uc/item/4q41361g

Martino, W. (1995). Deconstructing masculinity in the English classroom: A site for reconstituting gendered subjectivity. *Gender and Education, 7*, 205–220. doi:10.1080/09540259550039121.

Mendez, L. M. R., Knoff, H. M., & Ferron, J. M. (2002). School demographic variables and out-of-school suspension rates: A quantitative and qualitative analysis of a large, ethnically diverse school district. *Psychology in the Schools, 39*, 259–277. doi:10.1002/pits.10020.

Nosek, B. A., Smyth, F. L., Hansen, J. J., Devos, T., Lindner, N. M., Ratliff (Ranganath), K. A., et al. (2007). Pervasiveness and correlates of implicit attitudes and stereotypes. *European Review of Social Psychology, 18*, 36–88. doi:10.1080/10463280701489053.

Nosek, B. A., Smyth, F. L., Sriram, N., Lindner, N. M., Devos, T., Ayala, A., et al. (2009). National differences in gender-science stereotypes predict national sex differences in science and math achievement. *Proceedings of the National Academy of Sciences, 106*, 10593–10597. doi:10.1073/pnas.0809921106.

Olson, M. A., & Fazio, R. H. (2003). Relations between implicit measures of prejudice: What are we measuring? *Psychological Science, 14*, 636–639. doi:10.1037/e633872013-734.

Parks, F. R., & Kennedy, J. H. (2007). The impact of race, physical attractiveness, and gender on education majors' and teachers' perceptions of student competence. *Journal of Black Studies, 37*, 936–943. doi:10.1177/0021934705285955.

Plant, E. A., & Peruche, B. M. (2005). The consequences of race for police officers' responses to criminal suspects. *Psychological Science, 16*, 180–183. doi:10.1111/j.0956-7976.2005.00800.x.

Plant, E. A., Peruche, B. M., & Butz, D. A. (2005). Eliminating automatic racial bias: Making race non-diagnostic for responses to criminal suspects. *Journal of Experimental Social Psychology, 41*, 141–156. doi:10.1016/j.jesp.2004.07.004.

Raymond, B. (2010). *Assigning police officers to schools*. Center for Problem-Oriented Policing. Retrieved February 23, 2015, from http://www.popcenter.org/Responses/school_police/print/

Renold, E. (2001). Learning the 'hard' way: Boys, hegemonic masculinity and the negotiation of learner identities in the primary school. *British Journal of Sociology of Education, 22*, 369–385. doi:10.1080/01425690123433.

Richardson, L. S., & Goff, P. A. (2015). Interrogating racial violence. *Ohio State Journal of Criminal Law, 12*, 115–152.

Riegle-Crumb, C., & Humphries, M. (2012). Exploring bias in math teachers' perceptions of students' ability by gender and race/ethnicity. *Gender and Society, 26*, 290–322. doi:10.1177/0891243211434614.

Skiba, R. J., Horner, R. H., Chung, C. G., Rausch, M. K., May, S. L., & Tobin, T. (2011). Race is not neutral: A national investigation of African American and Latino disproportionality in school discipline. *School Psychology Review, 40,* 85–107.

Skiba, R. J., Michael, R. S., Nardo, A. C., & Peterson, R. L. (2002). The color of discipline: Sources of racial and gender disproportionality in school punishment. *The Urban Review, 34,* 317–342. doi:10.1023/A:1021320817372.

Talley, A. E., & Bettencourt, B. A. (2008). Evaluations and aggression directed at a gay male target: The role of threat and antigay prejudice. *Journal of Applied Social Psychology, 38,* 647–683. http://dx.doi.org/10.1111/j.1559-1816.2007.00321.x

Tiedemann, J. (2000). Gender-related beliefs of teachers in elementary school mathematics. *Educational Studies in Mathematics, 41,* 191–207. doi:10.1023/A:1003953801526.

Tiedemann, J. (2002). Teachers' gender stereotypes as determinants of teacher perceptions in elementary school mathematics. *Educational Studies in Mathematics, 50,* 49–62. doi:10.1023/A:1020518104346.

Van den Bergh, L., Denessen, E., Hornstra, L., Voeten, M., & Holland, R. W. (2010). The implicit prejudiced attitudes of teachers: Relations to teacher expectations and the ethnic achievement gap. *American Educational Research Journal, 47,* 497–527. doi:10.3102/0002831209353594.

Vandello, J. A., & Bosson, J. K. (2013). Hard won and easily lost: A review and synthesis of theory and research on precarious manhood. *Psychology of Men and Masculinity, 14,* 101–113. doi:10.1037/a0029826.

Vandello, J. A., Bosson, J. K., Cohen, D., Burnaford, R. M., & Weaver, J. R. (2008). Precarious manhood. *Journal of Personality and Social Psychology, 95,* 1325–1339. doi:10.1037/a0012453.

Wallace Jr., J. M., Goodkind, S., Wallace, C. M., & Bachman, J. G. (2008). Racial, ethnic, and gender differences in school discipline among U.S. high school students: 1991-2005. *The Negro Educational Review, 59*(1–2), 47–62.

Weaver, J. R., Vandello, J. A., Bosson, J. K., & Burnaford, R. M. (2009). The proof is in the punch: Gender differences in perceptions of action and aggression as components of manhood. *Sex Roles, 62,* 241–251. doi:10.1007/s11199-009-9713-6.

Willer, R., Rogalin, C. L., Conlon, B., & Wojnowicz, M. T. (2013). Overdoing gender: A test of the masculine overcompensation thesis. *American Journal of Sociology, 118,* 980–1022. doi:10.1086/668417.

CHAPTER 12

Discipline Disparities for LGBTQ Youth: Challenges that Perpetuate Disparities and Strategies to Overcome Them

Shannon D. Snapp and Stephen T. Russell

Emerging evidence indicates that lesbian, gay, bisexual, transgender, and queer (LGBTQ) students are disproportionately suspended and expelled in comparison to their straight and gender-conforming peers (Burdge, Hyemingway, & Licona, 2014; Burdge, Licona, & Hyemingway, 2014; Himmelstein & Bruckner, 2011; Snapp, Hoenig, Fields, & Russell, 2015). Although the over-use of punitive disciplinary measures for students of color and students with disabilities is now well documented, comparatively little attention has been paid to the particular challenges facing students whose self-expression may violate gender norms (e.g., a boy who wears hair extensions) or who engage in public displays of affection with same-gender partners. Not only are these students at added risk of bullying from peers, they may also face disapproval from school faculty who fail to intervene to prevent bullying and instead punish students for behavior

This project was an effort of the Crossroads Collaborative, which included Adela C. Licona, Hilary Burdge, Amanda Fields, Sarah Gonzalez, Zami T. Hyemingway, and Jennifer M. Hoenig. This work was supported by a grant from the Ford Foundation.

S.D. Snapp (✉)
Department of Psychology, California State University, Monterey Bay, CA, USA

S.T. Russell
Human Development in Family Sciences, University of Texas, Austin, TX, USA

© The Author(s) 2016
R.J. Skiba et al. (eds.), *Inequality in School Discipline*,
DOI 10.1057/978-1-137-51257-4_12

207

they do not understand or condone. When LGBTQ youth are bullied and fight back, they may face punishment for behavior that was done in self-defense, and are in effect blamed by adults for having been victimized (Snapp, Hoenig et al., 2015).

Once excluded from school through these policies and practices, youth are more likely to encounter the juvenile and adult criminal justice systems, a process referred to as the "school-to-prison pipeline" (STPP; Burdge, Hyemingway et al., 2014; Burdge, Licona et al., 2014; Monahan, VanDerhei, Bechtold, & Cauffman, 2014). Evidence of the STPP for LGBTQ students can be found in disproportionate rates of discipline in schools (e.g., Himmelstein & Bruckner, 2011), their overrepresentation in the criminal justice system (Garnette, Irvine, Reyes, & Wilber, 2011), and other more restrictive or less desirable educational programs (e.g., alternative schools, General Education Development (GED) programs; Snapp, Hoenig et al., 2015; Tuck, 2012).

To date, much of the scant literature on LGBTQ students and school discipline has focused on documenting the existence of disparities and related consequences for young people (Himmelstein & Bruckner, 2011). While more research is needed in this area, there is also a need for research on how and why these disparities arise for LGBTQ students, and strategies that may reduce them (Carter, Fine, & Russell, 2014; Snapp & Licona, in press), especially from the perspective of those most impacted by disparate treatment in schools. This study offers a first step in that direction. We present the perspectives of LGBTQ youth and the adults who work with them on dynamics they believe contribute to the over-punishment of LGBTQ students in schools as well as the steps that must be taken to create more supportive and affirming environments.

METHODS

The Sexual Orientation, Race, and Gender Disparities in Discipline project emerged from the need to address the gap in knowledge regarding school discipline experiences of LGBTQ youth. The research team consisted of researchers and students from the University of Arizona, the Crossroads Collaborative (a think-and-do-research-tank that studies sexuality, health, and rights for youth), and the Gay-Straight Alliance (GSA) Network.

Data reported in this chapter was collected from youth focus groups and adult interviews. Youth participants were recruited based on their responses to an online and paper survey ($n = 322$) about school discipline that was administered by the GSA Network through its online network and Youth Empowerment Summit. Youth were invited to participate in a focus group if they reported experiencing exclusionary discipline in school (e.g., suspension, expulsion), self-identified as LGBTQ, were in grades 9–12, and provided contact information. A small number of straight youth were also invited to participate if they had witnessed disparate treatment or had information about LGBTQ peers who had been disciplined in school. A total of 31 youth participated in eight focus groups in Arizona, California, and Georgia. Youth-reported demographic information including sexual orientation, gender (identity), and race/ethnicity (see Table 13.1).

In addition, we conducted interviews with adults (n = 19) from across the USA who have direct knowledge of LGBTQ youth and school discipline. The research team used a snowball sampling strategy, beginning with an initial list of educators, policymakers, and personnel within community-based organizations (CBOs) known to be working on these issues, and identifying additional interviewees based on referrals from adult participants. Focus group and interview protocols probed factors that might contribute to or reduce discipline disparities for LGBTQ youth (for more information on focus group/interview protocol, see Snapp, Hoenig et al., 2015).

All focus groups and interviews were transcribed and data analyzed using MAXQDA, a qualitative software program. Drawing on grounded theory (Charmaz, 2000) and qualitative coding techniques (LeCompte, 2000), the research team developed a series of thematic codes and phrases that emerged from the data. Two trained coders independently read and assigned themes to the data, and, when necessary, a third coder resolved any discrepancies in coding agreement.

Perspectives on LGBTQ Youth and School Discipline

Youth and adults in our study shared numerous examples of factors that contribute to discipline disparities, as well as strategies to overcome them. Findings are organized conceptually using an ecological systems model (Bronfenbrenner, 1979) which focuses on factors closest to young people's experiences and then moves outward toward systemic factors such as school practices and policies. Quotes represent the range of participant responses. When relevant, we highlight differences in the responses of youth and adults.

Factors that Contribute to Discipline Disparities

Excessively punitive discipline and security measures. Research shows that exclusionary discipline, arrests, and ticketing in schools are negatively associated with students' engagement, attendance, and academic achievement (Fine et al., 2003; Skiba & Knesting, 2001). Study participants agree that while punitive discipline and related surveillance and security measures are generally ineffective in establishing a safe and supportive climate in schools, they are particularly problematic for LGBTQ students. For example, one adult from Georgia explains how the use of metal detectors resulted in unnecessary punishment for one gay student:

> A gay young man was going through metal detectors, and he was detained for like half a day…because he had nail polish in his backpack. Now if someone saw this nail polish at a school that did not have metal detectors and school safety officers, you know maybe he would have been ridiculed, maybe he would have gotten it taken away from him, but [he] certainly wouldn't have been taken out of class for more than half of day.

Indeed, nail polish is generally not prohibited on school grounds, and the student's possession of it should not have warranted extra attention from school security personnel. However, the combination of heightened surveillance and adult biases about appropriate gender expression resulted in this student facing an unnecessary and excessively punitive disciplinary response.

Zero-tolerance policies often lead to automatic suspensions and/or expulsions for fighting, even in the event of self-protection, and these punishments are compounded when police are in schools. "We did have a lot of zero-tolerance policies … if you were caught fighting … they would not only automatically suspend you, but they would also call the police. You could automatically press charges as a student against another student" (Youth, Arizona). This quote represents the potential for double punishment when youth fight in school, in that they are punished once by the school and then again by police. When schools rely on exclusionary discipline and police, all students, regardless of sexual orientation and gender identity, may face double punishment. However, excessive and punitive discipline can create additional harm for LGBTQ students if the student is also "outed" through the disciplinary process (Snapp, Hoenig et al., 2015).

Once students have been disciplined, it becomes difficult to return to school without being labeled as "troublemaker" and the stigma of discipline can have a lasting effect. An adult from Louisiana describes this cycle: "You get in trouble at school. You're suspended. You come back. Now you're the troublemaker, and everything you do is under the microscope." In addition, because students are often unaware of the school's code of conduct delineating consequences for acts of misbehavior, they may not realize when a punishment given by the school is atypical or excessive, and may lack recourse in responding. One adult in D.C. explains: "[I] make sure they [students] understand the code of conduct and understand the consequence [s]... that if you curse somebody out ... you're not supposed to get suspended for five days. But that's what often happens, because they [students] are unaware."

In addition, punitive discipline may not address the underlying causes of bullying and, in some cases, may further aggravate the temperament of the student who engaged in bullying behavior. An adult from Illinois observed:

> [What] I hear from a lot of young people about why punitive discipline doesn't work is: 'because I reported that I was being bullied, that person was given a suspension for three days and then they came back...they've had three days to stew on the fact that I got them in trouble, and so now they're really going to beat the crap out of me.'

Adults and youth reported that because LGBTQ students are at greater risk of bullying, they are especially at risk of retribution. Fear of retribution can discourage students from reporting bullying. A youth from California explains, "It's not that I don't want to tell anybody [about bullying]. I just don't want to face anything else."

These quotes from youth and adults illustrate how punitive discipline can fail to create safe and supportive environments for LGBTQ students. LGBTQ students may be punished disproportionately for their behavior; they also may be singled out for their self-expression and face increased risk of retribution if they report bullying, or double punishment if they choose to fight back.

Insufficient awareness and training of school staff. Disproportionate discipline and related differential treatment may be the result of school staff or teachers who are untrained, ill-equipped, or unavailable to appropriately address LGBTQ issues in schools. An adult from Arizona observes a general lack of knowledge of LGBTQ issues among the adults who work with youth, and as a result, "they don't necessarily know how to handle challenges that these students face."

Bias, homophobia and transphobia can further cloud educators' ability to recognize, intervene, and respond fairly to students. Reflecting on these dynamics, a youth recalls "a lot of bullying towards LGBTQ people and it not being dealt with at all … it's part of the culture at this school." Another explains:

> I just think personally that if someone like, an instructor or a teacher or anything, has any kind of homophobia or anything like that it is easier for them [school staff] to…I guess pick on a student who is LGBTQ. (Youth, Arizona)

Even when teachers are aware of bias, they may find it difficult to respond to every incident of bias-based bullying in a school where the overall climate is homophobic. As the students' comments suggest, in a context where homophobia and transphobia are prevalent, teachers often cannot (or will not) intervene in every instance of biased behavior.

While school staff can certainly contribute to inequities for LGBTQ students (Snapp, Burdge, Licona, Moody, & Russell, 2015), youth also recognize that teachers and support staff are often underpaid and stretched beyond their limits. One young person from Arizona observed: "Some teachers are cool but … what are they supposed to do?" Faced with few resources and supports, as well as the pressure of preparing students to score highly on standardized tests, teachers may have little time or capacity to attend to students' overall well-being (Fine, 1991; Tuck, 2012). The combination of a homophobic school culture and an untrained and over-extended school staff can create a situation where LGBTQ students are treated differently from their peers. This differential treatment may also be heightened in a school that lacks other necessary supports for LGBTQ youth.

Lack of school-based supports for LGBTQ youth. Compounding the challenges of culture and staffing, under-resourced schools often have insufficient social-emotional supports for students, and this can be particularly problematic for LGBTQ youth. An educator from Louisiana explains:

> When we start eliminating guidance counselors, social workers. . .you know we're gonna push out a whole hell of a lot of kids, especially kids who are

dealing with identity issues. When we start eliminating those positions, we eliminate very crucial support systems for kids.

Another adult describes how the additional support systems that can help LGBTQ youth are often lacking in schools: "In terms of the climate of schools for queer youth, those schools are less likely to have enumerated anti-bullying policies, they're less likely to have Gay-Straight Alliances, and they're less likely to have a supportive teacher" (Adult, Georgia). When schools have anti-bullying policies that are enumerated to include sexual orientation and gender identity among the potential biases that may lead to bullying behavior, they communicate clearly that anti-LGBTQ bullying is unacceptable. These enumerated anti-bullying policies, in addition to supports such as supportive teachers, LGBTQ-inclusive curriculum, and Gay-Straight Alliances (GSAs), are associated with a host of positive outcomes for LGBTQ youth as well as heterosexual students (Horn, Kosciw, & Russell, 2009; Snapp, Burdge et al., 2015; Snapp, Hoenig et al., 2015).

Underfunded and under-implemented legislation and policies. Even, in schools where administrators, faculty, and the larger community recognize and endorse supports for LGBTQ students, implementation can be a problem. A youth leader from Arizona observed, "We have this policy that no one knows about. And, if you don't know about it, you don't have to implement it."

Ongoing professional development and monitoring are needed to enforce implementation of supportive policies for LGBTQ students, as is adequate funding. An educator from California recounts: "I can say unequivocally that we [school district] have fabulous plans to really meet the needs of these students, but [they've] been jeopardized by funding cuts ... Professional development on a regular and systematic basis is just impossible ..." Without close attention to policy implementation and sufficient funding, school-based supports for LGBT students cannot be implemented, and student needs continue to be unmet.

Inadequate data collection on sexual orientation and gender identity. Study participants identified the lack of data collection on students' sexual orientation and gender identity (SOGI) as a systemic impediment to protecting the rights of LGBTQ students. At present, sexual orientation and gender identity are not protected categories against discrimination in Title VI of the Civil Rights Act.[1] As a result, federal agencies are limited in their ability to investigate and seek recourse for acts of discrimination.

One adult from Washington, D.C., explains implications of this lack of protection:

> LGBT youth experience what's called disparate impact with regard to the school discipline… [but] because sexual orientation and gender identity are not a part of our nation's civil rights code, we can't. . .do anything about disparate impact as it relates to those margins of difference.

Lack of protection within the civil rights code also means data collection is not required, as it is for other protected classes (racial/ethnic minorities, students with disabilities). Therefore, schools, as well as districts, states, federal agencies and the general public, are unable to identify and track discipline disparities based on those characteristics. As described by an adult from D.C., the lack of data contributes to the invisibility of LGBTQ youth: "Even though they're experiencing the same harsh push out scenarios that you see quantified in terms of racial metrics, they're just completely not being talked about." The failure to collect data on SOGI-related disciplinary incidents hampers the ability not only to document existing disparities, but also to fight for the intervention and prevention supports that would address the needs of LGBTQ students.

IMPLICATIONS FOR POLICY AND PRACTICE: STRATEGIES TO ADDRESS DISPROPORTIONATE DISCIPLINE

Our data points to a number of strategies that can be used to address and reduce discipline disparities for LGBTQ youth. First and foremost, a shift from punitive school discipline would reduce the risk of exclusion for all students and the marginalization of LGBTQ students in particular. There are also a number of school-based strategies that would positively affect the experiences of LGBTQ students, and create LGBTQ-affirmative spaces. Professional development to improve the competency of school staff, improve stakeholder engagement, and increase data collection and analysis are necessary steps to ameliorate discipline disparities. Each is expanded upon below.

Implement non-punitive models of discipline. Adults and students agree that schools should use positive youth development-oriented alternatives to respond to student misconduct. Restorative justice practices and Positive Behavioral Intervention Supports (PBIS), along with support from guidance counselors, social workers, and school psychologists, were identified as potential solutions by several study participants (see also Schotland et al., this volume).

> A lot of districts are implementing restorative justice. Folks get to talk about the root cause...and students really get to take responsibility for their actions and their lives. There's positive behavior support, school psychologists, and counselors... also I know a couple of schools that [refer students] to family resources. (Adult, Colorado)

Such a multi-faceted and non-punitive approach to support students has been shown to reduce misbehavior and address underlying issues that may not be dealt with through exclusionary discipline (Gregory, Bell, Pollock, 2014; Losen, Hewitt, & Toldson, 2014).

Similarly, participants stressed the importance of identifying the underlying reasons for students' behavior before meting out punishment, to ensure that vulnerable students are not further marginalized. A youth advised schools to "ask them to go to a counselor first ... to maybe get at the root of what the problem is, instead of immediately going to punishment" (Youth, Arizona). Another young person from Arizona suggested:

> "I'd like to see [school faculty and administrators] talk to students more. 'Cause I think, like, if you're ditching a class a lot, I think there's a deeper reason that you're doing it. They should probably send you to a guidance counselor and figure out, you know, the root of the problem."

Participants uniformly observed that when students acted out in schools, there were likely deeper issues that required attention and were unlikely to be addressed by punishment or police involvement.

Focus on improving school climate. As discussed previously, research has identified a number of school-based strategies that would improve the school climate for both LGBTQ and straight students, including supportive clubs and teachers, inclusive curriculum, and enumerated anti-bullying policies (Horn et al., 2009). Participants pointed to similar strategies to counter discipline disparities for LGBTQ students. Respondents argued that LGBTQ support clubs such as GSAs can "make schools safer for LGBT youth and [all] students" (Adult, Georgia), and felt that the inclusion of factual and positive LGBTQ curricula such as LGBTQ history would "provide a foundation for understanding" (Youth, Arizona). The addition of *supportive and allied teachers* creates a school climate where students feel "very safe" and "make sure everything's ok." (Youth, California). Finally, participants suggested that school policies that protect LGBTQ students, such as "comprehensive anti-bullying policies ... and restorative justice," can create supportive climates (Adult, Georgia). Research has indeed shown that inclusion of these strategies within schools is associated with reductions in bullying and improved safety, achievement, learning, and feelings of belonging in school for all students (Horn et al., 2009; Snapp, McGuire, Sinclair, Gabrion, & Russell, 2015; Snapp, Burdge et al., 2015). Since these strategies improve school climate (Horn et al., 2009), they may also reduce disproportionate discipline among LGBTQ students. For example, many LGBTQ youth report getting disciplined for missing school, often due to concerns of safety (Snapp, Hoenig et al., 2015). A safe and supportive school climate could improve attendance, and therefore limit sanctions against LGBTQ students.

Youth identified several concrete steps for creating more open and affirming learning environments for LGBTQ students. These included: revising dress codes and bathroom policies to be inclusive of gender nonconforming and trans*[2] students by, for example, allowing students to wear what they choose for their school portraits, and creating a gender-neutral bathroom to use. Additionally, for trans* youth, one Arizona youth suggested,

> Instead of calling out somebody's first name and last name, maybe only calling out their last name and allowing the student to provide a name. . .or even having a teacher go, 'Hi, my name is, my preferred pronouns are [he him his or she her hers].'

Young people suggest that by using these strategies, schools can help students to learn about and accept LGBTQ people, which may lead to a broader shift in attitudes and norms within and outside of the school.

> We start so young conditioning each other to say, 'Oh, this is wrong, this is wrong, this is wrong.' I think if somebody goes, 'Okay, we're going to condition the youth to say, 'This is acceptable...this is fine.' If it gets said enough, even if their parents are saying something different, you're spending more time in school at a certain age than you are at home. You're going to eventually...create an entire new generation of acceptance. (Youth, Arizona)

In sum, youth called on schools to create affirmative climates that accept LGBTQ youth and meet their developmental needs. By doing so, schools can serve not only as a refuge and safe haven for LGBTQ youth, but also as a means of building broader understanding, acceptance, and support for LGBTQ people in their communities.

Build the professional competency of school staff on LGBTQ issues. Training adults who work in schools in "LGBT 101," as an adult from Georgia put it, was identified as a crucial strategy for improving educators' awareness of LGBTQ issues and professional competency to establish a safe and supportive environment for their students. Respondents argued that this training should cover basic definitions and terminology in regard to SOGI and introduce teachers, administrators, school staff, and security/police officers to diversity within the queer community as well as the best practices to support LGBTQ students as they develop.

An Arizona youth also pointed out the importance of monitoring staff behavior toward students, and intervening with staff who disproportionately punish LGBTQ students:

> I had a high school math teacher my freshman year that, every time I would bring my girlfriend in front of the class[room] to you know, kiss her [and] give her a hug goodbye...I'd have to sit outside of the class. I failed math that year. He got fired, though, at the end of the year, because apparently it happened to other queer students. They reported it, so he got fired.

Professional development for educators and safety personnel could include information on anti-LGBTQ bias/prejudice, the harms to LGBTQ youth who experience biased-based harassment, as well as best practices to support students, such as the aforementioned strategies to create safe schools.

Engage in collaboration and advocacy across stakeholders. To reduce discipline disparities and end the school-to-prison pipeline, engagement from diverse stakeholders is needed—including policymakers, educators, community members and agencies, and young people themselves (Snapp & Licona, in press). Participating in diverse coalitions provides the opportunity to learn about the concerns of other community members and work together to address these concerns through changes to practice and policy. For example, an educator in Louisiana describes how one school plans to improve the climate for learning for LGBTQ students and advocate for supportive state policy.

> Going forward we are looking to do more real explicit integration of our
> LGBT [work]. . . so being very specific about training teachers on LGBT
> kids. . .and then moving forward and looking to enumerating a Safe Schools
> Act through the legislation.

Similarly, an adult community organizer from Colorado explains how
stakeholders were brought together to "change the conversation" about
the STPP. The conversation generated new recommendations for policy
change that were youth-informed and thus culturally relevant.

> We create[d] a study group bringing together all of the stakeholders who
> are involved in school discipline. . .which included legislators, police, school
> administrators, restorative justice practitioners, child advocates though fos-
> ter care, parents, students. Our students testified and shared their stories
> about how they have been pushed out before, and how they had seen other
> students from the state who had been pushed out, and they shared data, and
> [they] offered their recommendations of what should be in the law.

Participants also recognize that collaborations, particularly with youth,
may extend beyond the need to identify solutions to the STPP, but can
also teach youth activism and provide essential emotional support. "We're
teaching them [youth] how to do activism ... and [if] the parents aren't
supportive, then they're going to need other community advocates in
place that can help them" (Adult, California). Thus, engaging in collaboration and advocacy can maximize the potential for all relevant voices to be
heard and supported as shared concerns around the STPP are addressed.

Collect data on LGBTQ youth in schools. The need for educational data
that documents the experiences of LGBTQ students and is disaggregated
by sexual orientation and gender identity has been a consistent request
by researchers and advocates (Hunt & Moodie-Mills, 2012; Losen et al.,
2014; Snapp & Licona, in press). Data allows us to close a gap in our
knowledge about LGBTQ youth, track educational disparities, and ensure
LGBTQ youth are represented in research and policy (Cianciotto &
Cahill, 2012; Horn et al., 2009; Mustanski, 2011; Russell, Kosciw, Horn,
& Saewyc, 2010; Skiba, Arredondo, & Karega Rausch, 2014; Snapp,
Russell, Skiba, & Arredondo, in press). Additionally, data can serve as
markers of accountability for the well-being of LGBTQ youth in schools.
As one adult from D.C. observed, "It's not enough for them to say, 'Oh,
we don't have any gay kids in our school' ...or to say, 'Well we treat our
gay kids like we treat everyone else' [since] they don't have any metric[s]."

Researchers have identified strategies to collect this data (Mustanski, 2011; Snapp et al., in press) from new and existing sources. One strategy is to augment anonymous existing surveys that are administered at the school level to include SOGI questions. These questions could be included as additional demographic items in the surveys. Another strategy, in addition to expanded surveys, would be to require schools and districts to report on SOGI as part of their mandated reporting to states and federal agencies (Snapp et al., in press). To do so effectively, schools and school systems must be helped to develop strategies to ensure this information is kept private at the school level. A current tension in SOGI data collection in schools is that if this information is stored in student records, parents may have access to it. Researchers call for a revised system in which youth are given the agency to disclose their SOGI information (e.g., to support data tracking) or have that information kept private at their discretion (Snapp et al., in press). Data privacy and SOGI disclosure concerns have already been addressed in fields such as public health and juvenile justice and could serve as models for the field of education. For example, in the health sector, patient privacy is prioritized, especially for youth (Cahill & Makadon, 2014). Youth are ensured privacy (unless they indicate they are in harm or intend to harm another) and can disclose relevant sexual health information to their doctor (such as their sexual or gender identity) and receive sexually transmitted infections (STI) tests and birth control without parental involvement (Ford & English, 2002).

Collecting more and better data on SOGI is an essential step not only in reducing discipline disparities for LGBTQ students and dismantling the STPP (Carter et al., 2014; Snapp & Licona, in press) but also in creating equity in education. Growing awareness of this need has led to a new effort by researchers and educators to work together to inform survey questions and methods in federal data collection efforts in order to improve data collection on SOGI while ensuring that student well-being is not compromised in the process.

SUMMARY

This chapter draws on the voices of young people and adult allies to understand the work needed to both illuminate and eliminate discipline disparities for LGBTQ youth. Participants in our study identified challenges that give rise to and maintain differential discipline for LGBTQ students compared to their peers. They also proposed strategies to address these challenges, some of which have been highlighted in previous reviews (see Gregory & Bell, this volume; Snapp & Licona, in press). Importantly, because these recommendations focus on creating more caring and inclusive learning environments, with stronger social-emotional supports for students, they are likely to benefit all students who are pushed out of school and into the justice system, and not only LGBTQ students.

Participants agreed that punitive discipline is a major contributor to discipline disparities, but it is not the only one. Other contributors to discipline disparities include the limited support for LGBTQ students from school personnel and a lack of awareness of the experiences and needs of these students. Alternative models, such as restorative justice practices (see Gregory et al., this volume; Vincent et al., this volume) can help to create a new culture of positive discipline. School counselors can help uncover the "root" of the problem contributing to disciplinary infractions (e.g., skipping school) and conflict in the school.

In addition, study participants recommended that educators and other personnel in schools be trained on LGBTQ issues so that "good policies" are understood and implemented. A positive school climate also can be fostered by providing school-based supports such as GSAs and inclusive curricula, and creating affirmative spaces that recognize diversity in sexual and gender identity/expression. Finally, inclusion of SOGI measures in data collection efforts would enable identification of education disparities among LGBTQ youth and provide schools and districts with information for planning and accountability.

Disparate discipline among students is a growing concern in the USA (U.S Department of Education, 2014), and LGBTQ youth are among those who experience inequitable educational outcomes as a result of differential treatment (Himmelstein & Bruckner, 2011; Snapp, Hoenig et al., 2015). The challenges that perpetuate disparities have become clearer. The strategies outlined by youth and adults can serve as the next step in an ongoing effort to reduce disparities and create equity in education for all youth.

NOTES

1. For specifics on the U.S. Civil Rights Act and protected categories, see: http://www.stopbullying.gov/laws/federal/
2. Trans* is used as an umbrella term for people whose gender identity or expression is nonconforming. *See* http://www.pdxqcenter.org/bridging-the-gap-trans-what-does-the-asterisk-mean-and-why-is-it-used/ for more information.

REFERENCES

Bronfenbrenner, U. (1979). *The ecology of human development: Experiments by nature and design.* Cambridge, MA: Harvard University Press.

Burdge, H., Hyemingway, Z. T., & Licona, A. C. (2014). *Gender nonconforming youth: Discipline disparities, school push-out, and the school-to-prison pipeline.* San Francisco, CA: Gay-Straight Alliance Network and Tucson, AZ: Crossroads Collaborative at the University of Arizona.

Burdge, H., Licona, A. C., & Hyemingway, Z. T. (2014). *LGBTQ youth of color: Discipline disparities, school push-out, and the school-to-prison pipeline.* San Francisco, CA: Gay-Straight Alliance Network and Tucson, AZ: Crossroads Collaborative at the University of Arizona.

Cahill, S., & Makadon, H. J. (2014). Sexual orientation and gender identity data collection update: U.S. government takes steps to promote sexual orientation and gender identity data collection through meaningful use guidelines. *LGBT Health, 1,* 157–160. doi:10.1089/lgbt.2014.0033.

Carter, P., Fine, M., & Russell, S. T. (2014). *Discipline disparities series: An overview.* Bloomington, IN: The Equity Project. Available at http://rtpcollaborative.indiana.edu/briefing-papers/

Charmaz, K. (2000). Grounded theory: Objectivist and constructivist methods. In N. K. Denzin & Y. S. Lincoln (Eds.), *Handbook of qualitative research* (2nd ed., pp. 509–535). Thousand Oaks, CA: SAGE.

Cianciotto, J., & Cahill, S. (2012). *LGBT youth in America's schools.* Ann Arbor, MI: University of Michigan Press.

Fine, M. (1991). *Framing dropouts: Notes on the politics of an urban high school.* New York: State University of New York Press.

Fine, M., Freudenberg, N., Payne, Y., Perkins, T., Smith, K., & Wanzer, K. (2003). "Anything can happen with police around": Urban youth evaluate strategies of surveillance in public places. *Journal of Social Issues, 59,* 141–158. doi:10.1111/1540-4560.t01-1-00009.

Ford, C. A., & English, A. (2002). Limiting confidentiality of adolescent health services: What are the risks? *Journal of the American Medical Association, 288,* 752–753. doi:10.1001/jama.288.6.752.

Garnette, L., Irvine, A., Reyes, C., & Wilber, S. (2011). Lesbian, gay, bisexual, and transgender (LGBT) youth and the juvenile justice system. In F. T. Sherman & F. H. Jacobs (Eds.), *Juvenile justice: Advancing research, policy, and practice* (pp. 156–173). Hoboken, NJ: John Wiley.

Gregory, A., Bell, J., & Pollock, M. (2014). *How educators can eradicate disparities in school discipline: A briefing paper on school-based interventions.* Bloomington, IN: The Equity Project. Available at http://rtpcollaborative.indiana.edu/briefing-papers/

Himmelstein, K. E. W., & Bruckner, H. (2011). Criminal-justice and school sanctions against nonheterosexual youth: A national longitudinal study. *Pediatrics*, *127*(1), 49–57. doi:10.1542/peds.2009-2306.

Horn, S. S., Kosciw, J. G., & Russell, S. T. (2009). Special issue introduction: New research on lesbian, gay, bisexual, and transgender youth: Studying lives in context. *Journal of Youth and Adolescence*, *38*, 863–866. doi:10.1007/s10964-009-9420-1.

Hunt, J., & Moodie-Mills, A. C. (2012). *The unfair criminalization of gay and transgender youth*. Washington, DC: Center for American Progress.

LeCompte, M. D. (2000). Analyzing qualitative data. *Theory Into Practice*, *39*, 146–154. doi:10.1207/s15430421tip3903_5.

Losen, D., Hewitt, D., & Toldson, I. (2014). *Eliminating excessive and unfair exclusionary discipline in schools: Policy recommendations for reducing disparities*. Bloomington, IN: The Equity Project. Available at http://rtpcollaborative.indiana.edu/briefing-papers/

Monahan, K. C., VanDerhei, S., Bechtold, J., & Cauffman, E. (2014). From the school yard to the squad car: School discipline, truancy, and arrest. *Journal of Youth and Adolescence*, *43*(7), 1110–1122. doi:10.1007/s10964-014-0103-1.

Mustanski, B. (2011). Ethical and regulatory issues with conducting sexuality research with LGBT adolescents: A call to action for a scientifically informed approach. *Archives of Sexual Behavior*, *40*, 673–686. doi:10.1007/s10508-011-9745-1.

Russell, S. T., Kosciw, J., Horn, S., & Saewyc, E. (2010). Safe schools policy for LGBTQ students. *Society for Research in Child Development Social Policy Report*, *24*(4), 1–25.

Skiba, R. J., Arredondo, M. I., & Karega Rausch, M. (2014). *New and developing research on disparities in discipline*. Bloomington, IN: The Equity Project at Indiana University.

Skiba, R. J., & Knesting, K. (2001). Zero tolerance, zero evidence: An analysis of school disciplinary practice. *New Directions for Youth Development*, *92*, 17–43. doi:10.1002/yd.23320019204.

Snapp, S., Burdge, H., Licona, A. C., Moody, R., & Russell, S. T. (2015). Students' perspectives on LGBTQ-inclusive curriculum. *Equity and Excellence in Education*, *48*, 249–265. doi:10.1080/10665684.2015.1025614.

Snapp, S., Hoenig, J., Fields, A., & Russell, S. T. (2015). Messy, butch, and queer: LGBTQ youth and the school-to-prison pipeline. *Journal of Adolescent Research*, *30*, 57–82. doi:10.1177/0743558414557625.

Snapp, S., & Licona, A. C. (in press). The pipeline population: Interrogating the patterns and practices of its production, for. In S. T. Russell & S. Horn (Eds.), *Sexual orientation, gender identity, and schooling: The Nexus of research, practice, and policy*. New York: Oxford University Press.

Snapp, S., McGuire, J., Sinclair, K., Gabrion, K., & Russell, S. T. (2015). LGBTQ-inclusive curricula: Why supportive curricula matters. *Sex Education: Sexuality, Society, & Learning*, online, 1–17.

Snapp, S., Russell, S. T., Skiba, R., & Arredondo, M. (in press). A right to disclose: LGBTQ youth representation in data, science, and policy. In S. Horn, M. Ruck, & L. Liben (Eds.), *Equity and justice in developmental sciences: Theoretical and methodological issues*. Oxford, UK: Elsevier.

Tuck, E. (2012). *Urban youth and school push-out. Gateways, get-aways, and the GED*. New York: Routledge.

U.S. Department of Education. (2014). *Guiding principles: A resource guide for improving school climate and discipline*. Washington, DC: Author. Retrieved from http://www2.ed.gov/policy/gen/guid/school-discipline/guiding-principles.pdf

CHAPTER 13

From Punitive to Restorative: One School's Journey to Transform Its Culture and Discipline Practices to Reduce Disparities

Marieka Schotland, Harriet MacLean, Karen Junker, and Jean Phinney

Evidence from the past three decades shows that school disciplinary policy and practice focused on punitive and exclusionary punishment have not appreciably diminished disorder and violence, nor have they changed perceptions of school climate for the better (American Psychological Association Zero Tolerance Task Force, 2008; Skiba & Peterson, 2000; Stinchcomb, Bazemore, & Riestenberg, 2006). Punitive discipline has been shown repeatedly to disproportionately impact boys and students

---

The authors would like to thank Anne Gregory and Emily Ozer for their guidance and support, and Jenny Michaelson, Hannah da Cruz, Lia Poitras and Jackson Masters for their tireless efforts with data collection.

M. Schotland (✉)
Independent Consultant, Oakland, CA, USA

H. MacLean
San Rafael City Schools, San Rafael, CA, USA

K. Junker
Davidson Middle School, San Rafael, CA, USA

J. Phinney
Department of Psychology, California State University, Los Angeles, CA, USA

© The Author(s) 2016   225
R.J. Skiba et al. (eds.), *Inequality in School Discipline*,
DOI 10.1057/978-1-137-51257-4_13

of color (American Psychological Association Zero Tolerance Task Force, 2008; Gregory & Weinstein, 2008; Skiba, Michael, Nardo, & Peterson, 2002). In response, a number of schools have shifted the paradigm of discipline to emphasize restorative actions and interpersonal connections over punitive and retributive sanctions. These schools have shown promising reductions in rates of suspension (International Institute for Restorative Practices, 2009; Karp & Breslin, 2001), as well as in gender and racial/ethnic disparities in discipline (Gregory, Clawson, Davis, & Gerewitz, 2014; see also Gregory & Clawson, this volume).

Examining the implementation of restorative practices in schools is essential in order to fully understand the process and potential of a restorative approach to discipline. Through an in-depth evaluation of Davidson Middle School in San Rafael, California, we explore how one school made the shift to a more restorative and positive school discipline policy and the impact of this shift on the school and students. Through this example, we hope to inform other schools about what they can do to reduce suspensions and disparities in disciplinary exclusion.

PREVIOUS FINDINGS

Zero-tolerance discipline policies and practices used in US schools today are characterized by harsh and exclusionary consequences for rule breaking, often in the form of out-of-school suspensions and expulsions. This approach to discipline has been linked to lower levels of school bonding, higher dropout rates, increased rates of juvenile incarceration, and higher levels of delinquency (Gregory & Cornell, 2009; Skiba & Peterson, 2000). Zero-tolerance discipline has also been shown to contribute to gender, racial, and ethnic disparities in disciplinary exclusion from school (Gregory & Weinstein, 2008; Skiba et al., 2002). In particular, African American, Native American, and Latino students are often subjected to stricter controls in school environments and have a greater likelihood of receiving more punitive disciplinary sanctions (Gregory & Cornell, 2009; Payne & Welch, 2010).

In contrast, restorative practices seek to restore relationships and repair the harms caused by conflict. Arising from the criminal justice setting, restorative practices are a method of responding to crime or hurtful behavior (Stinchcomb et al., 2006). In educational settings, this approach seeks to engage students who have offended others through a process of conflict mediation and resolution. School discipline programs employing restorative practices generally use formal and informal conferencing and classroom or community conference circles to address discipline issues and promote trust and community building (Skiba, Shure, Middleberg, & Baker, 2011). Students are taught to take responsibility and accountability for their behavior rather than receiving punishments that exclude and isolate them. As such, restorative practices offer a means of rebuilding relationships that have been damaged and repairing harm that has been done to the school community as a whole (Amstutz & Mullet, 2005; Pranis, 1998).

Empirical research on the impact of restorative practices in school is growing. Evidence thus far suggests that, when implemented fully, restorative practices can reduce the number of disciplinary referrals and suspensions, as well as the number of incidents of violence, misbehavior, and physical aggression (International Institute for Restorative Practices, 2009; Karp & Breslin, 2001; Stinchcomb et al., 2006). These findings suggest that the use of restorative practices may have far-reaching positive impacts on school culture and climate in addition to reducing the gender and racial discipline disparity gap (Gregory et al., 2014). However, challenges to effective implementation include high levels of teacher and administrator turnover and the lack of alignment and integration of the program into larger school reform efforts (Skiba et al., 2011; Stinchcomb et al., 2006). By examining one school's successful implementation of restorative practices, this study provides a unique window into an effective program of this approach.

DAVIDSON MIDDLE SCHOOL

Davidson Middle School is located between a residential and a commercial district in an area of Northern California that is typically associated with upper- and middle-class families. Reflecting the socioeconomic diversity of the school's surrounding community, however, the school's student population consists largely of low-income Latino families and middle-income white families; more than 60% of students qualify for free/reduced lunch at the school.

Until recently, Davidson was considered a low-performing school, suffering from social discord and behavioral problems as well as low student achievement. The school had a high rate of suspensions, with disciplinary actions targeted mostly at Latino students, and students' social interactions were largely segregated by ethnic group. The use of academic tracking added a layer to the social segregation, creating two different school experiences. On the one hand, advanced classes were composed of mostly white, middle-to-upper class students, with an actively engaged parent community. Latino, working-class students were found primarily in standard or remedial classes, with a less active English-as-a-second-language parent community.

In 2008, a new principal, Dr. Harriet MacLean, joined the school and immediately began instituting changes to improve achievement, increase parent involvement, and build a healthier and more socially integrated school community. She began by de-tracking academic classes to provide a more heterogeneous academic and social experience for all students and to communicate the expectation of high achievement for every student. Other academic supports put in place included regular parent-teacher conferences, academic coaches, and college and career fairs. In conjunction with these academic changes, MacLean sought to increase family engagement. Monthly parent education nights were introduced and greater emphasis placed on parent volunteers, with the goal of having one parent volunteer in every classroom. In addition, parents were included in discipline processes for their students. These efforts produced an immediate impact, with achievement scores rising and suspension rates dropping in the following academic year.

Academic and parent involvement changes were only the beginning of the school transformation. Over two years, MacLean implemented six different programs to improve climate and culture in the school. Three programs specifically targeted social dynamics, and included a mentoring program for incoming 6th graders, a program to combat social isolation that used the motto "no one eats alone," and a gang deterrence program that supported one dozen youth most at risk for gang involvement. In addition, three programs were implemented to reduce suspension rates and shift discipline practices to a more restorative approach to discipline. These included (1) Restorative Circles to address relational issues;[1] (2) No Bully Solution Teams to reduce bullying; and (3) Peer Courts to provide a suspension diversion option. Complementing these programs, the school adopted the motto, "Suspension is the last resort," and sought to limit punitive discipline. The school also allocated funds for a half-time position to oversee implementation of these discipline programs. A part-time math teacher, who had been extensively trained in restorative practices, was hired to fill this position. This hire allowed for a facilitator dedicated to the implementation of the programs.

CURRENT STUDY

This study examined how Davidson Middle School successfully transformed its disciplinary approach, and the impact of its new programs and practices on suspension reduction, particularly by racial/ethnic group. The study was guided by three core objectives:

(1) to provide a process-based evaluation of how the three discipline programs worked in the school, drawing on in-depth observations of the programs;

(2) to understand the degree of integration and sustainability of the programs into the culture and climate of the school, based on student and teacher knowledge of and perspectives on the programs and concurrent school climate factors; and

(3) to assess the impact of the programs on suspension reduction, comparing suspension records before and after program implementation.

Embedded across these three areas of inquiry was the goal of understanding whether the discipline programs were experienced differently according to gender or race/ethnicity.

METHODS

Sample

The school population in the 2013–2014 school year, when the evaluation was conducted, was consistent with previous years, with a total population of 1062 students across three grades (6th = 369, 7th = 343, and 8th = 350). The demographic composition of the student body was also consistent with previous years; a majority of the students were Latino (N = 58%) or White (N = 31%) and were split fairly evenly by gender (Boys = 53%; Girls = 47%). Student academic achievement had improved substantially in recent years, with the school posting an Academic Performance Index (API) score of 829 in 2013 (year of evaluation) as compared to 748 in 2009 (prior to Principal MacLean's tenure). The API measures academic performance and growth in all California public schools and has a range of 200–1000, with the state-wide minimum target score being 800.

Data Collected

Qualitative and quantitative data were collected for the study, including observations of the three school discipline programs, interviews with key staff, administrative data on student discipline from the school district, and surveys of teachers and students. Student survey data were collected from a sample of the general student body as well as from students participating in the three programs. School-wide surveys from the general student body were administered to 368 students (34% of total school popula-tion), and split evenly across all three grades and genders. This school-wide student sample was racially and ethnically representative of the school (Latino = 53%, White = 30%, Asian = 5% and Other = 12%). Student program participant surveys were collected after researchers observed program meetings. There were 151 student program participant surveys completed, which, due to some students' repeat participation in programs, were completed by 100 students across the three programs (Restorative Circles = 31%, No Bully Solution Team = 20%, Peer Courts = 49%). Teacher surveys were completed by a sample of 50 teachers. This teacher sample was 56% female, and 80% White, 6% Asian, and 14% other. The average number of years teaching among teachers was 12 (SD = 7.7, Range = 1–34), with the average number of years at Davidson Middle School being 6 (SD = 5.6, Range = 1–23). About 20% of the responding teachers were in their first year of teaching.

Process-based evaluation. To assess program effectiveness, an adapted version of RP-Observe (Gregory, Gerewitz, Clawson, Davis, & Korth, 2013) was used to score observations. The measure assessed seven dimen-sions of implementation: program rules; adult-student respect and respon-siveness; student-student respect and responsiveness; autonomy; risk taking; problem solving; and student commitment. Observations were given a numeric score for each dimension on a scale from one (low) to seven (high) along with a written rationale and examples. Research team members received training on the codebook and the measure was piloted across all three programs. Teams of two researchers conducted the pro-gram observations, and their scores were averaged for each category to obtain a final score. For discrepancies larger than one, the research team members discussed observations in detail in order to reach agreement.

Because the programs were scheduled in response to a disciplinary issue, the research team usually received notice of a program meeting one or two days in advance. The short notice meant that not all of the programs were observed during the data collection time period. A total of 13 program observations were collected and coded using the RP-Observe instrument.

Integration and sustainability. To explore the integration and sus-tainability of the programs, student and teacher surveys probed general knowledge and perceived effectiveness of the programs, as well as percep-tions of discipline harshness, degree to which restorative practices were integrated into the school community, and support for cultural diversity. Table 13.1 lists each measure, the sample that was surveyed, the number of items, sample items, and reliability, when applicable.

Table 13.1 Measurement information for survey items

Measure and sample	# of items	Sample item(s)	Cronbach's alpha
General knowledge			
Students	1	I have heard about the following programs.	N/A
Teachers	1	I have initiated/requested the following programs.	N/A
Program effectiveness			
Program participants	8	I feel that the meeting was very helpful in handling the issue.	0.91
Teachers	3	Please rate how effective each program is.	N/A
Discipline harshness			
Students	5	The rules in this school are too strict.	0.67
Restorative practices			
Students	4	When a student misbehaves at my school, teachers and	0.82
Teachers	4	administrators ask questions in a respectful way.	0.85
Support for cultural Pluralism			
Students	4	Students of many different races and cultures are chosen to	0.73
Teachers	4	participate in important school activities.	0.69

Note: N/A—Not applicable if used for single item measures where Cronbach's Alpha cannot be calculated

New survey items were created to probe student and teacher general knowledge of the programs and perceptions of their effectiveness. In addition, the Discipline Harshness measure (Brand, Felner, Shim, Seitsinger, & Dumas, 2003) was used to elicit student perspectives about discipline. A measure developed by the International Institute of Restorative Practices (2010) was used to assess student and teacher perspectives on the extent to which the principles and behaviors of restorative practices were integrated into the school community. Finally, the Support for Cultural Pluralism measure (Brand et al., 2003) was administered to students and teachers to assess the extent to which the school's climate fostered integration and a respect for diversity.

Suspension reduction. Administrative records were obtained from the school on all of the suspensions that had occurred during the year of data collection (2013–2014), as well as the year before any school culture and climate programs were implemented (2008–2009). Records included grade, gender, race/ethnicity, California State educational code (reason) for suspension, and number of days suspended.

FINDINGS

A close examination of efforts at Davidson Middle School indicate a high degree of success in shifting the school from a paradigm of punitive discipline toward one that embodies restorative perspectives. The multi-faceted approach implemented by Davidson's principal successfully improved the school, both in academics and climate. Significant reductions in suspension rates and improvement in discipline disparities were associated with this holistic approach. Below is a detailed description of how these programs work, how the school community viewed them, and how parallel school climate components were perceived.

Program Observations

Restorative Circles

Restorative Circles were used to address issues related to social relationships between students—for example, when an argument or fight developed. Circles were also used to navigate conflicts between and among adults and students, although only circles involving students were observed in this study. Circles were set up at the request of staff or students. Some happened after teachers caught students in an altercation, while others were requested by the students themselves to resolve relationship issues. The facilitator gathered the students involved and asked them to take turns sharing their feelings and perspectives while maintaining an atmosphere of safety, decorum, and equality. Circle participants were asked to articulate and listen to ideas from peers about what could be done to repair the harm caused by conflict and how reparations could be made without resorting to a school-based punishment. Agreements were then made between the two students on further actions and next steps.

In the circles observed by the research team, students were initially reluctant to share their feelings openly, but gradually opened up to each other as the meeting progressed. The facilitator often started the circle by modeling the types of statements that could be made and students generally responded well to these efforts. Sometimes this happened after one student was willing to share more, or, in one case, began crying. In meetings where both students eventually opened up and shared, solutions were jointly generated and agreed upon. Students often admitted to wrongdoing and offered apologies on their own, without the facilitator prompting, after listening to and engaging with the offended student. In some cases, the conflicts leading to the circles were single events, while in others, the conflicts arose from long-standing problems between students that had recently escalated, and often involved multiple students. These more complex problems generally involved multiple circles with the various students. In situations where one or both of the parties involved was unresponsive, the facilitator took a more active role in forging agreements between students to address the issue. This was the case in one meeting about a boy who repeatedly threw a ball at a girl; the boy's behavior conveyed disinterested and low commitment to the program, despite repeated efforts by the facilitator. The circle eventually concluded with the facilitator creating action steps for both students.

No Bully Solution Teams

No Bully Solution Teams were convened when a student or a teacher witnessed or experienced bullying behavior. Prior to the initial meeting, the facilitator met with the targeted student to understand the actions of the bully. She then called a meeting with the bully, followers of the bully, and other class leaders, but not the targeted student. No information was provided to this group prior to the meeting. Using the targeted student's words, and without identifying the bully directly, the No Bully Solution Team heard about the targeted student's experience from the facilitator. Each member of the No Bully Solution Team then stated what they could do to prevent the behavior toward the targeted student from continuing, emphasizing a community effort to make a change. Each No Bully Solution Team reconvened twice more to assess what had been accomplished. In each of these follow-up meetings, the targeted student had the choice to participate or not.

The No Bully Solution Team meetings were characterized by a strong feeling of community. Although the facilitator never verbally identified the bully, students glanced at the bully when the behavior was being described. In one case, where the targeted student had expressed feeling sad and scared about being excluded during basketball games, students in the meeting were quick to offer ideas to prevent the negative behavior in the future. Each student seemed excited to add to the list of possible actions, all of which aimed to be more inclusive of the targeted student. The follow-up meeting was filled with students sharing the various actions they had taken to make the student feel more welcome during basketball games. The group effort was apparent, and the students worked together to make changes. Facilitator check-ins with the targeted student showed great improvement in the interactions.

Peer Courts

Peer Courts served as a suspension diversion program, and were called into action when the issue involving the student or students had progressed through either the Restorative Circles or the No Bully Solution Teams and had not been resolved, or if the student had committed one of the more serious actions listed on the California Education Code as reasons for suspension. The student was offered a choice of suspension or participation in the Peer Courts. During the course of the study, no student opted for suspension. The goal of the Peer Courts was to institute efforts to repair harm and make amends rather than suspend the student. The student, a parent, and a staff representative (typically a vice principal) were called before a panel of trained youth participants, guided by a facilitator. The panel then met privately, without the student, to decide on a contract of restitution to be completed in two weeks' time. After two weeks passed, the court met again to see if the student had fulfilled the contract, thus avoiding suspension. Completion of the contract also resulted in the offense being moved from the student's discipline record to the student's counseling record. Of the Peer Courts observed for this study, all students completed their contracts, although some needed a time extension.

In the Peer Courts, the inclusion of the family member and trained Peer Court members represented an additional dimension not typically seen in other discipline programs. One Spanish-speaking father shared through a translator how hard it was for him to take time off work to attend the Peer Court, while another mother broke down in tears about her son's behavior. In one situation in which a student had brought drugs to school, the father shared how the whole family had been impacted and that he had lost his trust in his son, whom he would no longer leave alone. These disclosures seemed to have an immediate and striking impact on the students, who exhibited feelings of shame and regret. Similarly, the trained Peer Court members often shared their own personal perspective on the situation. A student who was caught selling drugs had a friend serving on the Peer Court, and the Peer Court member shared how these actions hurt him. Members often offered support and guidance with statements such as, "We want the best for you," "We are here to help," and "You are too young to be involved in drugs." Resolutions proposed by the Peer Court were multi-faceted and typically restorative in nature. Most resolutions included a combination of academic supports (e.g., required tutoring), specific restitution efforts (e.g., apology letters), and more unconventional efforts, such as completing chores at home, joining a sports team, or reporting back to the Peer Court about various drug treatment programs.

One challenging aspect of the Peer Courts was the relatively frequent situation in which the student for whom the Peer Court had been called was defensive or reluctant to take responsibility for his or her actions. A staff representative sat with the student during the proceedings and offered ideas and suggestions for the student's responses. Despite this support, some students seemed to be caught off guard when facing a panel of their peers, especially when the peers were supportive rather than punitive. Students often responded minimally to questions, perhaps due to feelings of embarrassment. Despite this outward demeanor, all of the students agreed to the proposed resolutions and completed them.

Program Effectiveness

Overall, five Restorative Circles, one No Bully Solution Team, and seven Peer Court observations were coded on dimensions of effectiveness using the RP-Observe instrument (Gregory et al., 2013), and average scores are provided in Table 13.2. Most dimensions received relatively high scores, suggesting a high degree of program implementation. Student commitment in Peer Courts received the lowest rating (4.9 of 7), which may reflect the reluctance displayed by many of the students for whom the court was called. Over half the students in the seven Peer Courts observed were reluctant to acknowledge their wrongdoing and contribute substantively to solutions. However, despite these low scores, all of the students completed their contracts.

Sustainability and Integration

To understand how the three discipline programs were taken up and maintained in the school community, teachers and students in the school-wide survey were asked about their knowledge of the programs, specifically whether they had heard about the programs and utilized them. Slightly more than half (54%) of students sampled (N = 368) had heard of the Peer Courts program, while about one-third had heard of Restorative Circles (37%) and No Bully Solution Teams (35%). These percentages appear low given the number of years that the programs had been in place

Table 13.2   Mean scores for RP-observe coding

	Restorative circles (N = 5)	No bully solution teams (N = 1)	Peer courts (N = 7)
Program rules: Clear expectations and standards, facilitator fairness and consistency	5.6	6.0	6.3
Adults-student respect and responsiveness: Positive rapport and acceptance	6.0	7.0	5.7
Student-students respect and responsiveness: Positive rapport, empathy and acceptance	6.2	7.0	6.0
Autonomy: Student ownership of the process	5.4	–	5.8
Risk taking: Appropriate personal disclosure	5.4	7.0	5.6
Problem solving: Problem solving steps, collaboration	5.4	7.0	5.9
Student commitment: Student focus and engagement	6.0	7.0	4.9

Note: Range: 1–7

and the number of school-wide assemblies held to inform students about them. However, since these programs are utilized by students who get in trouble, the low level of awareness may represent that fact that most students had not had need of them.

Despite representing over 50% of the school population, Latino students were less likely than White students to have heard about Restorative Circles (28% vs. 54%; χ^2 (1, N = 307) = 19.11; $p < 0.001$) and Peer Courts (45% vs. 66%; χ^2(1, N = 307) = 12.37; $p < 0.001$), with no significant differences for the No Bully Teams. More girls than boys had heard of the Peer Courts (61% vs. 47%; χ^2 (1, N = 368) = 7.76; $p < 0.01$), which may be reflective of the slightly higher rate of female students that serve as trained youth court members. There were no gender differences for students who had heard of Restorative Circles or No Bully. Not surprisingly, teachers' knowledge of the programs was greater than students, with all or nearly all teachers having heard about all three (Peer Courts = 100%, Restorative Circles = 98%, No Bully = 80%).

Actual student participation in the programs was around 10% (Peer Courts = 11%, Restorative Circles = 9%, No Bully = 9%), with no significant differences by gender. Although Latino students were less likely than

White students to have participated in a No Bully Solution Team meeting (7%vs. 15%; χ^2 (1, N = 307) = 6.06; $p < 0.05$), there was no significant difference by ethnicity in Peer Courts or Restorative Circles. About 50% of the teachers had initiated a Restorative Circle, and 20% had initiated a Peer Court or a No Bully Solutions Team meeting.

Students and teachers rated all three programs favorably, suggesting they are viewed positively within the school. Student participants in the programs gave fairly high evaluations (Peer Courts: $M = 3.71$, $SD = 0.44$; Restorative Circles: $M = 3.35$, $SD = 0.66$; No Bully: $M = 3.49$, $SD = 0.58$; Range = 1–4), with no significant difference across the three programs. Teachers also rated program effectiveness highly (Peer Courts: $M = 3.51$, $SD = 0.71$; Restorative Circles: $M = 3.36$, $SD = 0.68$; No Bully: $M = 3.44$, $SD = 0.64$, Range = 1–4), with no significant difference between scores. These findings suggest strong buy-in among teachers and students for the programs.

To understand the programs' effect on the overall climate of the school, the survey probed perceptions of discipline, restorative justice, and support for cultural pluralism. Students rated discipline harshness moderately ($M = 2.31$, $SD = 0.50$, Range = 1–4). Although there were no differences by gender, Latino students rated the school's disciplinary approach more harshly than White students (2.36 vs. 2.23; $t(305) = 2.22$, $p < 0.05$). This finding may reflect the higher number of Latino students participating in the discipline process at the school.

Students' and teachers' perspectives on the integration of restorative practices into the school community were assessed with a four-item measure. Both students ($M = 3.15$, $SD = 0.66$, Range = 1–4) and teachers ($M = 3.09$, $SD = 0.40$, Range = 1–4) rated restorative justice efforts moderately high. Interestingly, Latino students' rating of restorative practices was significantly higher than White students (3.28 vs. 3.00; $t(303) = 3.67$, $p < 0.001$), suggesting that despite their experience of harsher discipline, they believed the discipline processes were more restorative in nature. There were also no differences by gender for perspectives on restorative practices.

School support for cultural pluralism was rated highly by students ($M = 3.38$, $SD = 0.57$, Range = 1–4) and teachers ($M = 3.28$, $SD = 0.45$, Range = 1–4). Support for cultural pluralism was rated significantly higher among girls compared to boys (2.45 vs. 2.31; $t(364) = 2.26$, $p < 0.05$). There were no differences in cultural pluralism by ethnicity.

Suspension Reduction

School discipline records for the time period during which restorative programs were utilized show reductions in both the number of suspensions in the school and the disparities in which groups received them as compared to previous years. During the 2008–2009 school year, prior to any school climate and culture reforms, there were 294 suspensions across 162 students. Five years later, by the 2013–2014 school year, the number of total suspensions had dropped to 73 across 48 students, a 75% reduction.

Importantly, Latino students' relative risk of being suspended was cut by more than half after the programs had been implemented, from 11 to 3 (see Table 13.3). In the 2008–2009 school year, 22% of the total Latino student population had experienced a suspension. By 2013–2014, that number had dropped to 3%. Across the same time period, White students risk of suspension dropped from 2% to 1%. The discipline gap had narrowed considerably, although Latino students continued to be at greater risk of suspension than their White peers.

CONCLUSIONS AND IMPLICATIONS

Our findings suggest that Davidson Middle School was successful not only in shifting discipline practices from a punitive to a restorative approach, but also in addressing disparities in the treatment of students. Through a multi-faceted strategy, the school was transformed from a place characterized by low academic achievement, high suspension rates, and persistent social discord into a vibrant environment for learning with high academic achievement, low rates of suspension, and a more harmonious culture and climate. By closely examining the three discipline programs implemented, a clearer picture emerges of how restorative approaches to discipline can help facilitate these changes.

Table 13.3 Risk index[a] and relative risk[b] for White and Latino students by year

		White	Latino	Relative Risk for Latino Students
2008–2009	Risk index	2%	22%	11.0
2013–2014	Risk index	1%	3%	3.0

[a]Represents the percentage of each group that experienced suspension in each year
[b]Latino students in comparison to White students

All three programs exemplified restorative justice practices. Restorative Circles sought to create an open dialogue between students in which the victim's voice and experiences were heard and appropriately addressed. When one or both students openly and honestly shared their emotions, these circles engendered genuine empathy and restitution efforts. No Bully Solution Teams proactively shared incidents of bullying to create a strong sense of community that fostered and affirmed a sense of inclusion and respect among students. The targeted students saw and felt changes in the behavior not only of the bully, but among the larger community of peers. Peer Courts that involved parents and peers in the proceedings had an emotional depth that struck a chord with most students. By hearing how friends and families were affected, students developed a better understanding of the repercussions of their actions.

Nonetheless, student knowledge of the programs and their use in the school were not as high as expected. Since the programs were initiated only in reaction to a discipline issue, the relatively low levels of awareness could reflect the reality of fewer disciplinary problems in the school as a result of the shift to restorative approaches to discipline problems. Higher levels of familiarity with Peer Courts could be related to those discipline problems being more extreme and thus more likely to be discussed among students. The finding that, although almost all of the teachers had heard about the programs, only 50% or less had actually utilized them may be a function of the programs' success and resulting lack of need for them. Alternatively, it may reflect a lack of uptake among the teaching staff.

Findings on Latino students are more difficult to explain. Latino students were less likely to have heard about the Peer Courts and Restorative Circles and to have participated in the No Bully Solution Teams. Future research should include student interviews to clarify how and which students learn about the programs. The disjuncture between Latino students' perceptions of harsher discipline in the school and their more positive views of restorative justice efforts in the school compared to White students also warrants further study. One explanation could be that while Latino students are still experiencing a disproportionate amount of discipline actions, they perceive these disciplinary actions to be handled in a restorative manner. This explanation is further supported by suspension data showing that despite reductions in the overall number of suspensions, Latino students continue to experience a disproportionate number of suspensions. The school's efforts to implement a more restorative discipline approach shows success, but more efforts are clearly needed to address remaining ethnic disparities. It is also worth noting that the levels of discipline were rated harshly across all students despite efforts to implement discipline programs grounded in restorative justice. Larger school-wide efforts to implement pro-active restorative justice practices, such as weekly classroom circles to address social issues, could promote a mindset more conducive to restorative practices in the school community, and result in discipline being viewed less harshly by students.

Although all three programs showed overall success, each faced hurdles. The Restorative Circles required facilitator leadership when one or both students refused to share their feelings honestly and openly. Despite the presence of parents and peers, many of the Peer Court students were reluctant and uncomfortable with the restorative nature of the program. Since middle school students' emotional development covers a wide spectrum with regard to empathetic efforts (Steinberg & Morris, 2001), these actions are not necessarily surprising, but do present a challenge for successful implementation. Middle school students' lack of emotional vocabulary and self-awareness may circumscribe the full dialogue needed for a feeling of restoration. In such cases, restorative processes may find better success if paired with other explicit strategies to foster students' social-emotional skills.

Moreover, these findings suggest that to fully integrate restorative practices into the school, teachers need to have full buy-in to the programs. Although most teachers knew about the programs, and there were no obvious barriers to their use of them, the uptake seemed low. The school was beginning to implement restorative practices training for the teachers, which may make this approach more tangible and thus increase usage and impact of the programs.

Overall, Davidson Middle School offers a promising example of the benefits of shifting punitive disciplinary policy and practice to a more restorative approach. The multi-faceted effort included a focus on de-tracking academics, increasing parent involvement, and implementing new school culture and climate programs. After five years, the school has successfully raised academic achievement, built an active parent community, and created a restorative disciplinary approach that has resulted in lower suspensions and less disproportionality in disciplinary actions. At a time when schools and districts across the country are seeking to shift from zero-tolerance discipline policies, Davidson provides a model of a restorative approach that educators can follow.

NOTE

1. Davidson Middle School used the term "restorative circles" to refer to both programs and meetings that, in the literature, are more typically described as "restorative conferences." Conferences generally are used in response to a discipline action, while circles refer to more pro-active relationship-building exercises.

REFERENCES

Amstutz, L. S., & Mullet, J. H. (2005). *The little book of restorative discipline for schools: Teaching responsibility, creating caring climate.* Intercourse, PA: Good Books.

American Psychological Association Zero Tolerance Task Force. (2008). Are zero tolerance polices effective in the schools? *American Psychologist, 63*(9), 852–862.

Brand, S., Felner, R. D., Shim, M., Seitsinger, A., & Dumas, T. (2003). Middle school improvement and reform: Development and validation of a school-level assessment of climate, cultural pluralism, and school safety. *Journal of Educational Psychology, 95*(3), 570–588.

Gregory, A., & Clawson, K. (in press, 2016). The potential of restorative approaches to discipline for narrowing racial and gender disparities. In R. J. Skiba, K. Mediratta, & M.K. Rausch (Eds.), *Inequality in school discipline: Research and practice to reduce disparities.* New York: Palgrave Macmillan.

Gregory, A., Clawson, K., Davis, A., & Gerewitz, J. (2014). The promise of restorative practices to transform teacher-student relationships and achieve equity in school discipline. *For a special issue on Restorative Justice in the Journal of Educational and Psychological Consultation.* doi:10.1080/10474412.2014.929.

Gregory, A., Gerewitz, J., Clawson, K., Davis, A., & Korth, J. (2013). *RP-Observe manual.* Unpublished.

Gregory, A., & Cornell, D. (2009). "Tolerating" adolescent needs: Moving beyond zero tolerance policies in high school. *Theory into Practice, 48,* 106–113.

Gregory, A., & Weinstein, S. R. (2008). The discipline gap and African Americans: Defiance or cooperation in the high school classroom. *Journal of School Psychology, 46,* 455–475.

International Institute for Restorative Practices (2010). *Restorative Practices Student Survey.* Bethlehem, PA: International Institute for Restorative Practices Graduate School.

International Institute for Restorative Practices (2009). *Improving school climate: Findings from schools implementing restorative practices.* Bethlehem, PA:

International Institute for Restorative Practices Graduate School. Retrieved from http://www.iirp.edu/pdf/ImprovingSchoolClimate.pdf

Karp, D., & Breslin, B. (2001). Restorative justice in school communities. *Youth & Society, 33*(2), 249–272. doi:10.1177/0044118X01033002006.

Payne, A. A., & Welch, K. (2010). Modeling the effects of racial threat on punitive and restorative school discipline practices. *Criminology, 48*(4), 1019–1062.

Pranis, K. (1998). *Guide for implementing the balanced and restorative justice model.* Washington, DC: Office of Juvenile Justice and Delinquency Prevention, U.S. Department of Justice.

Skiba, R. J., Michael, R. S., Nardo, A. C., & Peterson, R. L. (2002). The color of discipline: Sources of racial and gender disproportionality in school punishment. *The Urban Review, 34*, 317–342. doi:10.1023/A:1021320817372.

Skiba, R. J., & Peterson, R. L. (2000). School discipline at a crossroads: From zero tolerance to early response. *Exceptional Children, 66*(3), 335–346.

Skiba, R. J., Shure, L. A., Middleberg, L. V., & Baker, T. L. (2011). Reforming school discipline and reducing disproportionality in suspension and expulsion. In S. R. Jimerson, A. B. Nickerson, M. J. Mayer, & M. J. Furlong (Eds.), *The handbook of school violence and school safety: International research and practice* (2nd Ed.) (pp. 515–528). New York: Routledge.

Steinberg, L., & Morris, A. M. (2001). Adolescent development. *Annual Review of Psychology, 52*, 83–110.

Stinchcomb, J., Bazemore, G., & Riestenberg, N. (2006). Beyond zero tolerance, Restoring justice in secondary school. *Youth Violence and Juvenile Justice, 4*(2), 123–147.

PART III

Conclusions and Implications

Eliminating Excessive and Disparate School Discipline: A Review of Research and Policy Reform

Daniel J. Losen and Leticia Smith-Evans Haynes

Nearly 3.5 million public school students were suspended out of school at least once in 2011–2012 (U.S. Department of Education Office for Civil Rights, 2014). That is more than one student suspended for every public school teacher in America (Losen, Hodson, Keith, Morrison, & Belway, 2015b). The growing national awareness of the disparate treatment of students on the basis of race by law enforcement authorities was piqued most recently by the video images of a Black female student being thrown from her chair by a White school resource officer, prompted by her refusal to put her cell phone away during class. The officer not only arrested the girl, but also her classmate who videotaped the incident and protested what she was witnessing (Pérez-Peña, Hauser, & Stolberg, 2015). Incidents like these have provoked school authorities across the country to consider how race and gender bias might affect their perceptions of and response to student behavior (Smith-Evans, George, Goss Graves, Kaufman, & Frohlich, 2014). While harsh disciplinary approaches

D.J. Losen (✉)
The Civil Rights Project, UCLA, Los Angeles, CA, USA

L.S-E. Haynes
Office of Institutional Diversity and Equity, Williams College, Williamstown, MA, USA

© The Author(s) 2016   245
R.J. Skiba et al. (eds.), *Inequality in School Discipline*,
DOI 10.1057/978-1-137-51257-4_14

may be more common in schools serving high percentages of historically disadvantaged youth, biased perceptions in all schools can lead educators to respond more severely when the behavior of children of color is at issue (Okonofua & Eberhardt, 2015). Factors in the school setting, such as the presence of school police and other high-security measures, may further contribute to these disparate disciplinary responses and weaken the relationship between students and educators (Finn & Servoss, 2015).

Schools face the imperative of providing safety for all members of the community while also ensuring that children receive the level of support, freedom, and developmentally appropriate responses to behavior found in optimal learning environments. Although the topic of school discipline is often discussed as a safety issue, most suspensions are not responses to safety concerns. Rather, discipline policy and practice have much more to do with how schools manage the learning environment. For example, in Texas, serious violent acts and safety-related rule violations trigger a "non-discretionary" mandatory removal, but these represent less than 5% of all disciplinary removals from school (Fabelo et al., 2011). In contrast, removals are routine for minor offenses like tardiness, truancy, using foul language, disruption, defiance, or cell phone possession (Losen, Martinez, & Okelola, 2014). This excessive use of harsh discipline for minor offenses is highly problematic. As former United States Secretary of Education Arne Duncan observed, "[A]s a nation, we are severely underestimating the traumatic impact of our children being subject to, or even just seeing or witnessing, unnecessary physical force and arrests in our schools and classrooms.... To do better, we also have to take a hard look at ourselves, our history, and the implicit bias that we all carry" (Duncan, 2015).

Of course, school authorities must address misbehavior, even if it does not raise immediate safety concerns. Removing a student from a classroom can be an appropriate response to help de-escalate a conflict or to access counseling and other support outside the classroom. Yet many of our nation's public schools are quick to remove students from school for relatively minor offenses (Losen, 2011). In some schools, harsh punishments are meted out even for minor, first-time rule infractions, while in others, repeated minor misbehavior can trigger automatic suspension, expulsion, or referrals to juvenile court to pay fines or serve jail time (Theriot, 2009). A growing body of research demonstrates that the most effective responses do not entail exclusion from school (González, 2015; Gregory et al., this volume). Rather, strategies like the Virginia threat assessment protocol help educators distinguish serious threats from more minor offenses, and ensure that the disciplinary response is both appropriate to the student's behavior and responsive to what they may need (Cornell & Lovegrove, 2015). Time spent in the classroom is one of the most consistent predictors of academic achievement (Ginsburg, Jordan, & Chang, 2014). Therefore, any unnecessary exclusion reduces the opportunity for learning, and undermines our national goals for educating all children.

Mounting evidence of the overuse of exclusionary discipline in our nation's schools, and the significant threat posed to students' opportunity to learn, has led to federal, state, and district action to shift policy and practice. This chapter reviews the status and consequences of discipline disparities, as well as policy efforts to curb overly punitive practices and their disparate impact on students of color.

EXCESSIVE DISCIPLINARY EXCLUSION HARMS SOME GROUPS OF CHILDREN MORE THAN OTHERS

A large proportion of public school students will be suspended during their middle and high school years, and Black students are most at risk. Most parents, school board members, and policymakers do not realize how often our public schools suspend students because these data are not published on an annual basis in the way that test scores and graduation rates are (Center for Civil Rights Remedies and Council of State Governments, 2013). Nonetheless, data suggests that suspension rates in many of America's schools are extremely high. While approximately 5% of students are suspended out-of-school during any given year (Losen & Gillespie, 2012), these rates have shown a steady rise since the early 1970s, when the number of students suspended was about half of what it is today. Further, the 5% risk in a given year does not capture the high likelihood of suspension that accrues over the course of a student's school career. New longitudinal research findings using a national database indicates that between one third and one half of all students surveyed experienced at least one suspension at some point between Kindergarten and twelfth grade (Shollenberger, 2015).

Moreover, data for the 2011–2012 academic year shows that, nationally, Black students face the highest risk of out-of-school suspension, followed by Native Americans and then Latinos, at both the elementary and secondary levels (Losen et al., 2015b). As depicted in Fig. 14.1, Black students in elementary school were suspended out of school at a rate that is 6 percentage points higher than their White peers. This Black/White gap expanded almost threefold as they moved into secondary (middle and high) school, resulting in a nearly 17-percentage point difference. Indeed,

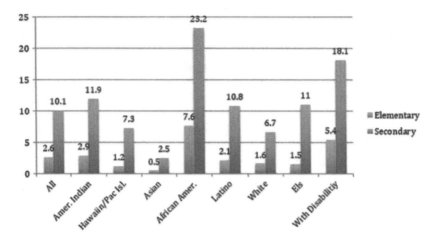

Fig. 14.1 Elementary and secondary suspension rates by subgroup, 2011–2012

across the nation, in just one year—2011–2012—nearly one of every four Black secondary school students was suspended at least one time.

These national averages do not fully capture the extent of the problem, given the wide variation in disciplinary approach within and across schools and districts. While many districts have low numbers of suspensions, others have staggering rates such as those in which well over 50% of the enrolled population are suspended in a single year (Losen et al., 2015b).

A cross-sectional analysis of gender and disability data shows extreme disparities. Data from the 2011–2012 school year shows that 34% of all enrolled Black male students with disabilities at the secondary level were suspended at least once (Losen et al., 2015b). Black female students also face significant disparities, and are at equal or greater risk of suspension compared with males of other racial/ethnic groups (Losen et al., 2015b). These disparities by race, gender, and disability status raise serious concerns about the extent to which some schools are meeting their legal obligation to educate all students.

Profound disparities are evident in rates of expulsion and school-based arrests, where the life consequences are severe. Compared to out-of-school suspensions, far fewer students are expelled, referred to law enforcement, or arrested, and the overall risks for these categories are typically no larger than 1% of any groups' enrollment (U.S. Department of Education National Projections, 2015). However, expulsion and arrest have much greater and more immediate impact, and the data are clear that Black students are disproportionately punished. While Black students represent 18% of enrolled public school students, they represent 39% of students expelled and 42% of referrals to law enforcement from school. Together, Black and Latino students represent 42% of the student body, but account for 72% of the students who are arrested for school-related offenses (U.S. Department of Education Office for Civil Rights, 2014).

These patterns mirror disparities in the juvenile justice system, where Black and Latino youth represent two-thirds of all those in detention and correctional facilities, despite comprising only one third of the country's adolescent population (National Council on Crime and Delinquency, 2007). In addition, data from a nationally representative population-based sample of adolescents indicate that LGBT youth are also at greater risk for expulsion than their heterosexual peers and are approximately 50% more likely to be stopped by the police than other youth (Himmelstein & Bruckner, 2011). Non-heterosexual girls, in particular, experienced about twice as many arrests and convictions as other girls who had engaged in similar transgressions.

RESEARCH SHOWS THAT THE HARM IS EXTENSIVE AND EXPENSIVE

The negative social and academic consequences of the over-reliance on exclusionary discipline to manage behavior are important for policymakers and practitioners to understand.

Frequent suspensions increase dropout risks and juvenile justice involvement. The potential impact of being suspended, even once, can be devastating. For example, a study tracking all ninth graders throughout high school and post-graduation in Florida found that being suspended just one time in Grade 9 was associated with a two-fold increase in the risk of dropping out, from 16% to 32% (Balfanz, Byrnes, & Fox, 2015). The *Breaking Schools' Rules* study that tracked Texas middle school students for six years (Fabelo et al., 2011) found that being removed on disciplinary grounds for a discretionary violation was associated with a nearly threefold increase in the likelihood of future contact with the juvenile justice system. In addition, a national longitudinal study revealed that suspension from school tended to precede serious delinquency, especially for Black and Latino children (Shollenberger, 2015).

The hidden costs of school exclusion are high. Out-of-school suspensions produce economic and social costs that are less obvious but enormously burdensome for school systems. For example, economists in Texas estimated a 13% increase in dropouts from the widespread use of suspension across the state, based on the *Breaking Schools' Rules* finding that 60% of all Texas middle school students had been suspended from the classroom. As a result, the state incurred between 700 million and 1 billion dollars annually in lost tax revenue and additional years of instruction for retained students (Marchbanks et al., 2015). Moreover, removal of students from the classroom can also negatively affect opportunities for higher education, since a significant number of colleges consider student school discipline records as part of the admissions process. A survey of colleges and universities found that 89% of institutions of higher education that collected school discipline records from prospective students used this information in their admissions decision making (Weissman & NaPier, 2015).

SCHOOL FACTORS, INCLUDING BIAS, CONTRIBUTE TO DISPARITIES IN DISCIPLINE

Behavioral differences do not explain the disparities. Research indicates that Black students are often disciplined more harshly than their White peers, even when engaging in the same conduct (Nicholson-Crotty, Birchmeier, & Valentine, 2009. Several studies indicate that racial disparities are far more likely to be found in the minor subjective offense categories (Fabelo et al., 2011), and that the racial disparities in suspensions are not sufficiently explained by differential misbehavior (Finn & Servoss, 2015; Skiba, Shure, & Williams, 2012) or poverty (Fabelo et al., 2011).

Data on disparities raises questions about the influence of stereotypes and unconscious bias. The hard-to-measure nature of implicit or unconscious bias makes it very difficult to prove a causal connection, but emerging research findings strongly suggest that bias may be one of several contributing factors to disparities in discipline (see e.g., Akalis, Banaji, & Kosslyn, 2008; Goff, Eberhardt, Williams, & Jackson, 2008). The clearest study indicating racial bias by teachers that affects disciplinary actions was recently reported by Okonofua and Eberhardt (2015), who found that when teachers of all races were each given the same narrative about a student's behavior, with the student's race randomly varied, those judging what they believed was a Black student's second misdeed were more likely to call for a suspension than if they believed the second time offender was White. Okonofua and Eberhardt suggest that, over time, with repeated exchanges, students may pick up on even subtle differences in treatment, which may in turn inspire repeated misbehavior and disengagement from school. Exactly how much influence bias has on teachers' and administrators' discipline decisions is just beginning to be explored. Given the research findings, it seems likely, however, that subtle forms of bias can affect whether the observed behaviors of different groups are perceived as differentially problematic, and can also influence the subjective decision regarding the appropriate response.

Differences in discipline may be reinforced by structural disparities. Many Black and other students of color attend schools that rely so heavily on safety and surveillance measures that they resemble correctional facilities more than educational institutions. Nationwide, 26% of Black students report passing through metal detectors when entering school compared with 5.4% of White students (Toldson, 2011). At the same time, Black students are significantly more likely to report feeling unsafe at their school. Civil rights advocates have long expressed concerns that the emphasis in funding and policy on putting police in schools might exacerbate extant disparities in referrals to law enforcement and school-based arrests (Toppo, 2015).

Effective and Promising Alternatives to Exclusionary Discipline and Interventions Can Reduce Racial Disparity

More effective practices can be found in thousands of schools across the country. Schools and districts vary widely in their use of suspensions, and many are successful in creating orderly, safe, and productive learning environments without excessive disciplinary exclusion. A national analysis of high- and low-suspending secondary schools suggests that 60% of schools employ more effective alternatives (Losen, Ee, Hodson, & Martinez, 2015a). In sheer numbers, approximately 8000 secondary schools from nearly 4,000 districts suspended fewer than 10% of every major subgroup enrolled (Losen & Martinez, 2013).

Greater awareness on the part of educators is already helping reduce excessive removals. In response to the concerns about exclusionary discipline, a number of states and districts have begun to change their practice. A preliminary analysis of data from these jurisdictions indicates a decline in suspension rates may already be occurring. For example, data on the 2011–2012 school year from Maryland, (Maryland State Department of Education, 2015), Wisconsin, (Wisconsin, Department of Public Instruction, 2015) and Connecticut (Connecticut State Department of Education, 2013), reports based on state-collected data from the 2011–2012, and in California, the 2013–2014, school year, show declining suspension rates for all students. Notably, in California, two consecutive years of reduction were observed for all racial and ethnic groups with lower suspensions for the catch-all category of disruption/defiance driving the downward trend (Losen, Keith, Hodson, Martinez, & Belway, 2015c).

Safe and effective schools are characterized by strong teacher-student and teacher-parent relationships and low suspension rates. A recent district-wide study of Chicago schools, controlling for student demographics and the safety of the neighborhood of the attending students, found that the quality of teacher-student and teacher-parent relationships was the strongest predictor of a strong sense of safety in the school building (Steinberg, Allensworth, & Johnson, 2015). While poverty and the crime levels in the community mattered, the study also found that lower suspension rates were correlated with the higher safety ratings found for "strong-relationship" schools serving students from high-crime neighborhoods.

A CHANGE IN DISCIPLINARY APPROACH IS UNDERWAY

Increasingly, federal and state policymakers are taking steps that de-emphasize student removals from school, yet help reduce disruptive behavior. State and federal efforts have included policy and legislative initiatives to expand and improve discipline data collection, analysis, and reporting; reform truancy laws; and limit out-of-school suspensions.

Federal Efforts

Among the most notable federal actions is the issuance in 2014 of guidance from the Department of Education's Office for Civil Rights (OCR) and Department of Justice (U.S. Department of Education, Office for Civil Rights and U.S. Department of Justice, 2014). That guidance alerted states and school districts to the harm that results from disciplinary disparities, and warned that failure to change harsh policies and practices in the face of more effective alternative approaches could constitute a violation of civil rights. Schools and districts whose patterns of disparity would support a finding of a disparate impact violation pursuant to federal regulations are obligated to use more effective methods that do not harm some groups of children more than others. Beginning in 2009, OCR expanded the school discipline data that school districts are required to report. It also negotiated more than 55 settlements with districts in response to complaints of racial disparity from advocates or prompted by federal compliance review, and at least 30 new complaints have been opened for investigation (Losen et al., 2015b).

In March 2015, members of Congress introduced the Supportive School Climate Act of 2015 to reduce suspensions, expulsions, and other overly punitive school disciplinary actions to improve youth outcomes. The Act would permit the use of federal funds for Positive Behavior Interventions and Supports (PBIS) when states do the following: (1) ensure that school discipline policies align with civil rights laws and are applied equally to all students; (2) provide technical assistance to state and local education professionals, including training on trauma-informed approaches; (3) coordinate efforts with local education agencies to maximize reintegration of students involved with the criminal and juvenile justice systems; (4) strengthen laws governing the coordination between school systems and correctional facilities, ensuring that once students are incarcerated, they have a meaningful opportunity to turn their lives around when released; (5) establish systems for sustained family and community engagement in schools; and (6) provide transparent reporting of data on suspensions, expulsions, disciplinary transfers and referrals, seclusion, restraint, and school-based arrests at the state and local level in both aggregated and disaggregated forms.

A May 2015 Report of the President's Task Force on 21st Century Policing called on law enforcement and school officials to work collaboratively to keep students in the classroom and ensure appropriate alternatives to suspension and expulsion are available. In addition, the Task Force encouraged the use of discipline as an instructional tool; the development of partnerships with community members, families, schools, and law enforcement; and minimizing law enforcement policies and procedures that stigmatize youth and marginalize their participation in schools and communities.

State Efforts

Following the 2011 *Breaking Schools' Rules* report, the Council of State Governments launched a consensus-building initiative among experts and stakeholders to identify and describe effective disciplinary practices and policy. The resulting *School Discipline Consensus Report* (Morgan, Salomon, Plotkin, & Cohen, 2014) highlights reform efforts by state policymakers as examples for others to follow. For example, Connecticut legislators passed a law requiring out-of-school suspension be used as a measure of last resort (Connecticut State Department of Education, 2013). In Colorado, state policymakers directed state education dollars to expand from a pilot program to system-wide implementation of restorative practices in Denver (González, 2015). And the state of Virginia mandated the formation of school-based teams to implement threat assessment protocols designed to prioritize prevention over punishment (Virginia Code § 22.1-79.4, 2013).

In September 2015, a law decriminalizing truancy in the state of Texas went into effect (Associated Press, 2015). As more than 100,000 students in the state were prosecuted for truancy-related misdemeanors in 2013 alone, these efforts stand to impact a significant number of students (Associated Press, 2015). April 2015 also marked a stay in the operations at one large Texas school district's truancy court, pending a review of the district's truancy procedures for disproportionality in the treatment of Black and Latino students (Elliott, 2015). Shortly thereafter, the Texas State Senate also voted to ease zero-tolerance policies in favor of helping students learn from minor infractions (Savage, 2015).

In March 2015, the Governor of West Virginia signed a truancy reform bill requiring school-based interventions before a student is referred to court for truancy and doubling the number of absences required before a referral is issued. The effort was made in response to a large increase in the number of children referred to the judicial system and the high costs of removing students from their home for missing school (Burdette, 2015). Shortly thereafter, the Governor signed a juvenile justice reform bill creating a $4.5 million initiative on restorative justice programs across the state (Jenkins, 2015).

In 2014, California lawmakers eliminated suspensions and expulsions of students in grades K-3 for "disruption or willful defiance," a category of behavioral offense that in 2011–2012 accounted for nearly 50% of all suspensions in the state K-12 schools (California Education Code § 48900, 2014). That same year, the Maryland Department of Education adopted new regulations requiring school districts to review data for significant disparities by race and student disability status, and to take steps to eliminate these disparities in three years (Blad, 2014). Local school districts were also required to reduce long-term out-of-school suspensions and expulsions, beginning with the 2014–2015 school year (Maryland State Department of Education, COMAR 13A.08.01, 2014). Similarly, in

Massachusetts, a new discipline reform law took effect in July 2014 that makes exclusion from school a last resort, and requires districts to provide academic assistance to students for the first ten days of exclusion, regardless of the offense. In addition, the law requires the collection, analysis, and dissemination of discipline data, disaggregated by race and ethnicity. Furthermore, where discipline disparities based on race and disability status are evident, the law requires that corrective action be taken.

In addition, two other states pushed for changes. Georgia altered its zero-tolerance weapons policy to refer only to firearms and gave boards of education discretion to modify expulsion or discipline of students who violate it (Georgia, Title 16, Act 575, 2014). In June 2014, the Louisiana State Legislature adopted SCR 134, a resolution urging schools to examine their discipline policies in light of the disproportionate impact on students of color (Broome, 2014).

And, beginning in 2014, Arkansas has required an annual report on school discipline, including data disaggregated by race and other factors (Arkansas Act 1329, 2013). In Texas, beginning in 2013, HB 2651 directs the commissioner of education to review school suspension/expulsion procedures with opportunity for public comment (Texas H. B. 2651, 2013). Washington State also made changes to its student discipline laws, in particular those that relate to re-engaging students after suspension (Washington State Legislature RCW 28A.600.022, 2013).

District Efforts

Federal guidance on "disparate impact" may have spurred better district practices. District actions in 2015 suggest that enforcement efforts and public reporting are succeeding in encouraging a shift in disciplinary approach. For example, the superintendent of the Oklahoma City Public Schools pledged to change disciplinary practice in response to an OCR investigation and news reports placing the district among the highest suspending in the nation (Wendler, 2015). While reform initiated in response to civil rights actions is encouraging, measures addressing the harmful and disparate impact of excessive suspension have been adopted without such pressure by school and district leaders who have come to realize the costs of the status quo and the benefits of alternative practices. For example, although not prompted by federal investigation, the Superintendent of the Visalia Unified School District in California took action to improve the school environment through non-punitive strategies that address and reduce the overuse of exclusionary discipline. Observing a decline in suspension rates, Superintendent Wheaton explained: "We did it on our own: We didn't jump into all of this to get this data to change … But obviously somewhere along the way, some of our initiatives started paying off … We need to think about suspension and when it's used and why it's used and what is the most effective way to change the behavior" (Paulson, 2015). Individual schools have made dramatic progress as well; Garfield High School in Los Angeles, for example, recently announced it had nearly eliminated all suspensions while improving graduation rates (Anderson, 2015).

CONCLUSION

Research, practice, and the actions of federal, state, and local leaders make it clear that schools can successfully and substantially reduce exclusionary and punitive discipline rates and racial disparities. Doing so in a manner that keeps students in the classroom and builds positive relationships among students and faculty can enhance teaching and learning and lead to better academic outcomes—in short, improving educational equity in both opportunity and outcomes. While more research on disciplinary alternatives is needed to further refine these reform efforts, there is enough information for policymakers to act now. Three essential steps will be important for federal, state, and local policymakers to take:

1. *Collect, analyze and report discipline data to the public at least annually.* Discipline data can help to gauge the quality of the school environment for students as well as educators. When reported annually, this data can help educators and the public to identify patterns of disciplinary exclusion and to assess the kinds of alternative interventions and practices that are needed. Reports should include the number of students that are suspended in-school, suspended out of school, arrested or referred to law enforcement, as well as the counts of suspensions, broken down by reasons for removal, and days of lost instruction. To monitor disparities, it is essential that data be disaggregated by race/ethnicity, gender, English Learner status, and disability status, and provided to the public in a manner that facilitates cross-sectional analyses (e.g., Black students with disabilities). Public reporting of state and local expenditures for resource officers and high-security measures can further help to inform policymakers' decisions. Educators at all levels also need to fully implement provisions of Individuals with Disabilities Education Act (IDEA) regarding the review of racial disparities in discipline for

students with disabilities and the triggering of resources for early intervening services. More frequent data collection and analysis throughout a school year may provide critical opportunities for intervention to reduce disparities and the number of suspensions overall.

2. *Invest in alternatives to punitive exclusion.* Funding for alternatives must include: training for teachers and administrators, revising codes of conduct, supporting students with special needs who exhibit behavioral challenges, and expanding monitoring and enforcement by federal and state civil rights agents. Research suggests that teacher in-service preparation should build skills in promoting higher levels of student engagement (see Gregory, Bell, & Pollock, this volume). In addition, all school employees who interact with students should be trained on the impact of explicit and implicit or unconscious bias.

3. *Align discipline policies, practices, and responses with the educational mission.* With accurate information in hand and funding available to support meaningful reforms, educators can evaluate whether school discipline policies and practices are aligned with the educational mission of public schools and are successfully fostering student engagement. Leaders at all levels of the educational system should routinely review and revise policies where necessary to eliminate racial disparities or reduce the number of exclusions from the classroom.

REFERENCES

Akalis, S. A., Banaji, M. R., & Kosslyn, S. M. (2008). Crime alert!: How thinking about a single suspect automatically shifts stereotypes toward an entire group. *Du Bois Review: Social Science Research on Race, 5,* 217–233. doi:10.1017/ S1742058X08080181.

Anderson, M. D. (2015, September 14). Will school-discipline reform actually change anything? *The Atlantic Magazine.* Retrieved from http://www.theatlantic.com/ education/archive/2015/09/will-school-discipline-reform-actually-change-anything/405157/

Arkansas Act 1329. (2013). Retrieved from ftp://www.arkleg.state.ar.us/ acts/2013/Public/ACT1329.pdf

Associated Press. (2015, June 20). Texas law decriminalizes school truancy. *The New York Times.* Retrieved from http://www.nytimes.com/2015/06/21/ us/texas-law-decriminalizes-school-truancy.html?_r=0

Balfanz, R., Byrnes, V., & Fox, J. (2015). Sent home and put off track: The antecedents, disproportionalities, and consequences of being suspended in the 9th grade. In D. J. Losen (Ed.), *Closing the school discipline gap: Equitable remedies for excessive exclusion* (pp. 17–30). New York: Teachers College Press.

Blad, E. (2014, January 29). Maryland adopts new discipline rule to address racial disparities, suspensions. *Education Week.* Retrieved from http://blogs.edweek. org/edweek/rulesforengagement/2014/01/maryland_adopts_new_discipline_rule_to_address_racial_disparities_suspensions.html

Broome, S. W. (2014). Louisiana Senate Concurrent Resolution No. 134. Retrieved from http://www.legis.la.gov/legis/ViewDocument.aspx?d=903045

Burdette, W. (2015, March 2). House passes truancy bill doubling number of allowed absences. *Charleston Daily Mail.* Retrieved from http://www.charlestondailymail.com/article/20150302/DM0104/150309861

California Education Code § 48900. (2014). Retrieved from http://leginfo.legislature.ca.gov/faces/billNavClient.xhtml?bill_id=201320140AB420

Center for Civil Rights Remedies and Council of State Governments. (2013). *Nation-wide survey of state education agencies' online school disciplinary data for students with disabilities (summer 2014).* San Francisco: Center for Civil Rights Remedies and Council of State Governments. Retrieved from http://civilrightsproject.ucla.edu/resources/projects/center-for-civil-rights-remedies/school-to-prison-folder/online-data-resources/nation-wide-survey-of-state-education-agencies2019-online-school-disciplinary-data

Connecticut State Department of Education. (2013). *Connecticut education data and research: Data tables for 2011-12 and 2012-13.* Hartford, CT: Connecticut State Department of Education. Retrieved from http://sdeportal.ct.gov/Cedar/WEB/ct_report/CedarHome.aspx

Cornell, D., & Lovegrove, P. (2015). Student threat assessment as a method of reducing school suspensions. In D. J. Losen (Ed.), *Closing the school discipline gap: Equitable remedies for excessive exclusion* (pp. 180–191). New York: Teachers College Press.

Council of State Governments (CSG). (2015). *Fifty-state survey of state education agencies' online school disciplinary data.* Washington, DC: Council of State Governments (CSG). Retrieved from http://csgjusticecenter.org/youth/school-discipline-consensus-project/online-school-disciplinary-data/

Duncan, A. (2015, October 30). Statement of U.S. Secretary of Education Arne Duncan on school discipline and civil rights. [Press release]. Retrieved from http://www.ed.gov/news/press-releases/statement-us-secretary-education-arne-duncan-school-discipline-and-civil-rights

Elliott, R. (2015, April 27). Fort Bend ISD suspends truancy procedures. *The Houston Chronicle.* Retrieved from http://www.chron.com/neighborhood/fortbend/news/article/Fort-Bend-ISD-suspends-truancy-procedures-6226182.php

Fabelo, T., Thompson, M. D. Plotkin, M., Carmichael, D., Marchbanks, M. P., & Booth, E. A. (2011). *Breaking schools' rules: A statewide study of how school discipline relates to students' success and juvenile justice involvement.* New York: Council of State Governments Justice Center, and College Station, TX: A&M University: Public Policy Research Institute. Retrieved from http://knowledgecenter.csg.org/kc/system/files/Breaking_School_Rules.pdf

Finn, J. D., & Servoss, T. J. (2015). Security measures and discipline in American high schools. In D. J. Losen (Ed.), *Closing the school discipline gap: Equitable remedies for excessive exclusion* (pp. 44–58). New York: Teachers College Press.

Georgia, Title 16, Act 575. (2014). Retrieved from http://www.legis.ga.gov/ Legislation/20132014/14sumdoc.pdf

Ginsburg, A., Jordan, P., & Chang, H. (2014). *Absences add up: How school attendance influences student success.* Attendance Works. Retrieved from http:// www.attendanceworks.org/wordpress/wp-content/uploads/2014/09/ Absences-Add-Up_September-3rd-2014.pdf

Goff, P. A., Eberhardt, J. L., Williams, M., & Jackson, M. C. (2008). Not yet human: Implicit knowledge, historical dehumanization, and contemporary consequences. *Journal of Personality and Social Psychology, 94,* 292–306. doi:10.1037/0022-3514.94.2.292.

González, T. (2015). Socializing schools: Addressing racial disparities in discipline through restorative justice. In D. J. Losen (Ed.), *Closing the school discipline gap: Equitable remedies for excessive exclusion* (pp. 151–165). New York: Teachers College Press.

Himmelstein, K. E. W., & Bruckner, H. (2011). Criminal-justice and school sanctions against nonheterosexual youth: A national longitudinal study. *Pediatrics, 127*(1), 49–57. Originally published online December 6, 2010. doi:10.1542/ peds.2009-2306.

Jenkins, J. (2015, April 2). Juvenile justice system going from patchwork to teamwork. *West Virginia Metro News.* Retrieved from http://wvmetronews. com/2015/04/02/juvenile-justice-system-going-from-patchwork-to-teamwork/

Losen, D. J. (2011). *Good discipline: Legislation for education reform.* Boulder, CO: National Education Policy Center. Retrieved from www.nepc.colorado. edu/files/NEPC-SchoolDiscipline-Losen-2-LB_Final.pdf

Losen, D. J., & Gillespie, J. (2012). *Opportunities suspended: The disparate impact of disciplinary exclusion from school.* Los Angeles, CA: The Center for Civil Rights Remedies at The Civil Right Project/Proyecto Derechos Civiles. Retrieved from https://civilrightsproject.ucla.edu/resources/projects/center-for-civil-rights-remedies/school-to-prison-folder/federal-reports/upcoming-ccrr-research/losen-gillespie-opportunity-suspended-2012.pdf

Losen, D. J., & Martinez, T. E. (2013). *Out of school and off track: The overuse of suspensions in American middle and high schools.* Los Angeles: The Center for Civil Rights Remedies at The Civil Right Project/Proyecto Derechos Civiles. Retrieved from https://civilrightsproject.ucla.edu/resources/projects/center-for-civil-rights-remedies/school-to-prison-folder/federal-reports/ out-of-school-and-off-track-the-overuse-of-suspensions-in-american-middle-and-high-schools

Losen, D. J., Ee, J., Hodson, C., & Martinez, T. (2015a). Disturbing inequities: Exploring the relationship between racial disparities in special education identification and discipline. In D. J. Losen (Ed.), *Closing the school discipline gap: Equitable remedies for excessive exclusion* (pp. 89–106). New York: Teachers College Press.

Losen, D. J., Hodson, C., Keith, M. A., Morrison, K., & Belway, S. (2015b). *Are we closing the school discipline gap?* Los Angeles: Report by Center for Civil Rights Remedies at the Civil Rights Project of UCLA. Retrieved from https://civilrightsproject.ucla.edu/resources/projects/center-for-civil-rights-remedies/school-to-prison-folder/federal-reports/are-we-closing-the-school-discipline-gap

Losen, D. J., Keith, II, M. A., Hodson, C. L., Martinez, T. E., & Belway, S. (2015c). *Closing the school discipline gap in California: Signs of progress.* Los Angeles: Center for Civil Rights Remedies at UCLA's Civil Rights Project. Retrieved from http://static.politico.com/38/c7/1289eff0461fbd85a9f94a3ee7cf/ucla-closing-the-gap-suspension-report.pdf

Losen, D. J., Martinez, T. E., & Okelola, V. (2014). *Keeping California's kids in school: Fewer students of color missing school for minor misbehavior.* Los Angeles: The Center for Civil Rights Remedies at the Civil Rights Project of UCLA. Retrieved from https://civilrightsproject.ucla.edu/resources/projects/center-for-civil-rights-remedies/school-to-prison-folder/summary-reports/keeping-californias-kids-in-school

Marchbanks III, M. P., Blake, J. J., Booth, E. A., Carmichael, D., Seibert, A. L., & Fabelo, T. (2015). The economic effects of exclusionary discipline on grade retention and high school dropout. In D. J. Losen (Ed.), *Closing the school discipline gap: Equitable remedies for excessive exclusion* (pp. 59–74). New York: Teachers College Press.

Maryland State Department of Education, COMAR 13A.08.01. (2014). Retrieved from http://www.marylandpublicschools.org/stateboard/boardagenda/01282014/Tab_H_COMAR_13A.08.01_DisciplineRegulations_Adoption.pdf

Maryland State Department of Education. (2015). *Suspensions, expulsions, and health related exclusions: Maryland Public Schools 2012–2013.* Retrieved from http://marylandpublicschools.org/MSDE/divisions/planningresultstest/doc/20122013Student/susp13.pdf

Morgan, E., Salomon, N., Plotkin, M., & Cohen, R. (2014). *The school discipline consensus report: Strategies from the field to keep students engaged in school and out of the juvenile justice system.* New York: Council of State Governments. Retrieved from https://csgjusticecenter.org/wp-content/uploads/2014/06/The_School_Discipline_Consensus_Report.pdf

National Council on Crime and Delinquency. (2007). *And justice for some: Differential treatment of youth of color in the justice system.* Oakland, CA: National Council on Crime and Delinquency. Retrieved from http://www.nccdglobal.org/sites/default/files/publication_pdf/justice-for-some.pdf.

Nicholson-Crotty, S., Birchmeier, Z., & Valentine, D. (2009). Exploring the impact of school discipline on racial disproportion in the juvenile justice system. *Social Science Quarterly, 90*(4), 1003–1018. doi:10.1111/j.1540-6237.2009.00674.x.

Okonofua, J. A., & Eberhardt, J. L. (2015). *Two strikes: Race and the disciplining of young students. Psychological Science, 26*(5), 617–624.

Paulson, A. (2015, February 23). Schools' reliance on suspension expulsion isn't necessary report finds. *The Christian Science Monitor.* Retrieved from http://www.csmonitor.com/USA/2015/0223/Schools-reliance-on-suspension-expulsion-isn-t-necessary-report-finds

Pérez-Peña, R., Hauser, C., & Stolberg, S. G. (2015, October 28). Rough student arrest puts spotlight on school police. *New York Times.* Retrieved from http://www.nytimes.com/2015/10/29/us/police-officers-in-schools.html?_r=0

President's Task Force on 21st Century Policing. (2015). *Final report of the President's Task Force on 21st Century Policing.* Washington, DC: Office of Community Oriented Policing Services. Retrieved from http://www.cops.usdoj.gov/pdf/taskforce/taskforce_finalreport.pdf

Savage, J. (2015, April 23). Senate votes to loosen school zero-tolerance policies. *Texas Observer.* Retrieved from http://www.texasobserver.org/senate-votes-to-loosen-school-zero-tolerance-policies/

Shollenberger, T. L. (2015). Racial disparities in school suspension and subsequent outcomes: Evidence from the national longitudinal survey of youth. In D. J. Losen (Ed.), *Closing the school discipline gap: Equitable remedies for excessive exclusion* (pp. 31–43). New York: Teachers College Press.

Skiba, R. J., Chung, C. G., Trachok, M., Baker, T., Sheya, A., & Hughes, R. (2015). Where should we intervene? Contributions of behavior, student, and school characteristics to out-of-school suspension. In D. J. Losen (Ed.), *Closing the school discipline gap: Equitable remedies for excessive exclusion* (pp. 132–146). New York: Teachers College Press.

Skiba, R. J., Shure, L., & Williams, N. (2012). Racial and ethnic disproportionality in suspension and expulsion. In A. L. Noltemeyer & C. S. Mcloughlin (Eds.), *Disproportionality in education and special education* (pp. 89–118). Springfield, IL: Charles C. Thomas Publisher, Ltd..

Smith-Evans, L., George, J., Goss Graves, F., Kaufman, L. S., & Frohlich, L. (2014). *Unlocking opportunity for African American girls: A call to action for educational equity.* New York: NAACP Legal Defense and Educational Fund, and Washington, DC: National Women's Law Center. Retrieved from http://www.nwlc.org/sites/default/files/pdfs/unlocking_opportunity_for_african_american_girls_report.pdf

Steinberg, M. P., Allensworth, E., & Johnson, D. W. (2015). What conditions support safety in urban schools? The influence of school organizational practices on student and teacher reports of safety in Chicago. In D. J. Losen (Ed.), *Closing the school discipline gap: Equitable remedies for excessive exclusion* (pp. 118–131). New York: Teachers College Press.

Supportive School Climate Act of 2015, S. 811, H.R. 1435, 114th Cong. (2015). Retrieved from https://www.govtrack.us/congress/bills/114/s811

Texas H. B. 2651. (2013). Retrieved from http://www.legis.state.tx.us/tlodocs/83R/billtext/pdf/HB02651I.pdf

Texas SB107, 2015-2016, 84th Legislature. (2015, June 20). LegiScan. Retrieved from https://legiscan.com/TX/bill/SB107/2015

Theriot, M. (2009). School resource officers and the criminalization of student behavior. *Journal of Criminal Justice, 37*(3), 280–287.

Toldson, I. A. (2011). *Breaking barriers 2: Plotting the path away from juvenile detention and toward academic success for school-age African American males.* Washington, DC: Congressional Black Caucus Foundation, Inc., Center for Policy Analysis and Research. Retrieved from http://www.cbcfinc.org/oUploadedFiles/BreakingBarriers2.pdf

Toppo, G. (2015, October 28). Civil rights groups: Cops in schools don't make students safer. *USA Today.* Retrieved from http://www.usatoday.com/story/news/2015/10/28/school-resource-officer-civil-rights/74751574/

U.S. Department of Education, National Projections. (2015). *2011-12 Discipline Estimations by State, 2011-12 Discipline Estimations by Discipline Type, 2011-12 Discipline Estimations by Disability Status, 2011-12 Discipline Estimations by Enrollment.* Retrieved from http://ocrdata.ed.gvo/StateNational/Estimations/Projections_2011_12

U.S. Department of Education Office for Civil Rights. (2014). *Civil rights data collection. Data snapshot: School Discipline.* Washington, DC: U.S. Department of Education Office for Civil Rights. Retrieved from http://ocrdata.ed.gov/Downloads/CRDC-School-Discipline-Snapshot.pdf

U.S. Department of Education, Office for Civil Rights and U.S. Department of Justice. (2014). *Dear colleague letter: Nondiscriminatory administration of school discipline.* Retrieved from http://www2.ed.gov/about/offices/list/ocr/letters/colleague-201401-title-vi.pdf

Virginia Code § 22.1-79.4. (2013). *Threat assessment teams and oversight committees.* Retrieved from http://law.justia.com/codes/virginia/2013/title-22.1/chapter-7/section-22.1-79.4

Washington State Legislature RCW 28A.600.022. (2013). Retrieved from http://apps.leg.wa.gov/rcw/default.aspx?cite=28A.600.022

Weissman, M., & NaPier, E. (2015, May). Education suspended: The use of high school disciplinary records in college admissions. Brooklyn, NY: Center for Community Alternatives. Retrieved from http://www.communityalternatives.org/publications/publications.html

Wendler, E. (2015, March 25). *High suspension rates at Oklahoma City Public Schools trigger systemic changes. KOSU.* Retrieved from http://kosu.org/post/high-suspension-rates-oklahoma-city-public-schools-trigger-systemic-changes#stream/0

Wisconsin Department of Public Instruction. (2015). *ACT participation continues steady increase.* Madison, WI: Wisconsin Department of Public Instruction. Retrieved from http://wisedash.dpi.wi.gov/Dashboard/portalHome.jsp

CHAPTER 15

Conclusion: Moving Toward Equity in School Discipline

Russell J. Skiba

We stand at a critical juncture in the struggle for civil rights in our nation. White House initiatives addressing excellence in African American and Latino programming, removal of Confederate flags and symbols in states throughout the South, and a rapid national shift in attitudes toward sexual orientation—all of these bespeak a new openness in the national dialogue to confronting and addressing issues of inequity. Yet we see dramatic and often tragic evidence of continuing discrimination on almost a daily basis. Between April 2014 and November 2015, there were at least 16 nationally publicized incidents where an apparently unarmed Black man, woman, or child has been killed by police or in police custody—including the shooting of Michael Brown by Officer Darren Wilson in Ferguson, Missouri on August 9, 2014. The actual number of deaths is probably higher.[1]

The same paradox is apparent on a day-to-day basis in the treatment and outcomes of school discipline. Numerous federal and state initiatives have called for reductions in the rate of exclusionary discipline, and highlighted the importance of closing the discipline gap. Initiatives such as the Discipline Disparities Research to Practice Collaborative and the Council for State Government's School Discipline Consensus project have created momentum for national and local policy reform. Millions of students continue to be removed from school for disciplinary reasons each year,

R.J. Skiba
The Equity Project, Indiana University, Bloomington, IN, USA

© The Author(s) 2016
R.J. Skiba et al. (eds.), *Inequality in School Discipline*,
DOI 10.1057/978-1-137-51257-4_15

263

however, despite evidence that suspension and expulsion are ineffective and create short- and long-term risks for excluded students. Moreover, the differential use of exclusionary discipline by race has grown substantially in the past 40 years, and we now know that this unequal treatment extends to gender, disability, and sexual orientation as well.

Yet the chapters in this book also hold out grounds for hope, providing important new directions in interventions intended specifically to address inequities in school discipline. They describe approaches from restorative justice to implicit bias training, specific programs and comprehensive school-wide strategies, that hold promise for closing the discipline gap. Across the three years of study that these chapters represent, what have we learned?

PROXIMATE CAUSES OF DISPARITIES IN DISCIPLINE

What Is the Role of Poverty and Misbehavior in the Discipline Gap?

The poverty hypothesis. Poverty is a deep dividing line in our society. There is a profound gap experienced by rich and poor students in the safety of their neighborhoods, the personal traumas they endure on a daily basis, and the availability of community opportunities. These burdens of inequality serve as powerful barriers to school success, and these disadvantages are further exacerbated by schools with poor facilities, few resources, and a transient and less highly qualified teaching force.

So it is no surprise that low-income students face discipline more frequently, and are consistently over-represented in the use of out-of-school suspension (Brantlinger, 1991; Noltemeyer & Mcloughlin, 2010). A variety of variables typically associated with poverty, including presence of mother or father in the home, number of siblings, and quality of home resources, are significantly associated with the likelihood of suspension (Hinojosa, 2008). The rapidly growing field of trauma-informed care has at its heart the notion that students bearing the brunt of family and community poverty must be supported, and services provided to address the trauma left in the wake of poverty and extreme disadvantage.

Yet there is something more at work than poverty in explaining widespread disparities in the use of out-of-school suspension and expulsion. Although poverty influences rates of suspension and expulsion, multivariate analyses have shown that race remains a significant predictor of Black over-representation in suspension, even after holding poverty constant (see Skiba et al., this volume). While African American students in poverty are more likely to be suspended than poor White students, middle- and upper-class Black students are also more likely to be suspended than their peers at the same demographic level.

Blake and her colleagues' data once again reaffirm this finding in their chapter. In their analyses, controlling for a wide variety of sociodemographic variables, both race and poverty remain, independently of one another, among the strongest predictors of discipline. To be clear, this means that poverty is a risk factor for school discipline, but that race, *in and of itself*, is also a powerful predictor of school exclusion, regardless of level of poverty or a host of other factors. This data once again support Noltemeyer and Mcloughlin's (2010) conclusion that "there is something above and beyond poverty that explains disciplinary differences" (p. 33).

Differential behavior or differential treatment? School discipline is often assumed to be a straightforward linear process, in which students who disrupt schools or classrooms are referred to the office to be processed by administrators bound by a standard code of conduct. Yet in reality, the line from student behavior to classroom referral to office discipline is complex and non-linear, dependent on teacher tolerance, classroom management capabilities, administrator preference, and variations in school and district policy (Morrison et al., 2001).

In the same way, higher rates of suspension by race, gender, or sexual orientation are often viewed as a sign that those groups are engaging in differential rates of disruption. Yet to date there has been little or no support in the research literature for the notion that disproportionality in suspension for some groups is due to more severe behavior on the part of those students. As Skiba and colleagues (this volume) note, Black students are referred more frequently to the office, even when statistically controlling for misbehavior, and receive harsher punishments for the same or lesser behavior: Racial differences in discipline appear to be caused less by type of behavior or student characteristics than by school factors such as perspective on discipline.

In this volume, Poteat and his colleagues use discipline data for LGBT students to conduct one of the most sophisticated analyses to date, comparing the contributions to disciplinary disparities by both student behavior and systems characteristics. Drawing upon minority stress theory, Poteat et al. argue that the harsh and negative climate faced by non-heterosexual students increases their chances of engaging in behaviors—such as drinking or weapon-carrying—that are more likely to be disciplined. Yet, the statistical findings suggest that the contribution of differential student behavior is significant but not strong. There is stronger support for the differential processing hypothesis—once referred to the office, LGBT students are more likely to receive more serious consequences for the same or similar infractions. Poteat and colleagues' findings join other work (see e.g., Skiba et al., 2014) in suggesting that although student behavior clearly makes a contribution to determining who will be disciplined, decisions at the administrative level are as strong or stronger in predicting disciplinary disparities.

The School Climate for Marginalized Students

School climate and student perceptions of it are key factors in predicting learning outcomes. Student perceptions of a positive school climate have been found to be associated with higher academic achievement (see e.g., Brand, Felner, Shim, Seitsinger, & Dumas, 2003). Students who rate their school's climate more positively engage in fewer risk-taking and violent behaviors (Resnick et al., 1997) and show lower rates of problem behavior in general (Brand et al., 2003; Wang, Selman, Dishion, & Stormshak, 2010).

The advent of zero-tolerance philosophy and steady increases in the use of suspension and expulsion created a shift in many schools toward a more punitive and exclusionary orientation, with a corresponding negative effect on perceptions of school climate (see e.g., Steinberg, Allensworth, & Johnson, 2015), especially for students of color. Schools rated by their students as having low levels of support and academic expectations evidence the highest rates of suspension and the largest Black-White suspension gap (Gregory, Cornell, & Fan, 2011). African American students hold more negative perceptions of school climate and racial fairness than their White peers; these negative ratings have been associated with higher rates of detention and suspension (Kupchik & Ellis, 2008; Mattison & Aber, 2007).

One of the more disturbing findings in this volume is the negative, indeed hostile, climate that frequently greets students of differing sexual orientation or gender identity. Across three chapters, the experiences of LGBT/queer youth were documented through individual interviews (Bellinger and colleagues), focus groups (Snapp and Russell), and a mixed method approach involving both survey and follow-up interviews

(Chmielewski and colleagues). In all three, the voices of LGBT youth are strikingly consistent in describing school climates that not only fail to support them, but often actively single them out for harassment and punishment.

School environments that are unsafe for LGBT students. Across their surveys of youth, Chmielewski and her colleagues found that LGBTQ students of color, regardless of their gender, felt less safe in schools. Respondents in all three chapters reported verbal harassment and even physical attacks by their peers. Unfortunately, threats to the safety and well-being of LGBT youth may come not only from other students, but sometimes from school staff as well. Students interviewed by Bellinger and colleagues' reported hearing words like "fag" or "queer" from school security agents or administrative deans. In one startling incident described by Chmielewski and colleagues, a lesbian student reported being taunted by a police officer while she was handcuffed to a railing. Such reports of verbal or even physical aggression by school staff cannot be taken lightly, especially given the consequences of such treatment. Reports by the students in these chapters of mental health issues and higher rates of school dropout echo previous literature on the higher risk of a range of mental health issues for LGBT students subjected to verbal and physical harassment (Russell, Everest, Rosario, & Birkett, 2014).

Failure to report. Non-heterosexual students may not feel safe in reporting incidents of bullying and harassment in part because, as Bellinger and colleagues point out, they feel that nothing will be done about it. Without adequate response from school officials in the face of bullying and harassment, there is no protection for the victims. Indeed, LGBT students who spoke with Snapp and Russell reported that they feared retribution from the students who had harassed them if they did report.

Differentially disciplined. Although the disciplinary environment in our nation's schools has become more punitive over time for all students, marginalized students, whether by race/ethnicity, disability, or sexual orientation, are at even greater risk of being disciplined in punitive environments. Chmielewski and colleagues found that gender non-conforming LGBQ girls had the highest rates in their sample for both in- and out-of-school suspension. Queer students interviewed by Bellinger et al. reported that the same infractions that led them into the discipline system were ignored when committed by male, heterosexual students. Snapp and Russell, recounting the story of a young man kept out of class for most of the school day when he was found with nail polish passing through a metal detector, suggest that the differential discipline of LGBT students falls at the intersection of "heightened surveillance and adult biases about appropriate gender expression" (p. 210).

The intersection of race and sexual orientation. As in research on the intersection of race and disability (see Losen and Smith-Evans Haynes, this volume), risks of differential treatment appear to be additive when one is a gay or lesbian student of color. In Bellinger et al., queer students reported that schools were more likely to respond negatively to non-heteronormative gender expression for students of color than for White students. At the same time, Chmielewski and colleagues' surveys revealed that LGBT youth of color were 1.5 times more likely to be suspended than straight youth of color.

Lack of supports for students. The students who spoke in these chapters were not merely passive victims—some actively pressed for policy reform or helped found a Gay Straight Alliance (GSA) at their schools. But that initiative is frequently offset by continuing declines in the availability of mental health resources for all students, while the absence of support networks and policies countering bullying and harassment constitute a more specific lack of support for LGBTQ students. Snapp and Russell suggest that climates hostile to LGBT students may be due to a combination of insufficient training and homophobia, while Bellinger and colleagues recommend training all school personnel in recognizing and responding in an appropriate manner to issues of gender and gender non-conformity.

Cultural Synchrony and Implicit Bias

To what extent do cultural mismatch or bias contribute to unequal discipline in our schools? Directly addressing the topic of race is awkward and uncomfortable, and can create its own resistance and pushback, especially from educators who fear being labeled as racist (Trepagnier, 2006). Yet, given a long national history of deeply entrenched individual and institutional racism and stereotyping, the possibility that cultural mismatch or historical biases persist must be explored.

While school populations become progressively more diverse, the teaching force in most areas of the nation remains overwhelmingly White and female (King, 2005), begging the question whether this mismatch contributes to the discipline gap. Blake et al. begin that exploration in their study of cultural synchrony, the theory that disciplinary disparities are due in part to a mismatch of race/ethnicity between students and school staff, leading to misunderstanding and the possibility of bias.

Across a comprehensive longitudinal database, they found that Black and Latino students, as well as female students, were more likely to be referred for disciplinary action in schools characterized by a lack of congruence between students and teachers. In particular, Black students in schools with fewer Black staff were 44% more likely than their peers to be disciplined, at least between 7th and 12th grade. Certainly, these data suggest the need for redoubling efforts to diversify our nation's teaching force and for the innovative tiered approach to teacher training the authors suggest to improve the cultural responsiveness of all school staff.

Numbers indicating a lack of staff-student congruence do not in and of themselves prove that bias or stereotype is responsible for discipline disparities; yet evidence that bias and stereotype do contribute to racial disparities continues to build. Kahn and colleagues, reviewing extensive literature on stereotype and bias, found that although explicit racial stereotypes and bias may be in retreat, a) extensive research using the Implicit Association Test (see e.g., Nosek et al., 2007) has found that the majority of Americans hold some form of pro-White, anti-Black bias, often unconscious and unintentional; b) that such biases have been documented in law enforcement, influencing key decisions (e.g., shoot/no shoot) in video simulations; and c) that such stereotypes have been documented among teachers, affecting their judgment about school achievement among different groups.

As of now, it is difficult to estimate what proportion of disparity in school discipline is due to bias or stereotype. Yet a deep history of vicious and corrosive stereotypes for non-White and non-heteronormative groups, and steadily accumulating evidence that those stereotypes remain embedded in our consciousness today (Carter, Skiba, Arredondo, & Pollock, 2014), make it a topic of key importance. For victims of police over-reaction in cities across the nation, the results of lingering stereotypes have too often been deadly. In our nation's schools, it is plausible that the enactment of bias places far too many young people at risk for school exclusion, seriously harming their chances of success in school and in life.

WHAT ARE THE MOST PROMISING DISPARITY-REDUCING STRATEGIES?

One of the key goals of the Discipline Disparities Research to Practice Collaborative when first convened in 2010 was to address the significant shortage of research-based intervention strategies for reducing inequity in school discipline. At the time, although programmatic strategies such as Positive Behavioral Interventions and Supports, restorative justice, and social-emotional learning were identified as promising means of reducing suspension and expulsion (Osher, Bear, Sprague, & Doyle, 2010), there were virtually no tests of these or any other strategy targeted specifically at closing the discipline gap. Fortunately, in the intervening period, there has been substantial growth in the availability of intervention strategies specifically intended to do just that.

Gregory, Bell, and Pollock (2014) outline the most comprehensive model to date to guide educators in addressing and reducing disparities in school discipline. Drawing upon both evidence-based interventions such as My Teaching Partner, restorative justice, and threat assessment, and practical and common sense strategies for teachers and administrators, Gregory and her colleagues argue that both *conflict prevention* and *conflict reduction* are needed to reform school discipline and reduce disparities.

The five chapters in this volume describing specific disparity-reducing interventions are the result of intervention research commissioned by the Discipline Disparities Collaborative. Some of those chapters (Gregory and Clawson; Vincent et al.) provide empirical tests of the efficacy of intervention programs for disparity reduction, while others (Schotland et al.; Yusuf et al.) describe school-based strategies for changing school or teacher practice. Kahn and her colleagues describe a model for training police officers, teachers, and school administrators in recognizing and overcoming implicit bias and masculinity threat. Some clear and consistent themes emerged across these important new approaches:

The importance of multicomponent interventions. Disciplinary disparities are complex, driven by behavior, student, and school characteristics, suggesting that intervention strategies to reduce disparities must also be complex and multifaceted. Schotland and colleagues described a three-part strategy that included Restorative Circles, No Bully Solution Teams, and Peer Court to reduce the use of school suspension at Davidson Middle School. Similarly, Vincent and her colleagues combined two strategies—restorative justice and School-wide Positive Behavioral Interventions and Supports (SWPBIS)—to achieve more promising results in terms of disparity reduction.

Relationships are key. The importance of relationship-building—between educators, students, and parents—has been one of the more significant recent findings in the field of school discipline, often spelling the difference between de-escalation and problem-solving within the classroom, and confrontation that cycles up to school exclusion or even the use of force or arrest. Gregory and Clawson found that those teachers who engaged in affective statements to build interpersonal relationships with their students were more effective than their peers in reducing or even eliminating discipline gaps by race and sexual preference. Similarly, the success of the restorative interventions at Davidson Middle appeared to be built to a large measure on relationships—from parents who expressed their disappointment in their son or daughter in Peer Court, to improved student-teacher relationships in classrooms implementing Restorative Circles.

Not yet elimination, but clear reductions in disparities. All of these chapters describe implementation over a relatively short term—sometimes only one year. So it is not surprising that these interventions all reduced disparities, but did not always eliminate discipline gaps. Schoolwide Positive and Restorative Discipline (SWPRD) eliminated the gap in racial fairness between White and Latino students, and the gap in perceptions of the extent of bullying and harassment between LGBT and heterosexual students; all racial/ethnic groups saw decreases in their rates of Office Disciplinary Referrals (ODRs), and the gap between White and Latino ODR rates closed. Neither Schotland nor Gregory and Clawson reported a complete elimination of racial/ethnic disparities. Yet these chapters also document that schools dedicated to rethinking discipline also showed reductions in inequity: Davidson Middle School's programs cut Latino/White disciplinary inequity in half, while Gregory and Clawson found that those teachers who implemented Restorative Practices (RP) with greater fidelity were able to reduce African American and Latino disparities in defiance referrals for males, and completely eliminate those gaps for African American and Latino females.

Effective programs demand educator buy-in and time for reflection. Systems reform is challenging, and cannot be accomplished without buy-in from frontline educators and law enforcement personnel, who need time to reflect on why change is important, as well as sufficient resources and training to implement alternative approaches. The reform efforts described in these chapters suggest that implementation of new initiatives may grow slowly, or even face resistance, if teachers are not sufficiently engaged in the process of reform. Yet when frontline education and criminal justice personnel participate in the design and execution of reform, their engagement in the change process can yield creative and promising results. The facilitated discussion highlighting discipline disparities led by Yusuf and colleagues allowed teachers to reflect on their own responsibility for the discipline gap, and generate a response grid focused on reducing the use of exclusionary and punitive approaches to discipline. Kahn and colleagues have delved deeply into the research on implicit bias to design a comprehensive training program for police, teachers, and school administrators to raise awareness and reduce the influence of implicit bias and masculinity threat. Their promising pilot results suggest that it is possible for educators and law enforcement personnel to identify their own biases and stereotypes, and, more importantly, keep those from affecting their interactions with students who are otherwise at risk of facing disproportionate discipline.

How Do We Get to Enduring Change and Disparity Reduction?

As Losen and Smith-Evans Haynes note in their chapter on policy, the recent pace of policy change in school discipline has been remarkable. Strong new policy changes at the federal, state, and district levels have called for limiting the use of suspension to only the most serious infractions, and have begun to provide support for a range of more effective and equitable practices.

Yet, although the enunciation of policy change at the federal, state, or even district level provides a basis for change, it in no way guarantees effective reform at the local school level. Media reports have already documented pushback from local educators concerned that rhetoric may not be backed up by resources (Sperry, 2015). To ensure sustainable change, federal and state policies must translate into school-based implementation, training, and resources for educators dealing with day-to-day discipline issues. Recommendations for policy, practice, and research have been made throughout this volume, across the following dimensions:

Expand the Availability and Use of Data for Documenting Disciplinary Disparities

The continuing availability of comprehensive, universal, and disaggregated discipline data serves as the keystone for monitoring and remediating disproportionality. State, district, and school data can provide information for those seeking to understand or change disciplinary practices. Yet the lack of local availability or lack of use of that data suggests a number of recommendations:

- *Ensure that disaggregated suspension and expulsion data are available for all states, districts, and schools.* The collection of disciplinary data varies greatly, even at the state level. While most districts and schools collect disciplinary data, it is often difficult for community members to access it.

- *Continue to study all groups for whom there is disproportionality in discipline.* African American males remain the group most likely to be harmed by the overuse of exclusionary discipline. Yet it is striking how many other groups—students with disabilities, African American females, Latino and American Indian students, LGBT students—are also at a disproportionate risk of removal from school for disciplinary reasons. The true extent of these disparities calls into question the inclusiveness and responsiveness of our educational systems for large numbers of students caught up in the web of disciplinary exclusion.
- *Expand data collection and availability for LGBT students.* The fear of identifying students as LGBT who may not have as yet self-identified is clearly a barrier to collecting reliable data on discipline and harassment by sexual orientation. Yet, while the concern for the right of privacy is important, the threats of bullying and disparities in discipline suggest that another right—namely the right to have inequitable treatment documented—may be violated by failing to collect and report such data (see e.g., Snapp, Russell, Skiba, Arredondo, & Gray, in press).
- *Provide guidance on using and understanding data.* The availability of data does not always ensure that such data will be used or understood. Institutionalization of data analysis, one of the key features of school discipline reform in systems such as School-Wide Positive Behavior Interventions and Supports (Sprague & Horner, 2007), can help ensure that data are part of a self-reflective process for creating and monitoring the impact of school reform. In particular, resources that train practitioners and policymakers in the meaning of disproportionality data[2] are useful in empowering local schools and communities to understand and utilize trends and patterns in their own findings.

Continue to Test, Refine, and Support Interventions, Including Local Initiatives

As findings on the ineffectiveness and inequity of punitive and exclusionary discipline continue to drive policy reform, pressure will build on schools and school districts to replace exclusion with more effective and equitable practices. The research presented in this volume represents a quantum leap forward in testing interventions designed specifically to reduce disparities in discipline. Scale-up and more sophisticated randomized treatment-control studies are obviously needed, but so is research that, in a period of rapid change, can document the process and outcomes of local reforms:

- *Study how local schools and districts implement disciplinary reform.* Although evidence-based research validating disparity-reducing interventions is critical, the presence of such research does not guarantee that schools can or will implement such alternatives with fidelity (see Yusuf and colleagues, this volume). More research is needed highlighting exemplars who have undertaken change "from the ground up." School-based implementation research at sites like Davidson Middle School provide a rich guide for educators and advocates seeking practical strategies for changing disciplinary outcomes in their own community. Ultimately, districts that currently have lower rates of exclusion and lower rates of suspension/expulsion have much to teach others on how effective reform might be implemented.
- *Provide sufficient resources to support change.* Without adequate understanding of the need for change or sufficient training and resources to accomplish it, successful reform may be unattainable. Federal initiatives such as the Supportive School Discipline Initiative, the *National Leadership Summit on School Discipline*, the White House *Rethink School Discipline*, and school discipline/school climate grants from the Department of Justice and Department of Education have provided a promising start.

To Reduce and Eliminate Racial Disparities, It Is Necessary to Confront the Topic of Race

Inequities documented in our schools and society are rooted in a 400-year history of oppression and discrimination that has left us with stereotypes and biases that remain embedded in our personal and collective consciousness (see Carter et al., 2014), acted out in both tragic deadly encounters in our communities and in micro-aggressions in our classrooms and schools (Howard, 2008). The difficulty and awkwardness of talking about race, disadvantage, and privilege has been widely documented (Pollock, 2009; Singleton & Linton, 2005; Solomon et al., 2005). Yet it is not possible to close achievement or discipline gaps without confronting and working through issues of race and other differences. To avoid what Pollock (2009) has referred to as "clumsy race talk" and to create safe spaces for school personnel to openly discuss issues of race and difference inherent in many disciplinary incidents, Carter et al. (2014) provide a number of recommendations:

- Model a willingness to ask awkward and difficult questions (Pollock, 2009).
- Acknowledge that mistakes will be made when speaking about race (Tatum, 2006).
- Acknowledge that participants will experience discomfort while considering and discussing experiences/perspectives different from their own (Singleton & Linton, 2005).
- Use "race teachable moments" (Border Crossers, 2011), when students' comments, questions, and classroom incidents about race or racism surface, to sustain critical conversations about inequity.

CONCLUSIONS

A national consensus has begun to emerge that over-reliance on disciplinary removal is ineffective and reinforces inequity in our society (American Psychological Association Zero Tolerance Task Force. 2008), and that it is time to take positive steps to close the discipline gap. Reflecting federal guidance on the need for more effective methods to build positive school climates, many states, districts, and schools are beginning to search for evidence-based strategies to make that consensus a reality. The interventions and recommendations contained within this volume represent promising paths toward the goal of fairness in disciplinary treatment for all students.

Yet more is needed if the good intentions of policy are to be successfully translated into practice in our nation's schools. First, there must be a willingness to admit that students or their families do not hold full responsibility for differential outcomes in school discipline, but that important sources of differential treatment continue to exist within our institutions. Sustainable change can occur only when those participating in our institutions are willing to move beyond deficit thinking (Valencia, 1997) to reflect on the ways that institutions and the actors within them continue to contribute to the perpetuation of age-old inequality and stereotypes.

Second, changes in disciplinary outcomes are more likely to occur by establishing a clear focus on actionable factors within the purview of schools and educators. Educators cannot change the sociodemographic challenges that students bring with them; they can however, commit to establishing positive rather than punitive school and classroom environments, engaging in problem solving rather than exclusion, and consciously increasing the cultural responsiveness of pedagogy and school discipline.

Finally, change requires resources. Although the notion of spending new money on social programs has become almost taboo in the current political climate, any policy that requires a significant shift in school policy—including new disciplinary paradigms—cannot be implemented on the backs of teachers and administrators. This is not a matter of resource availability, but rather a question of priorities. None of the interventions described in this volume are out of reach of federal or state education budgets; the ultimate question is whether there is sufficient will to bring school-based inequity to an end.

Our nation has set and continues to set high goals for excellent outcomes for all students, yet it has become increasingly clear that reliance on exclusionary discipline is a path that is incompatible with reaching those goals. Bringing promising discipline reform initiatives to fruition in our nation's schools will almost certainly require partnerships between educators and communities, between researchers and practitioners, between advocates and administrators, to develop new models that recognize that student learning requires engagement and instruction, not exclusion. Those who have already begun to engage in that process have demonstrated that safety and educational opportunity are not mutually exclusive, and that schools are abundantly capable, with appropriate support, of developing instructional settings that preserve a commitment to both excellence and equity.

NOTES

1. Data drawn from Quahand Davis (2015). *Here's a timeline of unarmed black men killed by police. Buzzfeed.* Downloaded from http://www. buzzfeed.com/nicholasquah/heres-a-timeline-of-unarmed-black-men-killed-by-police-over#.pe1RndVbP. A full listing of deaths of unarmed persons of color by police may be found at: *The Counted: People killed by police in the U.S.* (2015).*The Guardian.* Downloaded from http://www.the-guardian.com/us-news/ng-interactive/2015/jun/01/the-counted-police-killings-us-database# suggests that the number may be much higher.

2. See, for example, *Addressing the Root Causes of Disparities in School Discipline An Educator's Action Planning Guide* (Osher et al., 2015).

REFERENCES

American Psychological Association Zero Tolerance Task Force. (2008). Are zero tolerance polices effective in the schools? *American Psychologist, 63*(9), 852–862.

Border Crossers. (2011). *Talking about race with K-5: Honoring teachable race moments in your classroom.* Retrieved from http://issuu.com/bordercrossers/docs/talking_about_race_with_k-5/1?e=0

Brand, S., Felner, R. D., Shim, M., Seitsinger, A., & Dumas, T. (2003). Middle school improvement and reform: Development and validation of a school-level assessment of climate, cultural pluralism and school safety. *Journal of Educational Psychology, 95*(3), 570–588.

Brantlinger, E. (1991). Social class distinctions in adolescents' reports of problems and punishment in school. *Behavioral Disorders, 17*, 36–46.

Carter, P., Skiba, R. J., Arredondo, M. I., & Pollock, M. (2014). *You can't fix what you don't look at: Acknowledging race in addressing racial disparities.* Bloomington, IN: The Equity Project at Indiana University. Retrieved from http://rtpcollaborative.indiana.edu/briefing-papers/

Gregory, A., Bell, J., & Pollock, M. (2014). *How educators can eradicate disparities in school discipline: A briefing paper on school-based interventions.* Bloomington, IN: The Equity Project at Indiana University. Retrieved from http://rtpcollaborative.indiana.edu/briefing-papers/

Gregory, A., Cornell, D., & Fan, X. (2011). The relationship of school structure and support to suspension rates for black and white high school students. *American Educational Research Journal, 48*(4), 904–934. doi:10.3102/0002831211398531.

Hinojosa, M. S. (2008). Black-white differences in school suspensions: Effect on student beliefs about teachers. *Sociological Spectrum, 28*, 175–193.

Howard, T. C. (2008). Who really cares? The disenfranchisement of African American males in Pre K-12 schools: A critical race theory perspective. *Teachers' College Record, 110*, 954–985.

King, J. E. (Ed.) (2005). *Black education: A transformative research and action agenda for the new century.* Mahwah, NJ: Lawrence Erlbaum Associates for the American Educational Research Association.

Kupchik, A., & Ellis, N. (2008). School discipline and security: Fair for all students? *Youth & Society, 39*, 549–574.

Mattison, E., & Aber, M. S. (2007). Closing the achievement gap: The association of racial climate with achievement and behavioral outcomes. *American Journal of Community Psychology, 40*(1), 1–12.

Morrison, G. M., Anthony, S., Storino, M., Cheng, J., Furlong, M. F., & Morrison, R. L. (2001). School expulsion as a process and an event: Before and after effects on children at-risk for school discipline. *New Directions for Youth Development: Theory, Practice, Research, 92*, 45–72.

Noltemeyer, A., & Mcloughlin, C. S. (2010). Patterns of exclusionary discipline by school typology, ethnicity, and their interactions. *Perspectives on Urban Education, 7*, 27–40.

Nosek, B. A., Smyth, F. L., Hansen, J. J., Devos, T., Lindner, N. M., Ratliff (Ranganath), K. A., Banaji, M. R. (2007). Pervasiveness and correlates of implicit attitudes and stereotypes. *European Review of Social Psychology, 18*, 36–88. doi:10.1080/10463280701489053.

Osher, D., Bear, G. G., Sprague, J. R., & Doyle, W. (2010). How can we improve school discipline? *Educational Researcher, 39*(1), 48–58. doi:10.3102/0013189X09357618.

Osher, D., Fisher, D., Amos, L., Katz, J., Dwyer, K., Duffey, T. et al. (2015). *Addressing the root causes of disparities in school discipline: An educator's action planning guide.* Washington, DC: National Center on Safe Supportive Learning Environments. Retrieved from http://safesupportivelearning.ed.gov/sites/default/files/15-1547%20NCSSLE%20Root%20Causes%20Guide%20FINAL02%20mb.pdf

Pollock, M. (2009). *Colormute: Race talk dilemmas in an American school.* Princeton, NJ: Princeton University Press.

Quah, N., & Davis, L. E. (2015) Here's a timeline of unarmed black men killed by police. *Buzzfeed.* Retrieved from http://www.buzzfeed.com/nicholasquah/heres-a-timeline-of-unarmed-black-men-killed-by-police-over#.pe1RndVbP

Resnick, M. D., Bearman, P. S., Blum, R. W., Bauman, K. E., Harris, K. M., Jones, J., et al. (1997). Protecting adolescents from harm: Findings from the National Longitudinal Study on Adolescent Health. *Journal of the American Medical Association, 287*, 823–832.

Russell, S. T., Everett, B. G., Rosario, M., & Birkett, M. (2014). Indicators of victimization and sexual orientation among adolescents: Analyses from youth risk behavior surveys. *American Journal of Public Health, 104*, 255–261. doi:10.2105/AJPH.2013.301493.

Singleton, G. E., & Linton, C. (Eds.) (2005). *Courageous conversations about race: A field guide for achieving equity in schools.* Thousand Oaks, CA: Corwin Press.

Skiba, R. J., Chung, C. G., Trachok, M., Baker, T. L., Sheya, A., & Hughes, R. L. (2014). Parsing disciplinary disproportionality: Contributions of infraction, student, and school characteristics to out-of-school suspension and expulsion. *American Educational Research Journal, 51*, 640–670.

Snapp, S., Arredondo, M., Russell, S.T. & Skiba, R. (in press). A right to disclose: LGBTQ youth representation in data, science, and policy. In S.Horn, M. Ruck,

& L. Liben (Eds.), *Equity and Justice in Developmental Sciences: Theoretical and Methodological Issues.* Oxford, England: Elsevier.

Solomon, P., Portelli, J., Daniel, B.-J. & Campbell, A. (2005). The discourse of denial: How white teacher candidates construct race, racism, and "white privilege." *Race Ethnicity and Education, 8*(20), 147–169.

Sperry, P. (2015, March14). How liberal discipline policies are making schools less safe. *New York Post.* Retrieved from http://nypost.com/2015/03/14/politicians-are-making-schools-less-safe-and-ruining-education-for-everyone/

Sprague, J., & Horner, R. (2007). School wide positive behavioral support. In S. R. Jimerson & M. J. Furlong (Eds.), *Handbook of school violence and school safety: From research to practice* (pp. 413–428). Mahwah, NJ: Erlbaum Associates, Inc..

Steinberg, M. P., Allensworth, E., & Johnson, D. W. (2015). What conditions jeopardize and support safety in urban schools? The influence of community characteristics, school composition and school organizational practices on student and teacher reports of safety in Chicago. In D. J. Losen (Ed.), *Closing the school discipline gap: Equitable remedies for excessive exclusion* (pp. 118–131). New York: Teachers College Press.

Swaine, J., Laughland, O., Lartey, J., & McCarthy, C. (2015). The counted: People killed by police in the U.S. *The Guardian.* Retrieved from http://www.theguardian.com/us-news/ng-interactive/2015/jun/01/the-counted-police-killings-us-database#

Tatum, B. D. (2006). *Can we talk about race?: And other conversations in an era of school resegregation.* Boston: Beacon Press.

Trepagnier, B. (2006). *Silent racism: How well-meaning white people perpetuate the racial divide.* Boulder, CO: Paradigm Publishers.

Valencia, R. R. (1997). *The evolution of deficit thinking: Educational thought and practice.* Washington, D.C.: Falmer Press.

Wallace Jr., J. M., Goodkind, S., Wallace, C. M., & Bachman, J. G. (2008). Racial, ethnic, and gender differences in school discipline among U.S. high school students: 1991-2005. *The Negro Educational Review, 59*(1-2), 47–62.

Wang, M. T., Selman, R. L., Dishion, T. J., & Stormshak, E. A. (2010). A tobit regression analysis of the covariation between middle school students' perceived school climate and behavioral problems. *Journal of Research on Adolescence, 20,* 274–286.

INDEX

© The Author(s) 2016
R.J. Skiba et al. (eds.), *Inequality in School Discipline*,
DOI 10.1057/978-1-137-51257-4